Kailyard
and
Scottish Literature

Scottish Cultural Review of Language and Literature

Volume 8

Series Editors
John Corbett
University of Glasgow

Sarah Dunnigan
University of Edinburgh

James McGonigal
University of Glasgow

Production Editor
Rhona Brown
University of Glasgow

SCROLL

The Scottish Cultural Review of Language and Literature publishes new work in Scottish Studies, with a focus on analysis and reinterpretation of the literature and languages of Scotland, and the cultural contexts that have shaped them.

Further information on our editorial and production procedures can be found at www.rodopi.nl

Kailyard
and
Scottish Literature

Andrew Nash

Amsterdam - New York, NY 2007

Cover painting: Sir James Guthrie, *A Hind's Daughter*, 1883, Oil on canvas, ©National Gallery of Scotland

Cover design: Gavin Miller and Pier Post

The paper on which this book is printed meets the requirements of "ISO 9706: 1994, Information and documentation - Paper for documents - Requirements for permanence".

ISBN-13: 978-90-420-2203-4
©Editions Rodopi B.V., Amsterdam - New York, NY 2007
Printed in The Netherlands

To my parents

Contents

Acknowledgements

This book has its origins in a Ph.D thesis on J.M. Barrie and the Kailyard written at the University of St Andrews. I owe a considerable debt to Robert Crawford who provided energetic and enthusiastic support for me and my work from the moment I began doctoral research under his supervision. I also benefited from conversations about the subjects of this book with Douglas Dunn, R.D.S. Jack, Murray Pittock and, especially, Ian Campbell, who really sparked my enthusiasm for Scottish literature. Vincent Giroud and the staff of the Beinecke Library, Yale University, were extremely helpful during my period of research there. The general editors at SCROLL, especially Sarah Dunnigan and Jim McGonigal, have been patient, helpful and accommodating. In completing the book I benefited from working with Adam White, who wrote an MA dissertation on Kailyard at the University of Reading in 2005. My thanks go to all and also to Jonathan Bell and, most of all, to the two people to whom the book is dedicated. Portions of Chapter 5 of this book appeared in an earlier form in an article in *Scottish Studies Review* (Vol. 5, No. 1, Spring 2004), and reappear here by permission of the editors and the Association for Scottish Literary Studies.

Introduction

What is Kailyard?

It may be that some apology is due by anyone who refers to the Kailyard. Most readers must be weary of the outworn word itself, as they are of the class of writing for which it stands. But the word has become part of the language, and will probably survive the books which it connotes. (Rix 1897)

So began an article published in the *Glasgow Evening Times* on 6 January 1897 by a writer signing himself "Rix". His words could hardly have been more prophetic. One hundred and one years later, Donald Dewar, then Secretary of State for Scotland, participated in a debate about the likely cultural effects of devolution and spoke of his fears that a devolved structure for Scottish radio and television might lead to the production of "Kailyard" broadcasting. Reporting on the debate for *Scotland on Sunday*, Magnus Linklater summed up the import of Dewar's use of the word:

Kailyard. The dread word floated in the BBC air like a bad smell. [...] An audible hiss of in-drawn breath ran round Broadcasting House. The K-word had been uttered; and by the Scottish Secretary at that. Of course, he had retrieved it at once. But just saying it was bad enough. (Linklater 1998)

The mention of the K-word by a modern politician, and the extremity of response it apparently provoked in an audience of the press, proves that "Rix" was right to suppose that the word would remain part of the language and survive the books which, in 1897, it served to connote. For over a century, Kailyard has been a key term in Scottish literary and cultural debate. Though originating in literary criticism it has come to be used in a variety of ways across a whole range of academic and popular discourse. The literal meaning of the term – cabbage patch – does little to explain why it has become central to the cultural vocabulary but the range of reference establishes at once the essential point about the subject and the point of departure for the present study. Although Kailyard is commonly understood as an event in Scottish literary history it is in fact a critical term that has been used in various ways to help structure the discussion of literature and culture in Scotland.

The term Kailyard was first applied to Scottish literature in 1895 by the critic J.H. Millar in an article published in W.E. Henley's avant-garde *New Review*. Millar characterised the contemporary literary impulse as "a revolt of the provinces against the centre":

Scarce a locality in these isles from Land's End to the Moray Firth has lacked a recorder of its darling idiosyncrasies. Cornwall has striven with Galloway to catch the public ear, and Troy Town with Thrums. In this cry of mingled dialects the Caledonian note has rung out with its customary clearness. (Millar 1895: 384)

The instigator of this Caledonian note was, according to Millar, J.M. Barrie, who "for all his genius may, without any grave impropriety, be termed the founder of a special and notable department in the 'parochial' school of fiction". Millar's concession to Barrie's "genius" is not the only qualification he serves on placing this author within his new critical context, but he is in no doubt about "the fact" that Barrie "is fairly entitled to look upon himself as *pars magna*, if not *pars maxima*, of the Great Kailyard Movement". The mock-heroic tone seems tongue-in-cheek but Millar's half-joking label set out a future critical agenda as the term soon became an institution of letters. Only two months later, a publication as specialist as the *Magazine of Music* referred to Ian Maclaren as "the Kail-yard man" (August 1895).

The immediate consequence of Millar's article was to fix in place a canon of authors. Of the many writers whom he saw as following Barrie and contributing to the "Great Kailyard movement" he drew attention only to S.R. Crockett and Ian Maclaren (the penname of the Rev. John Watson). The effect was to make Kailyard synonymous with the work of these three writers. Ever since Millar's article, Kailyard has come to be seen as an event in Scottish literary history, and Barrie, Crockett and Maclaren as forming a "school" of writers, pursuing similar ends and employing comparable literary techniques. The most recent book-length study of Kailyard, by Thomas Knowles, approaches the subject from this context. In an early attempt to define Kailyard Knowles maps out what he takes to be its classic form:

In its "classic" form, the Kailyard is characterised by the sentimental and nostalgic treatment of parochial Scottish scenes, often centred on the church community, often on individual careers which move from childhood innocence to urban awakening (and contamination), and back again to the comfort and security of the native hearth. (Knowles 1983: 13)

This "'classic' form" has been used by many subsequent critics as a definition of Kailyard. It is quoted, for example, by Gillian Shepherd in her essay in *The History of Scottish Literature*. Shepherd points out that "not all of the work" of Barrie, Crockett and Maclaren was written to the Kailyard "formula" which, she argues, required:

an omniscient narrator, an episodic format, a rural setting, an imprecise chronology, a Free Church minister and/or a lonely schoolmaster, both frequently "stickit" or failed and one or other usually assuming the narrator's role. (Shepherd 1988: 310)

The attempt to impose a "formula" on a set of literary texts indicates that Kailyard is a product of literary criticism.

One of the inevitable effects of this critical construction of a "movement" or "formula" has been to impose a constraint upon discussion of Barrie, Crockett and Maclaren. In the context of Scottish literature these writers have become trapped within the critical parameters offered by the term Kailyard and Barrie's fiction in particular has been much neglected and misrepresented because of it. The importance of Kailyard to Scottish literature and culture extends beyond an understanding of Barrie, Crockett and Maclaren, however. As Shepherd asks: why should a dozen books or so written by three Scotsmen in a single distant decade continue to attract critical attention?" (Shepherd 1987: 310). The answer is that, whilst these writers have remained indelibly associated with Kailyard, the term quickly transcended the context within which it was originally applied and came to be used in wider senses. One of the earliest indications of this can be found in J.H. Millar's later *Literary History of Scotland* (1903), where he describes John Wilson's *Lights and Shadows of Scottish Life* (1822) as "pure 'Kailyard'" (Millar 1903: 511). In this instance the term is being used not as a noun to refer to an event in literary history but as an adjective to make a qualitative judgement on a work from much earlier in the century. This particular understanding of the term is developed in full in Ian Campbell's book *Kailyard*

(1981), which is the study that best exemplifies the way the term has come to be used in recent decades as an adjective to make qualitative judgements on various aspects of Scottish literature. Campbell's book is not a detailed account of the fiction of Barrie, Crockett and Maclaren but an examination of attitudes towards Scotland conveyed in a range of texts from the late-eighteenth century onwards. In this context the term involves a critical judgement; the Kailyard faults are exposed as:

a gelling of attitude and myth, a freezing of the possibilities of change or redefinition, a tacit acceptance of a narrow range of character and activity within which to present "real" Scotland; above all, a total weakness in any attempt to challenge the reader into startling or threatening identification or redefinition. (Campbell 1981: 11)

Kailyard has come to be used in this way throughout literary criticism to sum up what critics take to be wrong ways of writing about Scotland, whether this be at the level of style, content or outlook on Scottish life.

One of the consequences of Millar's transformation of the term was that Kailyard came to refer to the whole Victorian period in Scottish literature. There was a reason for this. Writers and critics of the early twentieth century considered Victorian Scottish literature to be not only undistinguished in quality but evasive in form and, in marked contrast to the English novel, unrepresentative of industrial life in the nineteenth century. The fiction that Millar had labelled Kailyard seemed to encapsulate these negative qualities only to an excessive extent. It appeared the culmination of a whole tradition of Scottish writing that had been characterised by a provincial outlook, a predilection for romance over realism, an excessive focus on rural as opposed to urban settings, and a tendency to evade social and industrial issues. These critical concerns have become embedded in the Kailyard term and are always implicit whenever it is used in criticism. The most influential book in this context is George Blake's *Barrie and the Kailyard School* (1951). Although the title suggests a close focus on the 1890s and on Barrie's work in particular, Blake's book is really an exposure of what Andrew Noble has described as Scotland's "Urbane Silence" (Noble 1985). As a result, the work of Barrie, Crockett and Maclaren came to be placed as central to, and emblematic of, the whole Victorian period, in spite of the fact that their careers were confined to the latter decades of the nineteenth century and the early years of the twentieth.

The legacy of Blake's book can be found in any number of studies in Scottish literature which either refer to the Victorian period as Kailyard or use the term as the defining context within which to discuss literature of that period. William Donaldson, for example, uses "Kailyard" as the context for his analysis of *Popular Literature in Victorian Scotland* (1986), a book that discusses fiction serialised in Scottish newspapers over the period 1850–80. Similarly, in a discussion of the effects of eighteenth-century Scottish literature, K.G. Simpson argues that in the nineteenth century "Scotland missed out on Romanticism in its full flowering and wallowed in the kailyard instead" (Simpson 1981: 6). As F.R. Hart writes: for most critics Scottish Victorianism is "nought [...] but several generations of Kailyard sentimentalists" (Hart 1978: 84). Tom Nairn dates the "Scots 'Kailyard' tradition" to the 1820s onwards (Nairn [1977] 1981: 156). From having first been associated with a group of writers active in the 1890s, the term has here leapt to defining a tradition – and not simply a literary tradition – originating some seventy years before.

The association between Kailyard and the Victorian period owes much to the writing of Hugh MacDiarmid who took the term to the centre of his creative and critical programme for a Scottish Renaissance. Much of MacDiarmid's writing was devoted to correcting what he took to be misrepresentations of Scotland and the Scottish literary tradition and Kailyard was the word he used to sum up the rejected tradition. The enormous influence of MacDiarmid's writings on the development of twentieth century Scottish literature meant that Kailyard came to be used as a critical concept to help structure cultural debate. Much discussion of Scottish literature in the twentieth century has been structured around a Kailyard/anti-Kailyard axis. Studies of twentieth-century Scottish literature invariably begin by using Kailyard as a defining context, seeing it as a tradition against which modern writers are reacting.[1]

It is not just in literature that the term has been used to structure

---

[1] e.g. Murray and Tait 1984; Craig 1987; Schwend and Drescher, 1990.

critical debate in this way. In the final quarter of the twentieth century the term was taken to the centre of debates over Scottish nationalism, politics and film culture and it continues to be used in historical, political and sociological analyses of Scottish culture. It is this range of reference that is the key to understanding Kailyard's continued significance in debates over Scottish culture. It helps explain why the fiction of Barrie, Crockett and Maclaren can be seen both, in George Blake's terms, as Scotland's woeful alternative to Dickens and Gaskell (never mind the fact that these great English yardsticks were, respectively, eighteen and twenty three years dead by the time Barrie's *Auld Licht Idylls* was published in 1888), and, in Tom Nairn's terms, as the only thing Scotland could produce during the climate of European nationalist revolt.

In a footnote in *A Literary History of Scotland*, J.H. Millar wrote: "It is betraying no secret to mention that for this happy nickname, which has attained so much currency, the world is indebted to Mr W.E. Henley and to no one else" (Millar 1903: 511n). Neither he nor Henley could possibly have predicted in 1903 that by the end of the century the word would have attained so much currency and become an essential part of the Scottish critical idiom. It will be the task of the following chapters to bring this idiom into some sort of focus, and to begin we need to look at the context within which the term was first applied to discussions of Scottish literature.

Chapter One

The Invention of the Term

I

In August 1889 the Scottish writer and critic Margaret Oliphant was
much excited about the work of J.M. Barrie. In an unsigned article in
Blackwood's Magazine, she combined notice of Barrie's *A Window in
Thrums* with a review of *Ideala* – a novel published anonymously by
the New Woman novelist Sarah Grand – of which she thoroughly
disapproved. In contrast to the forced and artificial nature of Grand's
writing, Oliphant noted the "absolute truth of the Scotch village set
before us by Mr Barrie which is simple matter of fact, comprehended,
perceived, and understood by genius" (Oliphant 1889: 262). More
than anything, Oliphant was struck by the realism of Barrie's
depiction of Scottish life. She considered that Jess (the mother-figure
who was to become so roundly abused by later commentators) might
"in coarser hands" have become "a mere gossip" or "the sentimental
invalid of fiction", but under Barrie's pen was "an acute and clever
woman of true Scottish mould." The penultimate chapter, "The Last
Night", easily dismissed by twentieth-century critics as overly
sentimental, was to Oliphant "a perfect picture of a parting such as has
taken place in many a Scotch cottage, when little is said, but a
profound feeling, we might say of passion, of love and sorrow
pervades all" (Oliphant 1889: 263).

The validity of fictional representations of Scottish life was an
issue that had concerned Oliphant throughout her long career as a
writer. In the 1860s she had pursued an agenda in the pages of
Blackwood's to correct English misconceptions of Scottish national
character, and some of her own Scottish novels were designed "to set
the Sassenachs straight about their kin north of the Tweed" (Colby
1979: 93). But it was not just Barrie's realism that struck Mrs
Oliphant. She considered his writing to transcend mere observation:

No one who knows Scotland can miss the extraordinary literal truth of this little interior, so full of the highest restrained emotions, love, trust, and sublime faith. It might be a photograph, yet the truthfulness of it is of the profoundest poetry. It requires a very great gift to accomplish this [...] no book could be more deeply instinct with the poetry of real feeling, in which no fiction is, though it requires something which can only be called genius to reveal it to the world. (Oliphant 1889: 264)

In terms of the Kailyard debate, however, the most significant aspect of Oliphant's review is her placing of Barrie's book within the context of a national school of Scottish fiction. Although she demurred about Barrie's excessive use of dialect, she contrasted his work favourably with that of his contemporaries in the field:

it is difficult to view without some consternation the host of little books which are finding their way to immense popularity in Scotland with very little claim upon the attention beyond that which this dialect brings. [...] The books called "Carlowrie," "Aldersyde," "Blinkbonny," "Glenairlie," &c are cheap books, perfectly well adapted, with their mild love-stories and abundant marriages, for the simpler classes, especially of women whose visions are bounded by the parish, who know nothing higher in society than the minister and his wife, and believe that all the world lieth in wickedness except Scotland. [...] It is sad to be told that these productions are regarded as representatives of a national school and attain their popularity by dint of their dialect and by the very narrowness of their aim. (Oliphant 1889: 265–6)

The books Oliphant mentions were all published between 1882 and 1884 by the Edinburgh firm of Oliphant & Co. *Glenairlie; or the Last of the Graemes* (1884) was one of the best-known publications of Robina F. Hardy, a Christian missionary who lived in the heart of the Edinburgh slums. Although some of her other books, such as *Jock Halliday: a Grassmarket Hero* (1883) and *Katie: an Edinburgh Lassie* (1886) drew on her own experiences of life in the city, *Glenairlie* is a tale of village life with much dialogue in Scots. *Aldersyde: a border story of seventy years ago* (1883), by Annie S. Swan, betrays a debt to *Waverley* in its title, and focuses on a young gentlewoman who lives a life of self-sacrifice after her father's estate is entailed away, her lover jilts her and her flighty sister runs off with a foreigner. Swan, who was later to become famous for well over a hundred volumes of romantic fiction for women, began her career by writing novels with strongly regional settings, of which *Aldersyde* and *Carlowrie: or, Among*

Lothian Folk (1884) were typical. *Blinkbonny, or Bell o' the Manse* (1882), by John Strathesk, tells of life in an imaginary parish in the 1840s. The book was very successful, giving rise to a prequel, *More Bits from Blinkbonny* (1886), which took the story back to the 1830s where the narrator tells of his youth.

To judge from the quoted extracts printed as advertisements for each of these books, Oliphant was correct in stating that they were well received by the press. The *Athenaeum* considered *Carlowrie* "a treat to the lovers of Scottish fiction, the scenery and local truth of the dialect and 'modes of thought' are all that can be desired," whilst the *Courant* observed that "Parents of taste and intelligence will be glad to put such a book as this into the hands of their children." The *Kelso Chonicle* suggested that *Aldersyde* deserved "to occupy a prominent and permanent place among Scottish works of imagination" whilst the *Haddington Courier* applauded the "vigorous raciness with which the vernacular is employed." Strathesk's *Blinkbonny* was warmly received not only in Scotland but in England, North America, Australia and New Zealand as well. The *Huntly Express* thought the "representations" to "far excel those in *Johnny Gibb*" whilst the *Bristol Mercury* went so far as to conclude that "since the days of Sir Walter Scott there have been few more graphic or accurate sketches of Scotch peasant life." A French translation, *Le Pasteur de Blinkbonny* soon appeared.[1]

In contrast to such opinions, Margaret Oliphant foresaw in these books confirmation that Scottish literature had descended into provincial status:

We, who have larger boasts, who have in so many ways contributed to the greatness of the empire, and helped authoritatively in building up its fame, we, above all, who in the person of Scott have set the example and given the laws of noble fiction to all the world, that we should fall into this poor little local separateness, is most painful to every loyal sentiment. (Oliphant 1889: 266)

Such a reflection led Oliphant to seize on Barrie as a figure of salvation, a writer who might restore the "national school" of fiction

---

[1] All of these quotations are taken from the publisher's advertisements printed in the end papers of the third edition of Strathek's *More Bits from Blinkbonny* (1886).

to the heights it had once known. In contrast to Strathesk, Swan and Hardy, Barrie was "a disciple to whom Sir Walter would have held out his kind hand, and in whom we can take an honest pride." Nor was she the only Scottish writer to respond in this way. Robert Louis Stevenson wrote to Barrie from Samoa in December 1892 to say that *A Window in Thrums* gave him "a source of living pleasure and heartfelt national pride. There are two of us now that the Shirra might have patted on the head" (Stevenson 1995: VII: 447).

Though it predates the application of the term Kailyard by almost six years, Oliphant's lengthy appreciation of Barrie's book is significant because it anticipates the range of issues that would later become central to the Kailyard debate: the accuracy of national representation; the concern over the narrow range of themes and issues and the consequent appeal to a lowbrow audience and taste; above all the anxiety over the provincial status of Scottish literature – its "poor little local separateness." Her review shows clearly that the critical attitudes and opinions that would soon become embedded in the Kailyard term were already in the air when Barrie's early texts were being published, and were being directed against works of literature that had been in circulation for several years. In Oliphant's eyes, the books by Strathesk, Swan and Hardy misrepresent Scotland, exploit dialect for novelty, appeal only to a popular audience, and present a vision of life that is "bounded by the parish". These are exactly the criticisms that would later be brought against the work of Crockett and Maclaren, and, in the twentieth century, against Barrie as well.

In placing her approval of Barrie within the context of a "national school" of fiction, Oliphant's review also reflects the wider critical and institutional enquiry that was taking place at the time into the definition and understanding of Scottish literature. The last quarter of the nineteenth century marks a key moment in the shaping of the discipline within academia and the publishing world. There was an upsurge in the number of histories or surveys of Scottish literature that were published: Millar's *Literary History of Scotland* (1903) was preceded by John Veitch's *History and Poetry of the Scottish Border* (1878, revised and reprinted in 1893), J.M. Ross's *Scottish History and Literature to the Period of the Reformation* (1884), Hugh

Walker's *Three Centuries of Scottish Literature* (1893) and T.F. Henderson's *Scottish Vernacular Literature: A History* (1898). The 1880s also witnessed the founding of the Scottish History Society and the Scottish Text Society. Furthermore, as Robert Crawford has shown, there was a gathering interest within the universities in the academic study of Scottish literature as distinct from its place in the understanding of English or British literature. Scottish texts begin to appear with greater regularity on University syllabuses in the final decades of the century and in 1897 St Andrews changed the heading of their calendar entry from "English Literature" to "English and Scottish Literature" (Crawford 1998: 229). The application of the Kailyard term in 1895 thus took place at a time when ideas about the subject were being debated and approaches established. Compared to earlier in the century, there was a much greater chance of a critical marker like Kailyard taking root.

In her review, Oliphant can be seen to be making a small but significant contribution to this preoccupation with the shaping of Scottish literary history by demanding the construction – or deconstruction – of ideas about national schools. And within this context the nature of her approval is all the more important. Like many other contemporary commentators, Oliphant separated Barrie off from "the host of little books" that she might have termed Kailyard had the epithet been hers. Beth Dickson misrepresents this point in her discussion of Oliphant's review, arguing erroneously that "Oliphant distances herself intellectually from the phenomenon [of popular fiction] as seen in the fiction of Barrie and Swan" (Dickson 1997: 331). But at no point does Oliphant place Barrie's fiction alongside that of Swan; instead she mentions Swan's novels to point up the differences between her books and those of Barrie. Before the Kailyard term was applied in 1895, Barrie's work offered hope that tales of Scottish village life could reach a higher literary level than that achieved by novels such as *Aldersyde* and *Carlowrie*.

Mrs Oliphant was not the only critic to draw a sharp contrast between Barrie and his contemporaries. When *Auld Licht Idylls* appeared in 1888, it was hailed by reviewers as a landmark event in Scottish literature. The *Spectator* considered it to be "the most truly literary, and the most realistic attempt that has been made for years –

if not for generations – to reproduce humble Scotch life", and as such was "a complete and welcome contrast to the "paltry duds" which are nowadays printed by the dozen as pictures of humble and religious life in Scotland" (5 May 1888). Such comments make clear that, in its focus on the humble life of a small community in a largely rural region of Scotland, Barrie's early work was nothing new. Indeed, whilst Oliphant could read Barrie alongside existing trends in Scottish fiction it was just as easy to place his work within traditions of Scottish literature that had been established much earlier in the century. The presentation of life in a small town would have reminded readers of the fiction of John Galt, and particularly of his *Annals of the Parish* (1821), whilst the strong regional setting would have prompted comparison with the more recent novels of George MacDonald, published from the 1860s onwards. The focus on the role of the Church in the community would also have been recognised as part of a common concern of Scottish literature. The 1843 disruption in the Kirk had led to a number of books preoccupied with ecclesiastical affairs, the most notable of which was William Alexander's novel *Johnny Gibb o' Gushetneuk* (1871). Most significantly of all, however, Barrie's collection of stories would have struck a chord of familiarity because it corresponded with the prevailing idea of Scottish literature as essentially concerned with rural and domestic themes. In the nineteenth century, "pictures of humble and religious life" were not just a staple part of Scottish fiction and poetry, they were, to a considerable extent, the very life-blood of the form. A whole rhetoric of national and literary identity had been constructed around images that celebrated "humble and religious life" in Scotland.

II

The key event in this construction was the critical reception of the poetry of Robert Burns. An article in *Literature* entitled "The Heritage of Burns", published a few years after the phenomenal success of Crockett and Maclaren, attributed "the Kailyard School" to "a perverted worship of the memory of Burns":

Burns has come to represent Scotland, and only Scotland to be adored in Burns. Therefore we have to-day not only a constant and copious flow of tolerable dialect verse, but also a local school of novelists [...]. The writer, whether of prose or verse, is prevented by the necessities of his market, no less than the limitations of his art, from straying outside one range of subjects. [...] If he will interest his countrymen he must write about them; and everything tends to make him dwell most upon the peculiarities that distinguish them from other men, to put his best work into observing and describing these, and to slur over that description of humanity which is the only subject of permanent literary work. (17 September 1898)

Kailyard fiction is seen here as descending directly, not specifically from Burns's poetry, but from the identification of that poetry as the meaning of Scotland. I have argued in detail elsewhere that in the nineteenth century "The Cotter's Saturday Night", Burns's then most famous poem, became the canonical image of Scottish life, helping to promote an emphasis on rural and humble life as representative of Scottish national identity (Nash 1997). This image of "the lowly train in life's sequestered scene", with the "toil-worn cotter" returning home from a cold November day to join his contented family in a meal and a reading from the Bible, is celebrated in the poem by one of Burns's most famous lines: "From scenes like these, old Scotia's grandeur springs". To Burns's critics the word "old" was unnecessary. As early as 1793 this poem was being presented as a realistic presentation of life in Scotland. Patrick Heron argued that:

[it] proves that the manners of our rustics can afford subjects for Pastoral Poetry more elevated and more amiable than those which are exhibited in Gay's "Shepherd's Week"; that Pastoral Poetry needs not to employ itself upon the fictitious manners, and modes of life, but may, with higher poetical advantages paint the humble virtues, the simple pleasures, the inartificial manners of our peasantry, such as they actually exist. (cited in Low 1974: 97)

Such remarks, written shortly before Wordsworth's famous Preface to the *Lyrical Ballads*, indicate the importance of Burns's poetry to Romantic theories of poetic diction. But whilst Burns has come to be seen as an important figure in early Romanticism, the immediate effect of remarks like these was to set up "The Cotter's Saturday Night" as a transcript of Burns's life and thus of Scottish identity. To a Burns critic in 1849 the belief remained that "everything else that he wrote may be considered as auxiliary to the purpose shadowed forth in that poem", and that was a poem where "the rural scenes are real scenes" (Tyler 1849: 60, 55).

It is significant in this context that Duncan Macmillan has argued for Wilkie's painting *The Cotter's Saturday Night* (1837) as forming *"the* canonical image of Scottish art" (Macmillan 1994: 91 original italics). Nineteenth-century commentators were to make much of this canonical image which spread across disciplines and the effect was to consolidate as a representation of Scotland the sentimental celebration of rural and domestic life. In this context, the work of John Wilson is crucial. Wilson, who became Professor of Moral Philosophy at Edinburgh, acquired fame both for his essays and reviews and for his poetry and fiction. His writings have long been identified as foundational to the Kailyard. As already mentioned, J.H. Millar was quick to forge a link between Wilson and the contemporary scene in his *Literary History of Scotland*. His writings have come to be seen as part of a distorting tradition of Scottish literature in the nineteenth century, one that culminates in the Kailyard fiction at the end of the century. Andrew Noble sees Wilson as the founding father of that sorry school" (Noble 1988: 137) and Ian Campbell argues that "the themes of Wilson's fiction, which startlingly prefigure familiar themes of the kailyard" established a taste for Scottish fiction that was made to appear "indispensable" (Campbell 1981: 40). Explicit in Wilson's association with Kailyard are literary and political arguments that will be returned to in a later chapter; what I want to establish here is the extent to which Wilson's vision of Scottish national character created an identity for Scottish fiction rooted in rural and humble life.

As editor of Burns, Wilson perpetuated the view of the poetry as a transcript of Burns's life. In "The Genius and Character of Burns", Wilson's much-reprinted preface to the 1840 edition of Burns's works, he argued that the peasantry of Scotland was "not surveyed and speculated on" by Burns as "the field of poetry, but as the field of his own existence. […] Most other poets of rural life have looked on it through the aerial veil of imagination. He looked around him" (Wilson 1857: 1–2). This long essay (running to over 200 pages) was the culmination of what Andrew Noble has described as Wilson's "perversion of Burns's achievement" (Noble 1988: 148). As co-editor of, and chief contributor to, *Blackwood's Magazine*, Wilson used the pages of *Blackwood's* to set out an agenda for a national cultural renewal which had Burns at its centre. In an article of 1819 he used Burns's status as a peasant poet to mark off Scotland from England, arguing that Scotland possessed a "depth of moral and religious feeling in the peasantry of Scotland" which could not be found in England:

The fireside of an English cottage is often a scene of happiness and virtue; but unquestionably, in the "Cotter's Saturday Night" of Burns, we feel, that we are reading the records of a purer, simpler, more pious race; and there is in that immortal poem a depth of domestic joy – an intensity of the feeling of home – a presiding spirit of love – and a lofty enthusiasm of religion, which are all peculiarly Scottish, and beyond the pitch of mind of any other people. (Cited in Low 1974: 309–10)

In a further article entitled "The Radical's Saturday Night", published later in the same year, Wilson repeated this observation and placed his reading of Burns within a context that reveals the cultural and political basis of his nationalism:

in Scotland alone, and I say so with a due sense of the virtues of England, does there exist among the peasantry a union of knowledge, morality and religion, so universal, so intense, and so solemn, as to constitute National Character. (Wilson 1819: 257)

The reference to National Character indicates Wilson's response to an established cultural idea. His theories of nationalism owe much to German Romanticism and in particular the writings of Johann Gottfried Herder. An admirer of James Macpherson's Ossianic texts, Herder's theories of national character and national genius are integral to Wilson's ideas on landscape and the *genius loci* and help explain why he should look to the rural poor for evidence of national distinctiveness.[2] But Wilson's view of Burns is also driven by an overt political stance. By arguing that "The Cotter's Saturday Night" represented Scottish national identity he was able to conclude that the "The Radical's Saturday Night would never be in Scotland anything more than – a dream" (Wilson 1819: 262). According to Wilson, in

---

[2] For an account of the development of cultural nationalism in the late eighteenth and early nineteenth centuries, see Smith 1991. For a discussion of Wilson's writings on poetry and landscape, see Nash 2000.

Burns's pictures of the poor you do not see "slaves sullenly labouring, or madly leaping in their chains but in nature's bondage, content with their toil, sedate in their suffering, in their recreations full of mirth [they] are seen as Free Men" (Wilson 1857: 224). This distorted view of Burns explicitly denies the radicalism that modern critics have rightly detected in Burns's poetry (McIlvanney 2002). Burns became the exemplum of Wilson's politically-motivated image of a Scottish national identity, one which Andrew Noble has termed an "ahistorical, apolitical image of a nation of pious, peasant communities" (Noble 1988: 135).

Wilson's fiction was equally influential in establishing ideas of Scottish national character. An anti-urban ethos rebounds throughout his work, nowhere more thoroughly than in *Lights and Shadows of Scottish Life* (1822), which, as Elsie Swann notes, "attained an amazing popularity by facile sentimentality and maudlin pathos" (Swann 1934: 114). A series of short stories designed to illustrate the spiritual integrity of the rural poor, the book presents a vision of the Scottish peasantry as contented with their lot and nobly resisting the corrupting world beyond. *The Trials of Margaret Lyndsay* (1823), a novel, traces the spiritual survival of Margaret as she is forced to leave the country and live in the sinful city. Wilson's fiction was extremely popular, going through a great many editions in the nineteenth century. Together with his enormously influential criticism, it helped consolidate the idea that the distinctiveness of Scottish literature lay in its focus on rural, peasant life.

The identification of Burns with Scotland had a powerful effect on the course of Scottish poetry. Writing in 1919, G. Gregory Smith argued:

the completeness of [Burns's] own triumph has probably done more than we can estimate in confirming his successors, great and small, in their liking for the intimate genre, and, in the changed circumstance of later Scotland, has given the excuse for a literary affectation in verse-making. (Smith 1919: 46–7)

Nineteenth-century Scottish poetry was indeed dominated by intimate and affected imitations of Burns, collected in such volumes as the various *Whistle Binkie* anthologies published in Glasgow in the 1830s and 40s and reissued throughout the century.[3] As Edwin Morgan has aptly summarised, these volumes were "carefully devised as instruments of social control" (Morgan 1988: 340). In a preface to the 1890s edition, the publisher celebrated the efforts to avoid the "filth" that had made the "pestilent" old chap-books so "coarse and indecent" (Robertson 1890: vi). An even more remarkable series was the volumes of *One Hundred Modern Poets*, described in J.H. Miller's *Literary History of Scotland* as "a monument of wasted toil" (Millar 1903: 665n). Prepared by D.H. Edwards and printed in Brechin, the first volume appeared in 1880, the eleventh in 1888 and the sixteenth in 1897. The verses in these anthologies were not the only poems published in Scotland in the Victorian period but they dominated ideas as to what constituted characteristic Scottish poetry, as much as the stories of Wilson dominated ideas about what constituted characteristic Scottish fiction.

The rhetoric of national literature and national identity that was constructed in the nineteenth century contributed to the development of a further branch of Scottish writing which represents another important context for understanding the application of the Kailyard term. The final decades of the century witnessed a quite extraordinary vogue for collecting reminiscences about Scotland – the precedent for which was E.B. Ramsay's enormously successful *Reminiscences of Scottish Life and Character*. First published in 1857, Ramsay's book went through twenty-two impressions within fifteen years and set out a trend that was to dominate Scottish publishing for a number of decades. His objective was "to fix and preserve a page of our domestic national annals which, in the eyes of the rising generation, is fast fading into oblivion" (Ramsay [1857] 1861: v). The effect was to precipitate an astonishing number of books in a similar vein that set out to record those fading annals. At a time when official parish histories were being published across the nation, individuals were also collecting and publishing sketches and stories containing anecdotes,

---

[3] The first *Whistle Binkie* volume appeared in 1832 (Glasgow: David Robertson) and various subsequent volumes were issued over the next fifteen years (the British Library holds volumes published in 1838, 1839, 1842 and 1846). The fruits of these publications were gathered together and issued in a collected volume in 1853, which was revised and enlarged in 1878 and 1890.

customs and reminiscences of their local regions. To list all of these volumes would be like reproducing a library catalogue, but the following are representative of the huge number of titles published in the fifteen years before *Auld Licht Idylls*: Rev. Walter Gregor: *An Echo of the Olden Time from the North of Scotland* (1874); Gordon Fraser: *Wigtown and Whithorn: Historical and Descriptive Sketches, Stories and Anecdotes, illustrative of the Racy Wit & pawky Humour of the District* (1877); J.S. Neish, *Reminiscences of Brechin and its characters. A series of sketches of well-known Brechin worthies* (1878); Rev. William Paul: *Past and Present of Aberdeenshire, or Reminsicence of Seventy Years* (1881); J.S. Neish, *In the By-ways of Life: A Series of Sketches of Forfarshire Characters* (1881); James Russell, *Reminiscences of Yarrow* (1886); J.M. M'Bain, *Arbroath: Past & Present. Being Reminiscences Chiefly Relating to the Last Half Century* (1887). The sheer number of these volumes – there was barely a single important town or county that escaped the trend – made the cultural idiom of the second half of the century one of ubiquitous nostalgia and provided the more immediate cultural climate within which *Auld Licht Idylls* would have been read and understood by contemporary readers.

A sense of nostalgia informs much Scottish non-fictional writing of the Victorian period.[4] In his *Reminiscences*, published in 1881, Thomas Carlyle paints a vivid picture of the enormity of change that had come over Edinburgh and Scotland during the course of half a century. Ostensibly an account of famous and influential acquaintances, from his wife, Jane Welsh, to Southey and Wordsworth, Carlyle's text offers the same nostalgic glance at the Scottish past that is captured on the pages of Ramsay's *Reminiscences*. Like many others of the time, Carlyle was writing out of a belief that an essential part of Scottish life and national identity was in the process of being eroded. That same belief informs the writings of his near contemporary, Henry Cockburn, who, in a much quoted phrase, wrote in 1852 of the earlier decades of the century as "the last purely Scotch age that Scotland was destined to see" (Scott 1988: 15).

---

[4] For a survey of non-fictional writing in this period see Campbell 1988a.

The books of reminiscences that flooded the printing presses in the final decades of the century were thus part of a larger consciousness of what Archibald Geikie identified in his *Scottish Reminiscences* as "the gradual decline of national peculiarities" (Geikie 1904: 7). Ramsay's pioneering book was crucial in encouraging a nostalgic stance towards Scotland and in perpetuating the emphasis on rural life. With a few exceptions, the volumes that his book inspired dealt mainly with rural settings. In J.S. Neish's *Series of Sketches of Forfarshire Characters* it was asserted that "the vast and houseless moors are more cheerful than the cities" and that "curiosities of human character are only to be met with in the 'by-ways of life'" (Neish 1881: iii). The significance of these volumes, however, in relation to the Kailyard texts, lies not simply in their nostalgic emphasis on the past; what is equally important is the way that the boundaries between fiction and history become blurred. Ramsay had identified his work as "contribut[ing] something to the materials of history, by exhibiting social customs and habits of thought which at a particular era were characteristic of a race" (Ramsay [1857] 1872: viii). Because most of the subsequent volumes dealt with specific counties, towns and villages, they made an immediate and explicit claim to historical and geographical fact. But the question of where facts ended and imagination began was one that writers felt compelled to discuss in the prefaces to their volumes. Some volumes eschewed the status of history. D. Croal noted in his *Sketches of East Lothian* that "the history of East Lothian has yet to be written" and made clear that his sketches made "no claim to absolute historical precision, or to minute topographical accuracy" (Croal 1873: 5). J.S. Neish, by contrast, was eager to confirm that the characters sketched in *Reminiscences of Brechin* were "real personages, and all well known in the localities where they lived" (Neish 1881: iii). Other writers argued that their compilations offered an alternative kind of history. J.M. Ferguson hoped that his "sketches and reminiscences" of *Auld Ayr* might "assist the future Historian" of the town (Ferguson 1884: preface) whilst D. Macara claimed that his "reminiscences of obsolete customs, traditions, superstitions and humorous anecdotes" of Crieff were "not the materials which are usually taken up by history but still they do throw some light upon history" (Macara 1881: v). Most commonly, however, writers emphasised the historical basis of their work but defended and made explicit their use of fiction and the imagination. M.F. Conolly declared his *Memorials of the East of Fife* to be "for the most part founded on facts" but at the same time "doubtless all more or less mixed up with what is fictitious and imaginative" (Conolly 1869: 5–6). Similarly, David Ogilvy Robertson's *Long Ago Legends of Clova* (1872) – a collection of stories set in the glen that J.M. Barrie would later transform into his Glen Quharity – is prefaced with a note pointing out that "the stories are to some degree founded on fact, though in embellishing them the author has endeavoured to throw into them as much of the characteristics of the glen folk as is possible" (Robertson 1872: i).

This blurring of fact and fiction characterises many of the volumes of reminiscences published around the same time as the early works of J.M. Barrie. A book such as James Thomson's *Recollections of A Speyside Parish Fifty Years Ago* (1887), for example, announces itself as a work of non-fiction but actually consists of a series of stories and sketches that use fictional forms. Alexander Lawson's *Legends and Traditions of Forfarshire* (1891) is a similar example but the most extraordinary book of this type is Hugh Muir's *Reminiscences and Sketches* of Rutherglen, which are composed in the form of a poem containing footnotes and endnotes which elaborate at length (covering more pages than the poetry) on the topographical and historical references made in the body of the poem. The preface, by W.F. Stevenson, makes absolutely clear the priorities of the text:

It is not claimed for these verses that they reach a very high standard of poetry. It is claimed for them that they record in a kindly way some of the best thoughts and deeds of those that have gone before [...] these pages will have served their end if they form a pleasing record of the places and persons that now, or in former years, have occupied the stage. (Muir 1890: x–xi)

By 1890, when this book was published, it had become common practice to present reminiscences in the form of fiction or poetry, regardless of the artistic merits of the work. A literary climate had been forged where factual anecdotes about real places could go together hand in hand with imaginative stories. As George Blake wrote in his attack on Barrie and the Kailyard in 1951: "There was nothing new, or anything in the least surprising, in the concentration of Scottish novelists on village and small-town humours" (Blake 1951: 17).

III

Once we take into account the literary context provided by these volumes of reminiscences, and recognise the extent to which imaginative literature was closely tied up with social history, it is easy to see how the realism and historical accuracy of the early fiction of Barrie, Crockett and Maclaren – all of it based on real identifiable places – became such an important issue for critics. It was almost certainly publications like those discussed above that the *Spectator* had in mind when it separated *Auld Licht Idylls* apart from the "paltry duds" being "printed by the dozen". Fictional tales of humble life in rural Scotland were indeed numerous at the time and in terms of content *Auld Licht Idylls* was nothing new. The difference, so far as contemporary commentators were concerned, lay in artistic qualities. And it is important to be clear that in their response to Barrie's work Scottish critics and reviewers were as fulsome in their praise as their southern counterparts. Reviewing *Auld Licht Idylls*, the *Glasgow Herald* wrote:

It is difficult to speak of this volume as it deserves without apparently laying oneself open to a charge of exaggeration, and yet to say in its class it is the most noticeable book of the year, or no transcript of Scottish life and character at once so truthful and poetic has recently been issued from the press, is to do it but meagre justice. (9 May 1888)

Nor was this an isolated response. The *Scottish Leader* felt Barrie "need fear no comparison with the very greatest of his predecessors" (25 October 1888) and the reviewer for the *Aberdeen Free Press* was in agreement about its importance:

Nothing has appeared for a long time so vivid and expressive in the way of description of Scottish social existence. Beyond anything else his [*sic*] charm of the book consists in its absolutely successful reproduction of an antique world that is fast passing away. (10 May 1888)

What is striking about these reviews is that they applaud Barrie for achieving precisely what he has since been charged with having failed to do – provide an accurate and realistic portrayal of Scotland. The *Herald* suggested that the book might explode a few myths, judging that "to an Englishman whose knowledge of rural Scotland has been picked up in brief summer tours, 'Auld Licht Idylls' must be both a surprise and a delight". The Free Press even considered that the book may be *too* realistic:

it may be that Mr. Barrie too disproportionately dwells on the wintry side of that world and revels in its dul[l]nes[s] and narrowness and perpetual struggle with a sordid poverty [...] this Dutch sombreness and realism excludes every suggestion of the ideal.

There is no criticism of false reality at this stage.

Barrie's success with *Auld Licht Idylls* prompted him to follow up the book with another account of life in his fictional village. *A Window in Thrums*, published a year later in 1889, had a more unified plot, telling the story of Jess and her son, Jamie, who returns to Thrums from his new home in London too late to see his family alive. The tone, which is charged throughout with pathos and sadness, is markedly different from the humour of *Auld Licht Idylls*. It was, nevertheless, an even greater critical success; the *Free Press* described it as "gold, pure gold" (11 November 1889) and the *Herald* commented that the book was "the art of a writer of the rarest insight, and genuine mastery of style" (14 November 1889).

The positive reception of Barrie by the Aberdeen and Glasgow newspapers is important because it contradicts the commonly held view that Scottish critics were against the work of Barrie, Crockett and Maclaren from the start. The failure to discriminate carefully between these three writers when making judgements on literary history has been one of the debilitating consequences of the Kailyard term. George Blake, for example, notes simply of all the Kailyard novels that "Scotland's two leading newspapers, the *Glasgow Herald* and the *Scotsman*, received the works with gravity, if with native caution" (Blake 1951: 88). But such a summary distorts the considerable differences in the way that the Scottish press received the works of Barrie on the one hand and Crockett and Maclaren on the other. Before the Kailyard term was applied in 1895, Barrie's work was held in high esteem by Scottish critics because it seemed to offer hope that tales of Scottish village life could reach a higher level of literary achievement than those attacked by Oliphant and others.

The success of Crockett and Maclaren in the mid 1890s provoked a different response from Scottish reviewers, who began to raise questions about literary value, originality and the accuracy of national representation. Margaret Oliphant was quick to express her criticism of the "romances in dialect [...] with which we are now overflooded". The artistic qualities that she detected in Barrie's writings were not matched by his followers who, in exploiting the vogue for dialect, were not fit to be considered artists at all: "we do not believe it is possible that it can last; and we hope that no more ministers or members of any other lawful profession will give up an honest trade for this whim of the public" (Oliphant 1895: 922). With the exception of *The Raiders*, which the *Evening Times* felt would "step at once into a foremost place among the novels of the modern national school" (17 March 1894), the Glasgow papers were equally unforgiving of Crockett and Maclaren. The *Herald* thought *The Stickit Minister* "a much over-praised book" (26 September 1895) and judged harshly of *The Lilac Sunbonnet*, commenting: "more is required of a good story than charming descriptions of scenery." The Glasgow papers were also at the centre of the accusations of plagiarism that were directed at Crockett, printing a number of reviews and letters that pointed out the similarity between his work and that of earlier books which Crockett had obviously trawled in search of local colour. Two anonymous letters printed in the *Herald* on 26 September 1895 and 12 October 1895 took up opposite positions on the question of Crockett's plagiarism. One correspondent pointed out remarkable instances of resemblance between *The Men of the Moss Hags* and three books of non-fiction, including Simpson's *Traditions of the Covenantors*; another argued that Crockett had transformed the material drawn from these books for his own artistic purposes.

In the review of *The Lilac Sunbonnet* quoted above, the *Herald* asserted that "Mr Crockett's peasants are sometime amusing; very often they are terribly tiresome, but once they are decidedly piquant, and that is when they plagiarise" (6 October 1894). When the same paper reviewed Maclaren's *Beside the Bonnie Brier Bush* just seven days later a similar charge of plagiarism was made. The task of reviewing two such books within a week prompted the paper to consider the development of what was by now a clearly identifiable genre of Scottish literature, though one as yet without a handy name to describe it:

> Mr Maclaren is a denizen of what may be called the literary parish of Barrie-cum-Crockett, and many of his pages are very pleasant reading, although all his characters, despite their living in Perthshire (as Mr Crockett's live in Galloway) are obviously cousins of the weavers of Thrums. Mr Barrie and his followers all look through the same window – but not all with the same glance; Mr Maclaren's glance is obviously an optimistic one [...] It is all idyllic but there are few Scotsmen knowing something of their own people who will believe in it at all. (13 October 1894)

The identifiable difference in "glance" between Barrie and his followers was a characteristic observation of early Scottish reviewers, who took the overtly idealist outlook of Maclaren in a more negative way than they had the realism of Barrie. The charge of imitation went hand-in-hand with the charge of plagiarism, showing the extent to which reviewers valued originality and artistic construction in their assessment of literary works. The *Herald*'s reviewer complained that "we should have a good deal more satisfaction in Mr Maclaren's pleasantry if we were sure it was not occasionally 'cauld kail het.' But some of his stories are certainly not new to print." The reviewer pointed out that the end of the chapter "Our Sermon-taster" was "very similar" to a passage in W.R. DeFann's *Seventy Years of Irish Life* and questioned the integrity of Maclaren's artistic achievement alongside that of Barrie:

> Where is all this to end? What one would like is that Mr Maclaren and other labourers in the same field, capable of admirable original work, should depict Scottish life *as they know it*. Some of them are not doing anything of the kind; and they are sweeping their note-books into print, and taking advantage of the renewed attention which Mr Barrie's books have directed to humble Scottish life. They are heedless of the fact that

any wandering is bound to be discovered. What need is there that such men should climb up behind Mr Barrie's dog-cart? (13 October 1894)

Not all the Scottish papers were against Crockett and Maclaren. The *Scotsman* considered that *The Raiders* would bring Crocket "at once into the front rank of the writers of the day who may be said to have founded among them a new school of Scottish romance".[5] Similarly, in its review of *Beside the Bonnie Brier Bush*, the paper commended Maclaren's "genuine gift of pathos" and "genuine gift of humour", and also found his depiction of character realistic:

He handles what may be called the domestic emotions with a power rare in modern fiction; and he understands thoroughly the religious aspects of that kind of Scottish character which is portrayed in the stories.[6]

The Glasgow papers, however, were noticeably less positive. When the *Herald* reviewed *The Days of Auld Langsyne* (1896) – the second dose of Drumtochty sketches – the judgement was unequivocal:

his book leaves one with the impression of having witnessed the working of a lucky vein to exhaustion. [...] Ian Maclaren, in the way of sentimentalising, really does not know where to stop, but moves gushingly on regardless alike of the facts of human nature and the canons of literary art. [...] Assuredly this is not Scottish nature, nor, indeed, is it the course of human life anywhere outside Drumtochty and the Sunday School books. Does any Scotchman, when in his tender moments, talk in this fashion? (7 November 1895)

Whereas six years earlier Barrie had been applauded for his realism and his restraint, Maclaren's books brought Scottish reviewers to judge harshly over the representation of Scottish life and character in fiction, so much so, that when the *Herald* came to review Henry Johnston's novel *Doctor Congalton's Legacy*, it praised its "admirable restraint in method – too rare a quality in the 'Kailyard' school" (26 March 1896).

Critical assault on the Kailyard thus only came about when a wealth of imitators followed Barrie's lead and provoked a critic like

---

[5] Quoted in an advertisement in the *Bookman*, April 1894.

[6] Quoted in an advertisement in *Bookman*, March 1895.

Millar into applying a derogatory label. In his later *Literary History of Scotland*, Millar confirmed that it was W.E. Henley who suggested the term, but the inspiration came from the epigraph in Maclaren's *Beside the Bonnie Brier Bush*:

"There grows a bonnier brier bush in our kail-yard
And white are the blossoms on't in our kail-yard"

As soon as Millar had applied his label the Glasgow papers seized on Kailyard as the word they had been looking for to describe a fictional genre. Although the *Herald* drew attention to Sabine Baring Gould's "distinct Dartmoor Kailyard flavour" when reviewing his *Dartmoor Idylls* (27 August 1896) the term took grip over Scottish fiction. Both the *Herald* and the *Evening Times* reviewed books by Scottish authors under the banner of Kailyard or Kailyard School throughout the second half of the decade and the term quickly acquired a pejorative edge. When reviewing a work by David Storrar Meldrum entitled *Greymantle and Gold Fringe*, the *Evening Times* concluded by saying that the author had "made a distinct addition to the literature of Scottish character at its best, and he will be a sour critic who discovers anything in it savouring of the weaknesses which have come to be slumped under the wide and not too well-defined epithet 'Kailyardism'" (26 April 1896). On 18 July 1896, the *Evening Times* announced "another addition to the kailyard literature" by Charles Aitken, "a well-known Vale of Leven man." One week later, however, the *Herald*, in its review of the work, poured scorn on what was patently an attempt to jump on a bandwagon:

It is Ian Maclaren watered to an unconscionable extent with the tears of many superfluous deathbeds. There are nine sketches in this book of 90 pages. In six of them there are eight deaths, all in the odour of sanctimoniousness. In none of them is there either plot or incident that could interest any person of the slightest intelligence, or character or observation of life or rural scenery. The book is simply written, and well printed, but it is difficult to see why it was written. (13 October 1894)

It was written because, for a time, authors and publishers recognised that there was a market for it, as there was for such volumes as John Menzies' *Our Toon and some of its People* (1894), Gordon Fraser's

The Whaups of Darley (1895), William Findley's *Ayrshire Idylls of other Days* (published under the pseudonym George Umber in 1896) and W.G. Tarbet's *In Oor Kailyard* (1897). The appearance of such volumes made even London critics tire of the Kailyard. William Wallace in the *Academy* called Fraser's book the "dregs of the Kailyard" and "one of the thinnest books that have had their origin in the new boom in Scottish fiction" (18 January 1896). The *Times* was particularly unforgiving about Tarbet's volume, which appears to be the only instance of an author actually using the word Kailyard in the title of his book:

His book is just like the other books of the species. We have the same canny people, with their humours, their sufferings, and their religious opinions. Mr Tarbet spells "to" as he ought to spell it, not "tae"; otherwise, for all that our critical instinct tells us, the work might be by Mr Ian Maclaren. [...] Is it easy to write this kind of book, so easy that every Scot can do it "if he abandons his mind to it"? (15 March 1897)

This is to touch only on those volumes that reached print. The archives of the publishing house of Macmillan revel the extent to which publishers were besieged with unpublishable manuscripts on similar themes. "I fancy people are growing rather weary of the kail-yard", wrote one Macmillan reader in February 1896, when confronted with another MS full of dialect. Neil Roy's "The Knights of the Mortar" was dismissed out of hand – "the whole Kailyard from Crockett upwards, or downwards, is nothing to it" – and J. McCartney's "The Learned Gowk" was also rejected:

This is a Scotch tale, and one of the Scotchest I have ever tried to read. Two young American girls spend a couple of months with some Scotch relations in a small Lowland town [...]. Every body talks all day long in the broadest Scotch, including the Yankee misses, when they are not singing Hail Columbia! And everybody is more or less of a sententious prig. [...] The mixture of the Kailyard and the star spangled banner is not very entertaining and the jocular parts of the dialogue are awful.[7]

As the number of imitations rose, the Kailyard novel became an established term in literary culture, allowing several writers to make

---

[7] The reports are dated 27 February 1896, 10 August 1896 and 7 January 1897. BL. Add. MS. 55977, 55954.

discreet – or indiscreet – use of its currency. In his novel *Redburn* (1895), Henry Ochiltree includes a chapter entitled "Beside the Bonnie Brier Buss" where an old "Grannie" tells her granddaughter of the "brier buss that smells sae sweetly" which was planted on the day when she first came to the farm of Redburn (Ochiltree 1895: 99). In a rather different vein, the detective novelist Clifford Ashdown (J. Austin Freeman) published a story entitled "The Kailyard Novel" in his collection *The Adventures of Romney Pringle* (1902). In this story Pringle, an eccentric private investigator, pretends to be a literary agent in order to disguise his covert operations. Unexpectedly, he receives a letter from an English pastor, who has resolved to write a Kailyard novel and intends to spend the summer on the Isle of Skye in order to acquaint himself with the Scots dialect, which he considers the only requirement to perform his task. Pringle is asked to find a replacement pastor to take up his vacated position. Unfortunately, the adventure itself carries the intrigue of the Kailyard novel no further.

The most striking contemporary response to the term, however, is an article entitled "An Interview with a Kailyard Novelist" by a writer signing himself T. Duncan published in the *Glasgow Herald* on 21 December 1895. Duncan records a chance meeting he had in London with Saunders McWhannel, a childhood friend from his home village of Drumwhinnie.[8] It emerges that Saunders had left his native place for London some years ago but had found success hard to come by and, as Duncan relates, "as we were all abject worshippers of success in Drumwhinnie we soon became content to forget Saunders' existence." It is with surprise, therefore, that Duncan encounters Saunders one day in London now lavishly dressed and frequenting fashionable clubs. Upon enquiring what has produced this dramatic turn in affairs, Saunders proudly announces: "I am a Kailyard novelist." In the long interview that follows, Saunders explains to Duncan that being a Kailyard novelist "is the brawest and easiest way o' makin' siller you are ever likely to run across":

---

[8] The names suggest that Crockett is the object of Duncan's satire. See the discussion in chapter 3.

"Oh! I just keep blethering awa' aboot a' the things that happened lang syne in Drumwhinnie. [...] A' that ye need to dae is to bring back to mind a' the auld clashes that were gaen aboot when you were a laddie at schule, and dress them up to hit the ideas o' the Cockney public."

Duncan, somewhat perplexed by all this, suggests that the "Cockney public" can hardly be expected to understand a word of the dialect, and Saunders replies:

"Neither they dae, but they like it a' better for that. The mair unintelligible it is the better they're pleased. I dinna ken the meanin' o' a wheen of the words I use mysell but I aye write wi' the Scotch Dictionary at my elbow."

That last remark, no doubt thought highly amusing, was, of course, prophetic, anticipating the artistic strategy Hugh MacDiarmid was to adopt in the twentieth century. The unintelligibility of the dialect is just one thing that explains the appeal according to Saunders McWhannel. He describes how easy it is to pretend that the population of Drumwhinnie are all humorous folk, something which strikes the narrator as dishonest. Saunders sticks to his guns:

"It's of nae consequence whether it exists or no. We maun purvey for the English public what the English public wants. They are awfu' pleased wi' it and the siller keeps rolling in."

The other principal agent which keeps the "siller" rolling in for Saunders is the "tear-drop": "we are awfu' for greeting in the Kailyard", he tells Duncan, and when he mentions his forthcoming novel "The Consumptive Probationer" he relates how he intends to "greet them a' blin'":

"[...] It'll bring tears to a North British Railway ticket-collector. The death-beds are a' just beautifu'. Ah! but its a gran' trade a Kailyard novelist, once you hae got a firm hand o' the machinary o' the teardrap."

Duncan's witty attack on Kailyard novels was written just six months after J.H. Millar had first applied the term. It shows how quickly Kailyard was absorbed into the popular vocabulary and how easily it acquired pejorative connotations. The criticisms of Kailyard

novels that Duncan makes in his sketch help bring into focus the
various subsequent attacks that have been made by other critics: the
ease with which novels could be produced; the sending-up of Scottish
people for swift financial gain; the cosmetic use of dialect; the ready
concession to the market; the betrayal of Scottish reality; the appeal to
an essentially "Cockney" – or rather Metropolitan – public; and the
misplaced emphasis on scenes of pathos. "I dinna see how it's
complimentary", Duncan concludes, in a phrase that unerringly
anticipates George Douglas Brown's famous remark in a letter that he
thought his novel *The House with the Green Shutters* "more
complimentary to Scotland" than "the sentimental slop of Barrie, and
Crockett, and Maclaren" (Veitch 1952: 153).

　　"An Interview with a Kailyard Novelist" shows that it was the
extent of imitation that altered the attitude among Scottish
commentators from positive to negative. At first Barrie was separated
off from Crockett, Maclaren and the others, but once the term
Kailyard gained a stranglehold in discussions of Scottish fiction he
was, in the words of one contemporary commentator, "brought
somewhat unfairly into the same gallery" (Rix 1897). A genre had
been identified and Barrie's role as precursor was too great to avoid
his being swept into its confines. Concern over the representation of
the nation and the demand for realist pictures of life in Scotland
overwhelmed his subsequent reputation within the context of Scottish
literature. The critical Kailyard had been invented.

IV

As these early reviews and articles show, the application of the
Kailyard term was prompted by certain critical anxieties about the
state of Scottish literature. If those anxieties had been anticipated in
Margaret Oliphant's review of *A Window in Thrums*, and expressed
satirically in T. Duncan's sketch in the *Glasgow Herald*, they were set
out authoritatively in the article that first applied the term. In "The
Literature of the Kailyard", J.H. Millar launched a wide-ranging
attack. As I mentioned in the introduction, although he looked upon
Barrie as the founder of a special and notable department in the

"'parochial' school of fiction", he makes a point of noting the "admirable qualities" of his work and reserves his more scathing judgement for Maclaren and (especially) Crockett. He dismisses both authors as "almost wholly the result of the modern method of reviewing" (Millar 1895: 393) and ridicules the way that both courted publicity and satisfied the "indecent curiosity of the public" by giving interviews about their lives and opinions – an aspect of contemporary literary culture that a periodical like the *New Review* would have looked upon with scorn. He criticises Maclaren's "diseased craving for the pathetic", finds Crockett "hopelessly at sea" when dealing with the upper classes and mocks his pretension to humour (Millar 1895: 385, 386). Most of all, however, he attacks Crockett's treatment of love, deploring what he calls the "perpetual flow of juicy bad-breeding which no American evangelist ever surpassed!" This was not a question of moral impropriety; Millar was "well aware that at the present day considerable license is granted to an author in this regard." What he objected to was Crockett's "clumsy and inartistic" language:

the very fact that authors are allowed a free hand imposes upon them a doubly stringent obligation to certain literary virtues: to tact, to reticence, to good feeling, to discretion. This obligation Mr Crockett consistently ignores; to these he is a total stranger. He touches courtship and love-making but to disfigure them with his heavy hand; he opens the sluices to an irresistible flood of nauseous and nasty philandering. (Millar 1895: 391)

The range of Millar's attack on Crockett and Maclaren provided the basis for the various criticisms that have since been made against Kailyard fiction and which have come to be embedded in the term. Chief among these was the attack on national representation, an issue that Millar discusses early on in his article and which quickly became integral to the Kailyard debate. As Millar makes clear, literature had the power to market and validate – particularly in the eyes of English readers – an authoritative identity for Scotland, something that made the accuracy of national representation a pressing critical concern. Millar noted that Barrie's writings were "eagerly devoured in England by people who, on the most charitable hypothesis, may possibly understand one word in three of his dialogue" and went on to summarise the likely effects wrought by the considerable sales of his books:

> and to the curious superstitions which the Southron breast has long nourished with regard to Scotland must now be added a new group of equally well-grounded beliefs; as, for example, that the Auld Lichts formed a large majority of the people of Scotland, and that the absorbing interest, if not the main occupation, of nine true-born Scotsmen out of ten is chatter about church officers, parleyings about precentors, babble about beadles, and maunderings about manses. (Millar 1895: 384)

The international success of Barrie's books, and even more so those of Crockett and Maclaren, raised this concern among Scottish critics that a partial, unrepresentative view of Scottish life was being marketed to an international audience. In 1897, John Buchan, then a student at Oxford University, proposed to the Oxford Union "This House Condemns the Kailyard School of Novelists". His speech was reported as "a striking exposition of the nature of the real Scotland, the romance and the pity of its history, which he placed in strong contrast with the narrow, parochial view of Scottish character spread by these writers" (Lownie 1995: 53).

It is noticeable that this issue of representation becomes more central to Millar's concerns in his *Literary History of Scotland* published eight years later. In this book Millar once again separates off Barrie from those writers who have "played 'the sedulous ape' to *him*". Although he observed a "cynical disregard of true art" in *The Little Minister*, he judges that Barrie was not merely "immeasurably greater" than these writers but "also greater from a literary point of view than the ablest of his countrymen who have betaken themselves to literature" (Millar 1903: 656). Significantly, he applauded the realism of Barrie's early work, arguing that he "portrayed human character as it presented itself in a Scotch provincial town with great fidelity and humour". Barrie's successors, however, were judged sorely principally for their misrepresentation of Scottish life:

> If the English and American public chose to pay for what they took to be accurate representations of the Caledonian on his native heath, why, it was no business of any "brither Scot" to dispel the illusion. (Millar 1903: 659)

In an article first published in 1899 but revised in 1904, the novelist J.H. Findlater articulated these concerns more strongly. To Findlater, novelists had fallen into a rut of national character-drawing, which could be produced to order "as a pudding is compounded from a recipe". Of the various national types, "none had been more thoroughly established in the popular mind" than the Scottish:

> To many Englishman there is but one Scotsman – the fictitious Scot – the Scot of fiction. He is a peculiarly odious person: grim, unmannerly, over-religious, hypocritical, grasping, coarse and miserly – a being to be shunned and feared alike. (Findlater [1899] 1904: 92)

Findlater outlined the "conventional life-story" of this "phenomenal and fictitious Scot" which, she argued, "with a few variations, has been described over and over again in fiction":

> He generally begins life as an intelligent herd-boy; then he has to go to school, so that that awful stock figure the Dominie may "walk on." A Scotch story without a dominie is extremely rare – I can remember eight dominies of curious similarity as I write. From the village school the herd-hero migrates to London with strange insistency. Before doing so, however, he must have fallen in love with the laird's daughter: this is a necessary part of the construction of the tale in every case. Arrived in London, the extraordinary career of this prodigy begins: the woolsack looms ahead; he maintains in the meantime all the frugal habits learned from home, always grudging even a sixpence for his own use but habitually posting his weekly savings to his saintly mother. (Those Scottish mothers). Struggles and parsimony are of course always in fiction crowned by success, whatever may be the case in fact; so we very speedily find our hero returning rich and distinguished to his native land and village to marry the laird's daughter, rescue the dominie from drink and despair, and fold the sainted mother to his heart in an ecstasy of filial devotion. Throughout this career the Scot of fiction keeps up the habit of church attendance in Babylon the great, and enters upon long discussions, in season and out, of predestination and election. (Findlater [1899] 1904: 93–4)

The conventional life story outlined here, like Findlater's conventional "Scot of fiction", is very much a composite creation, composed from various novels and involving far more than the fiction of Barrie, Crockett and Maclaren. Indeed, the features she outlines are more characteristic of those novels of Swan and Hardy mentioned by Margaret Oliphant. The commercial and critical success of Crockett and Maclaren must, however, have prompted Findlater to protest against a trend in Scottish fiction that she traced back to much earlier in the century. She places the blame for the stereotyping of Scottish character on John Galt, who, as well as being considered the "forerunner of the modern school of Scottish writers", is charged with having "gone far to establish the unpleasant popular idea of the Scottish character." Stevenson, likewise, is charged with propagating the "belief in Scotch meanness" and George Douglas Brown with committing "a libel not on Scotland only but on human nature" in trying to make us believe that the characteristics of the inhabitants of Barbie are universal and "may be found in many Scotsmen". Findlater found *The House with the Green Shutters* as false as *A Window in Thrums* – "they cannot both be true". Like Millar, she qualifies her criticism of Barrie by stating that she considered his books "delightful" and that she regretted quoting from them "in a seeming spirit of derision". Nevertheless, she found his emphasis on tenderness false in a comparison with Scott, who, as "the true observer of Scottish manners and characteristics" recognised that "the average Scot is nothing if not uncivil."

It is important to stress that what is being objected to here is not the realism of the work of Barrie, Galt, and Douglas Brown, but the status of that realism as *representative* of Scottish life. The emphasis is not primarily on fictional technique but on representation; on the way a picture of Scotland is marketed to an outside (and specifically English) audience. Moreso even than Millar's article, Findlater's essay points up the close relationship that existed between Scottish literature and Scottish national identity. I have argued elsewhere that in the nineteenth century the images of Scotland that were marketed through the popular and critical reception of Burns and Scott, as well as through tourism and the visual arts, were predominantly of literary provenance (Nash 2000). Literature had come to stand as the marker for Scottish national identity and every work of fiction carried the potential to validate a picture of Scottish life as a whole. It is for this reason that we find the local characteristics of the work of Barrie, Crockett and Maclaren largely ignored by critics who are more concerned with the way these characteristics could be taken by outsiders to stand for the whole of Scotland.

In Findlater's article Crockett and Maclaren are singled out for their over-emphasis on predestination and election. She considered their habit of making every character in their novels debate doctrinal points to be "a perfectly false and ridiculous misrepresentation":

You may travel from one end of Scotland to another and never hear predestination or election mentioned, yet conventions die so hard, that nothing will convince your average Englishman of this, and he will support his belief by pointing to certain novels. (Findlater [1899] 1904: 98–9)

These points about the inclusiveness of national representation were also made by R.B. Cunninghame Graham – another important contemporary critic of the Kailyard. In his article "A Survival", first published in the *Saturday Review* in 1896, Graham deplored the small range of interest covered by contemporary fiction and the limited options available for the Scottish writer. In order to be popular, he argued, Scottish writers had to adopt "the ruling fashion"; this meant they had "if possible [to] be clergymen and treat entirely of weavers, idiots, elders of churches, and of all those without aid" and "write a dialect which his reader cannot understand." (Cunninghame Graham [1896] 1899: 156). Graham did not want "Englishmen" to believe that "the entire Scotch nation is composed of ministers, elders, and maudlin whiskified physicians", but the success of Kailyard fiction had created that assumption (Cunninghame Graham [1896] 1899: 158). The "large sales and cheap editions" of the "Kailyarders" had created a situation where:

to-day a Scotchman stands confessed a sentimental fool, a canting cheat, a grave sententious man, dressed in a "stan o' black", oppressed with the tremendous difficulties of the jargon he is bound to speak, and above all weighted down with the responsibility of being Scotch. (Cunninghame Graham [1896] 1899: 152)

Graham's main concern in this article, however, was the assumption that might be drawn that everybody in Scotland came from the same religious stock and held the same religious inclinations as characters in Kailyard fiction. He concluded his article by drawing from his own experience characters who proved that "there still exist some few remains of the pre-Knoxian and pre-bawbee days, though fallen into decay" (Cunninghame Graham [1896] 1899: 164). Once again, it is not specifically the realism of Kailyard fiction that matters in this debate so much as the representative status of that realism. The anxiety among the contemporary critics of Kailyard was that the diversity of Scottish life was not being given cultural voice. William Wallace lamented the absence of a novel "representing Scottish life in all its breadth" (Wallace 1894: 50); Millar complained that "the 'Kailyard' writers, after all, have touched a mere fringe of the population" (Millar 1903: 680) and Findlater provided a succinct denunciation of Kailyard when she wrote: "the Scottish people remain" (Findlater 1904: 109).

By the end of the nineteenth century critics were beginning to demand that Scottish writers widen their scope and set their novels within a contemporary Scotland. Findlater considered that "the time is ripe for a new Scotch novelist who will write of Scotsmen as they are, and not as they are supposed to be" and Millar hoped that "some one else may have realised the immense amount of stuff, as yet practically untouched and lying ready to the novelist's hand, in the life of the Scottish professional, commercial, and middling classes" (Millar 1903: 681). In 1894 William Wallace, who had provided welcoming reviews of Barrie's early works in the *Academy*, drew attention to the absence of a contemporary setting as the main characteristic of "Scottish fiction of to-day". He argued that the tendency of Mrs Oliphant, Stevenson, Barrie, Henry Johnston, Sophie F. F. Veitch and Annie S. Swan was "to look askance at, if not to shirk, Scotland of to-day, and to let their imaginations have scope in the Scotland of yesterday, and still more of the day before yesterday" (Wallace 1894: 43).[9]

It was not absolutely the case that Scottish fiction in the final decades of the century ignored the urban milieu and shirked the "Scotland of to-day". Annie S. Swan did in fact write a story about a

---

[9] Wallace (1843–1921) was a Burns scholar who completed a new edition of Chambers's *Life and Works of Robert Burns* in 1896 and wrote *Burns and Mrs Dunlop* (1898). Having worked on the staff of the *Echo* and a number of other London papers, he became assistant editor of the *Glasgow Herald* in 1889 and then editor in 1906. He was, therefore, involved in providing the forum for the satirical attack on Kailyard, "An Interview with a Kailyard Novelist", discussed above.

strike in a Clydeside shipbuilding yard, *Who Shall Serve* (1891); Charles Gibbon, a prolific three-volume novelist of Scottish descent, published *A Princess of Jutedom* (1886), set in Dundee, and Sarah Tytler's *St Mungo's City* (1885) was set in Glasgow and dealt in part with the textile industry. Furthermore, as William Donaldson has shown, a whole host of serials novels with contemporary settings were published in various Scottish newspapers. The greater commercial success of the novels of Crockett and Maclaren, however, meant that the prevailing impression of Scottish fiction at this time was exactly as Wallace characterised it. In a later article in the *Bookman*, Wallace anticipated "the rise of a school of fiction dealing exclusively and even realistically with the Scotland of to-day" (Wallace 1900: 138). If he had lived to read George Blake's lament on the absence of realistic treatments of nineteenth-century Scotland, Wallace would have realised his hopes were not to be fulfilled.

Some twenty years after the contemporary Kailyard critics complained of the false representation of Scottish life, G. Gregory Smith began his book on the character and influence of Scottish literature by stating that "Englishmen think they know their Scot [...] In his literature [...] he stands so self-confessed that any man of intelligence can [...] discern the true Scottish note" (Smith 1919: 1). It is this process of validation of Scottish national identity that lies at the heart of the Kailyard term. Andrew Noble argues that Kailyard was "the notion that Scotland was an ahistorical collection of discrete if somewhat indiscreet small towns" (Noble 1985: 81). It is because Kailyard provides a "definition of Scotland" (Nairn [1977] 1981: 158) that it has been seen as so dangerous; that Angus MacDonald can refer to its "insidious poison" (Macdonald 1933: 156) and Gillian Shepherd can accuse the writers of "attempted national infanticide" (Shepherd 1988: 317). These accusations, cased in extraordinarily strong vocabulary, do not indicate the corrupting power of the rhetoric of individual writers; rather they signal the status which Scottish literature acquired as an indicator and commercial marketer of national identity. It has been largely within this preoccupation with national representation that the fiction of Barrie, Crockett and Maclaren was discussed in the twentieth century, and it is to the work of these writers that we must now turn.

Chapter Two

Regionalism, Representation and the Art of J.M. Barrie

An amusing and somewhat significant remark was recently overheard in the salon of Mudie's Library. Said a young lady, of the type upon which publishers of the ordinary three-volume novel flourish, "Will you please send me a new book, something very nice and interesting you know; but please not Scotch, everything is so Scotch just now" (Butcher 1897: 307).

I

In his social history of the English novel from 1875–1914, Peter Keating argues that "it was Scotland that came for a few years at the end of the century to typify regionalism in fiction" (Keating: 1989: 337). Much of the success of Barrie, Crockett and Maclaren undoubtedly turned on the prevailing taste for local colour. Reviewing Maclaren's *Beside the Bonnie Brier Bush*, the *Times* concluded: "Few things are more remarkable in the recent history of our literature, than the rise of a new school of Scottish fiction, drawing its inspiration from locality and national character" (19 January 1895). Regional fiction became a popular genre at the end of the century. The bibliographer Lucien Leclaire classifies the period after 1870 as "The Regional Novel Proper" and K.D.M. Snell notes that output of regional novels expanded rapidly after 1885 (Snell 1998: 270). Rural settings dominated and the use of dialect as a means of enhancing realism was common.

It is important to note, however, that the period at the end of the century also marked a change in attitude towards the regional or provincial in fiction. In 1871 George Eliot could subtitle *Middlemarch* "A Story of Provincial Life" without any fear that her work would be dismissed as parochial or marginal. Robin Gilmour has argued that the respectability of the regional novel diminished under the influence of Matthew Arnold, whose theories on provincialism were expressed in essays such as "The Literary Influence of Academies" (1864):

Arnold's formulation of Culture as a transcendent value is a crucial development, because it drove a wedge between regionalism and culture, stigmatising the one as enfeebled provincialism, and raising the other above the claims of time and place. (Gilmour 1989: 57)

Only after Arnold does the word "provincial" acquire the pejorative connotations it has come to hold. Implicit in the construction of "Culture as a transcendent value" is what Snell describes as "an assumed metropolitan arbitration of taste, the superiority of the metropolitan people over that of the merely 'local' person, whose criteria are 'only' those of the locality" (Snell 1998: 48).

This structural dynamic to regional fiction can be witnessed in the early critical reception of Barrie and his followers. The *London Quarterly Review* considered that *Auld Licht Idylls* would "introduce Southern folk to some quaint characters and customs which they will not easily forget" (December 1889) and another commentator shows how Barrie, Crockett and Maclaren were seen as articulating regional life for an outside audience:

Certainly within the last few years we have witnessed a new departure in fiction. We have been introduced to those who live "far from the madding crowd's ignoble strife," and to our surprise, we have found that their life is not entirely monotonous and wearisome [...] Thrums and Drumtochty and the Grey Galloway land are as familiar as those frequented holiday haunts to which we turn in longing desire, when the tired and jaded mind calls loudly for quiet and for rest. (Butcher 1897: 307)

The approval here is couched in terms that are at best condescending and at worst patronising. Regional writers at the end of the century faced this dilemma. Not only could their stories be interpreted as historical documents but they could also be seen as perpetuating stereotypes or disparaging the region. As we have already seen, this was a significant point for Scottish critics. Snell considers that "an important effect of regional fiction has been the articulation of regional stereotypes", often "through disinclination to break with tried and tested formulae" (Snell 1998: 36). The issues of stereotyping and exploitation of a formula are just two of the criticisms that lie embedded in the Kailyard term.

Linked to these issues is the use of dialect in fiction. Regional novels at the end of the century often depended for their distinctiveness on the extensive use of dialect. An article published in *Literature* in 1898 identified Kailyard fiction as part of "The Domination of Dialect" (14 May 1898) and the issue soon became a topic of satire. An article in the *Glasgow Evening Times* entitled "A Cockney's estimate of Crockett" cynically mocked the success of Kailyard by commenting: "there may be something else in the work of Messrs Crockett, Maclaren and Co. besides the dialect, but I for one have never been able to find it" (4 February 1897). Accusing the "Kailyarders" of palming off "a terrific amount of slushy rubbish on the public", the writer advised Crockett to "stick to your dialect [...] and the public will mistake your bad spelling for humour and pathos".[1] The biggest insult came in a *Punch* cartoon of 1895 entitled "The Latter-Day Taste." This featured a publisher being offered a collection of short stories and asking if they are "written in any unintelligible Scotch dialect". "Certainly not," replies the author. "Then", says the publisher, "I'm afraid they're of not the slightest use to us" (7 December 1895).

Scottish literature has a special relationship with the regional novel; indeed the origins of the genre have often been traced to the fiction of Walter Scott. More specifically, the conditions of cultural production that I detected in Chapter 1, where imaginative literature was closely tied to the recording of social history, meant that outside readers could easily respond to fictional depictions of regional Scottish life as documentary accounts. Furthermore, as Cairns Craig points out:

Regionalism is an almost all-embracing category in relation to the Scottish novel: simply by virtue of *being* Scottish, almost all Scottish novels will be identified as regional within the traditions of the *English* novel, rather than representing an alternative national tradition. (Craig 1998: 221)

As I discussed in the previous chapter, most of the criticism of the fiction of Crockett and Maclaren by contemporary Scottish writers was levelled at its status as representative of Scottish reality. Where a nation is involved it is perhaps inevitable that region is collapsed into

---

[1] It should be noted again that this contemporary commentator does not include Barrie with Crockett and Maclaren.

nation and the presentation of one part of national life taken to represent the whole.

In his recent overview of themes in the regional novel, Snell lays stress on the dangers of approaching regional fiction as a resource for history:

it is clear then that regional fiction is not an historical "resource" in the same form as historical "evidence", that it does not have a mimetic function, representing the structures of a pre-existent reality. Its role in representing "things as they are", for example, is often complicated through a juxtaposition with the rather different function of representing a didactic model of how things ought to be. (Snell 1995: 18)

Any account of the rhetoric and art of regional fiction has to begin from this premise. Nevertheless, when discussing the representation of place in Kailyard fiction it cannot be forgotten that one of the main reasons why this fiction became notorious was because of its representation of Scottish life. Whether writers intend their stories to have a mimetic function or not, the fact remains that regional fiction carries with it the capacity to be understood in such terms.

This point is particularly important when discussing fiction of the Victorian period, because the distinction between fact and fiction in literary discourse was not absolutely clear. Kenneth Graham notes that in criticism of the novel during the period 1865–1900 "there is a fairly common inability […] to distinguish between fiction and history, or biography." Kipling, for example, was "often valued mainly as a recorder of facts about Anglo-Indian society" (Graham 1965: 13). The absence of any explicit demarcation between fiction and non-fiction meant that any literature dealing with a recognisable geographical place was bound to be seen to some extent as a documentary, factual account. The important point is that this is of greater importance to Scotland than it is to Dorset or Devon, to take two obvious examples. Turning their regions into the pastoral world of *Under the Greenwood Tree* or the romantic fairy land of *Lorna Doone* was not likely to result in Hardy or Blackmore being seen as betrayers of the Dorset or Devonshire cause. Where the literary representation of a nation is concerned, however, accuracy of representation is more pertinent. Noticeably, critics of Irish literature adopted the same position as Kailyard critics. A correspondent to *Literature* in 1900 wrote in complaint of the fictional misrepresentation of the Irish peasant, and argued that it would be more valuable if the true "drab-coloured picture" was presented instead (5 May 1900). There was an anxious need for realism within fictional representations of the nation.

The early Thrums stories of J.M. Barrie – *Auld Licht Idylls* (1888), *A Window in Thrums* (1889) and *The Little Minister* (1891) – clearly fall within the context of regional fiction and were received by critics as realistic representations of Scottish life. In what follows, however, I want to argue that the rhetorical strategy of these early works is such that they do not attempt to give a documentary account of life in Scotland. As I will argue, the contexts of regionalism and Kailyard have resulted in the artistic strategies of Barrie's early fiction largely being ignored.

II

The stories in *Auld Licht Idylls* are based on the childhood memories of Barrie's mother and are set in the mid-nineteenth century. They are narrated by the dominie from the nearby glen and tell of life in "Thrums" – Barrie's fictional name for his native town of Kirriemuir. The stories focus in particular on the experiences of the Auld Licht congregation – a fiercely puritanical group that had seceded from the Established Kirk in 1733 but which had almost completely died out at the time of Barrie's writing.

It is clear that the narrator writes from the contemporary standpoint of the 1880s because he places the 1733 secession "a hundred and fifty years ago" (Barrie 1888: 60). On the other hand it is made absolutely clear that the picture described is not a contemporary one. The two main forces that shape the community's way of life – Auld Licht Presbyterianism and the handloom industry – are both presented as belonging to a past world: "There are few Auld Licht communities in Scotland nowadays" and "Until twenty years ago" a handloom filled "every other room" but now there are "two factories in the town" (Barrie 1888: 9, 11–12). The criticism that Barrie's fiction is unrepresentative of Scottish life in the late-nineteenth century is thus largely beside the point because he is openly writing about a time set in the past. Maurice Lindsay's judgement that the Kailyard writers – of whom he considers Barrie the "high priest" – " tried to give validity to a domestic present the outlines of which were already sixty years out of date when they began to write" is only one example of this widespread misjudgement (Lindsay 1961: 120). The charge remains, however, of whether Barrie writes of this world with no acknowledgement that it has past. But, as Eric Anderson has argued, *Auld Licht Idylls* is a series of vignettes illustrative of social change" (Anderson 1979: 132) and the presentation of a community in transition is a central part of the text.

Most of the impressions of social change come through the observations of the effects on the community of the decline of the handloom industry. "A railway line runs into Thrums now" and the town is "nowadays an agricultural centre of some importance" (Barrie 1888: 24, 37). The changes have brought shifts in the social life of the community. The account of the old post office illustrates how the simple innovation of the pillar box brought new codes of privacy and changes in the interaction of the community. Gone are the "sensational days of the post office", when "the letters were conveyed officially in a creaking old cart from Tilliedrum" and when the postmistress surreptitiously steamed open the letters (Barrie 1888: 24). There is also a growing interest in literature, books and the wider cultural world. In the past the postmistress kept a "bookseller's shop" where "the supply of books corresponded exactly to the lack of demand for them", but now the *Saturday Review*, the *People's Journal* and even a book of Darwin's can be found in the bothy (Barrie 1888: 51–2).

The emphasis is often on the erosion of a way of life by the infiltration of outside influences into the community. The old dominie, whose schoolhouse is now "a domicile for cattle", detests the modern improvements in the education system and sees the School Inspector from Oxford as his "natural enemy" (Barrie 1888: 132, 141). The changes have affected the town's environs as well. The lives of the "farmer-weavers" in the nearby glen, who were forced to combine two trades simply to survive, have been uprooted. The decline of the handloom industry has brought about the decline of their farms and a subsequent migration away from the glen:

When there was no longer a market for the produce of the hand-loom these farms had to be given up, and thus it is that the old school is not the only house in our weary glen around which gooseberry and currant bushes, once tended by careful hands, now grow wild. (Barrie 1888: 135)

The book abounds in such images of decay which generate the nostalgic tone, but at this stage in Barrie's career the dominant tone is humour. It must be asked to what extent Barrie turns his characters into caricatures. He certainly presents the idiosyncracies of the Auld Lichts comically. Take the description of the behaviour of Miss McQuhatty, an old woman who nearly "split the Auld Licht kirk" over the minister's introduction of the "run line" method of delivering the psalm:

Miss McQuhatty protested against this change, as meeting the devil half way, but the minister carried his point, and ever after that she rushed ostentatiously from the church the moment a psalm was given out, and remained behind the door until the singing was finished, when she returned, with a rustle, to her seat. Run line had on her the effect of the reading of the Riot Act. (Barrie 1888: 62–3)

In this instance the humour depends on the eccentricity of an old religious type; in the case of Snecky Hobart – who scaled the wall of his garden because he did not know there was a gate – it arises from the character's ignorance. In both cases the charge of exploitation stands but Barrie's comedy does not ridicule. As Eric Anderson notices, his humour "characteristically catches the reader by surprise, the sentences finishing in other manner than he has been led to expect" (Anderson 1979: 132). An example of this comes in the chapter "The Old Dominie" where we learn that "in its best scholastic days", the old school house "sent barefooted lads to college who helped to hasten the disruption" (Barrie 1888: 132). We anticipate a celebration of the virtues of the Scottish education system but the humour undercuts the expectation. The comic effect has much to do with the economical style of the writing. Barrie's qualities as a prose stylist have been underestimated – indeed largely ignored – by commentators. The actual writing in *Auld Licht Idylls* is impressive in the taut, crisp way in which it presents the characters and habits of the Auld Lichts.

F.R. Hart has argued that Kailyard fiction is "chiefly Victorian pastoral, sometimes neopagan (Crockett), sometimes elegiac (Maclaren), and sometimes ironic (Barrie)" (Hart 1978: 115). But whilst certainly there is irony in *Auld Licht Idylls* there is nothing pastoral about Barrie's treatment of the farming community. In his description of the bothy system, the narrator draws attention to the changes that have taken place in the way farm labourers are housed:

"Hands" are not huddled together nowadays in squalid barns more like cattle than men and women, but bothies in the neighbourhood of Thrums are not yet things of the past. [...] A few decades ago as many as fifty labourers engaged for the harvest had to be housed in the farm out-houses on beds of straw. There was no help for it, and men and women had to congregate in these barns together. Up as early as five in the morning, they were generally dead tired by night; and, miserable though this system of herding them together was, they took it like stoics, and their very number served as a moral safeguard. Nowadays the harvest is gathered in so quickly, and machinery does so much that used to be done by hand, that this crowding of labourers together, which was the bothy system at its worst, is nothing like what it was. (Barrie 1888: 48–9)

The past is not afforded uncritical nostalgic approval. Instead, the fading lifestyle of the bothy labourers is projected as one of harsh struggle. As yet there is very little of the sentimental Barrie so renounced by critical opinion.

Another charge frequently made against Barrie is that he glosses over the more unsavoury side of his material. Certainly he was no believer in the techniques of French naturalism but it is hard to mount a charge of evasion in relation to *Auld Licht Idylls*. As has often been pointed out, the use of the word "idylls" in the title is ironic, for there is nothing idyllic about Thrums or Barrie's manner of presentation. Life for the Auld Lichts is one of poverty "and their last years were generally a grim struggle with the workhouse" (Barrie 1888: 11–12). Violence is never very far from the surface and, as Anderson notes, it bubbles up in the description of the salmon-poaching at the end of chapter 2. When the neighbouring town break the Fast Day in "The Auld Lichts in Arms" it leads to open warfare, which is described in language that is as unsparing as the descriptions are explicit:

A stranger in the Tenements in the afternoon would have noted more than one draggled youth, in holiday attire, sitting on a doorstep with a wet cloth to his nose; and passing down the Commonty, he would have had to step over prostrate lumps of humanity from which all shape had departed. [...] It was in the square that the two parties, leading their maimed and blind, formed in force; Tilliedrum thirsting for its opponents blood, and Thrums humbly accepting the responsibility of punching the Fast Day breakers into the ways of rectitude. [...] The moment six o'clock struck, the upper mass broke its bonds and flung itself on the living barricade. There was a clatter of heads and sticks, a yelling and a groaning, and then the invaders bursting through the opposing ranks, fled for Tilliedrum. Down the Tanage brae and up the Brae-head they scurried, half a hundred avenging spirits in pursuit. (Barrie 1888: 121–2)

"On the Tilliedrum Fast Day", continues the narrator, "I have tasted blood myself" and with descriptions like these it is easy to understand how one critic judged: "it is a far cry from the demure and prim manners of Mrs. Gaskell's ladies to the rough vigour of Thrums" (Moffat 1910: 21).

"The Auld Lichts in Arms" concludes with an account of the meal-mob riots of the 1830s, where the people rose in revolt against the farmers who were increasing the price of meal. Again, the violence of the popular unrest is strongly evoked through the language:

The difference between the farmers and the town had resolved itself into an ugly and swollen hate [...]. The men, who were of various denominations, were armed with sticks, blunderbusses, anything they could snatch up at a moment's notice [...]. Some ugly cuts were given and received, and heads as well as ribs were broken. (Barrie 1888: 126–9)

Several reviewers criticised Barrie for the explicitness of his realism. The reviewer for the *Spectator* thought the picture too one-sided:

Auld Lichtism may seem petty and pitiable, and yet it must have had its redeeming virtues [...]. Mr. Barrie's picture of it is incomplete, because he does not give sufficient prominence to the spirituality and the faith which lay behind its censoriousness and poverty. (5 May 1888)

Only a few years later, the fiction of Ian Maclaren would lead commentators to make exactly the opposite criticism, that too much emphasis was given to matters of faith and spirituality.

Even accounting for this current of realism and the depiction of social change in *Auld Licht Idylls* there is a danger of overstating the relevance of social realism as a criterion for evaluation of this text, and even more so for Barrie's subsequent works. Closer examination of his early texts reveals that the rhetorical strategy employed is deliberately and consciously artificial. In his fiction Barrie gradually moved away from forms of realism towards a preoccupation with creativity and the construction of fictional reality – concerns that would find their richest expression in his plays and the various texts of *Peter Pan*. Inevitably, given the Kailyard context and the vogue for regional fiction, criticism of Barrie's fiction has focused too heavily on the extent to which it represents Scottish life. The subsequent international success of Crockett and Maclaren enforced this tendency as accuracy of national representation became the main critical concern. As a result, the artistic strategies of Barrie's early works have been downplayed. We can begin to understand these strategies if we look closely at the way *Auld Licht Idylls* was composed.

The book grew out of articles that Barrie had previously published in various London newspapers. Most of these appeared in the *St James's Gazette* and *Home Chimes* in a short flurry from November 1884 to March 1885. Shortly after moving to London, however, on 28 March 1885, Barrie abandoned the subject. In May he made a proposal to the firm of Macmillan for a book based on the articles but was dissuaded. He had been given an introduction to Alexander Macmillan by David Masson, his old Professor of Rhetoric and English literature at Edinburgh. On 6 May 1885, however, Macmillan wrote to Barrie:

I submitted your papers on the Auld Lichts to an English literary friend who has whole sympathy with, and knowledge of Scotland and its literature & thought. He sees no likelihood of even a small book proving attractive enough to an English audience to give any hope of an adequate sale. These short articles fulfil he thinks all the conditions that are hopeful.[2]

It was not until he had been discovered by William Robertson Nicoll over two years later that Barrie returned to the Auld Licht theme. Nicoll commissioned new sketches for *The British Weekly* and persuaded Barrie to make a book out of the material.

---

[2] British Library Add. MS 55419, fol. 1122.

Auld Licht Idylls has a diffuse quality that betrays its ancestry very clearly, but the changes Barrie made to the stories as he revised them for book publication are substantial and significant.[3] Chief amongst these was the insertion of long passages of dialogue in Scots and the addition of one complete story, "The Courting of T'nowhead's Bell". Barrie later revealed that he had found it difficult to get editors to accept articles containing Scots:

The magazines, Scotch and English, would have nothing to say to me – I think I tried them all with "The Courting of T'nowhead's Bell" but it never found shelter until it got within book-covers. (Barrie 1896c: viii)

Barrie's use of Scots has applauded for its "exceptional skill" in reproducing the pronunciation, vocabulary and idiom of the Angus region but criticised for its lack of social and generational differentiation (McClure 1995: 88–9). On occasions the meanings of Scots words are provided in parentheses in the text, a practice which is also found in some of George MacDonald's novels. Emma Letley considers this "a parading of linguistic local colour" (Letley 1988: 230) but it is worth pointing out that Barrie disliked this custom which was probably a requirement of his publishers. In 1892, he told J.A. Manson, his editor at Cassell and a fellow Scot, that "on the whole I don't care to insert meanings of Scotch words".[4] The artistic value of the Scots language was clearly something that Barrie saw as important to his stories.

For the most part, the newspaper sketches operate within an historical and factual paradigm that is loosened in the book version. In his revision of the chapter "The Old Dominie" Barrie removed a section from his original article in the *British Weekly* where he declared his sketch to be "no exaggeration picture, but a true flash into conditions of Scottish education twenty years ago" (16 September 1887). Similarly, in the story of "The Battle of Cabbylatch" discussed above, he omitted two paragraphs from the opening of the article that appeared in the *St James's Gazette* on 25 May 1885. Both of these had

---

[3] For a full bibliographical and textual analysis, see Nash (1998).

[4] Unpublished ALS to J.A. Manson, 24 January 1892 (New York Public Library).

served to place the story in a more precise time and space. The piece
begins:

The times are bad, trade is much depressed, there are far too many idle hands in the
community, and a vast deal of poverty and distress. But we ought not to forget that in
days not very far distant the lot of the poor was much harder than it is now. The story
of the fight at Cabbylatch illustrates a state of things very prevalent a few scores years
ago.

The style here is unmistakeably that of the journalist, and the
comparison between past and present places the story in a paradigm of
historical fact. In *Auld Licht Idylls* the rigidity of that paradigm is
loosened. As I have noted, throughout the book it is clear that the
stories are set in the past but it is never a precisely located past.
Similarly, Thrums and its surroundings are unmistakably Kirriemuir
and Forfarshire, but the geography is never explicitly set out. By
contrast, the newspaper article continues with a paragraph that locates
the story in a geographical framework which is designed to appeal to
the reader's armchair knowledge of Scotland:

The tourist seeking to reach Balmoral from the south by the shortest and most difficult
known route would leave the train at Forfar or Glamis and continue his journey on
foot or on horseback. In either case he would have to traverse the memorable field of
Cabbylatch – a low lying plot in the valley of Strathmore.

As Ian Carter reminds us, the end of the nineteenth century was a
period when Balmoralism was fervent and when Scotland was
becoming more of a tourist destination than ever before (Carter 1976:
3–4). Barrie's decision to delete all mention of Balmoral – another
reference was cut from the end of the sketch that became "The
Schoolhouse", the first chapter of *Auld Licht Idylls* – suggests that he
did not want his book to be reduced to that easy context.

In loosening the historical framework of his newspaper sketches
Barrie altered the narrative stance. In "An Auld Licht Community",
the very first article published in the *St James's Gazette* (17
November 1884), the narrator emerges as an outsider, new to
Scotland, reporting on the characteristics of an alien land:

Scotland had not been long known to me before I reached the conclusion that the scene of back-bent poverty-laden natives of the smaller towns, whose last years are a struggle with the workhouse, almost invariably constitute an Auld Licht congregation, of which a very young man is the minister.

This passage did not find its way into the book and nor did remarks like this: "the discreet man who sojourns in Scotland does on Sunday as Scotchmen do, without asking questions." As a result of these alterations, the identity and status of the narrator becomes more complex. Whereas in the articles he is an outsider, in *Auld Licht Idylls* (and even more so in *A Window in Thrums*) Barrie makes him both insider and outsider. He alternates between "we" and "they" when describing the community's characteristics and acts as a mediator for the reader, introducing the audience to the alien life of the Auld Lichts. But his role is an ambivalent one. Although he points up the trivialities of the community he also defends their profundities. As Cairns Craig suggests, this "strange ambivalence between the narrator and his subject-matter accounts for much of the tone of Barrie's writing" (Craig 1999: 59). He is thoroughly anglicised – as any dominie would be – and does not use the language of "these parts", placing his Scots words in inverted commas. But he is also a provincial, cut-off from the metropolitan world of the School Inspector, "fresh from Oxford", whose visit is impending: "I wonder what he would say if he saw me today digging myself out of the schoolhouse with the spade I now keep for the purpose in my bedroom" (Barrie 1888: 4).

The transforming role of the narrator helps place into perspective Barrie's relationship to his material and allows us to observe the way he constructs a picture of a fictional community in his early works. Although the narrator of *Auld Licht Idylls* is the dominie, at this stage in Barrie's evolving conception of Thrums he is not Gavin Ogilvy. "Gavin Ogilvy" was the pseudonym that Barrie used for his articles and stories in *The British Weekly* but he did not use that name for the earlier sketches in the *St James's Gazette* and *Home Chimes* (which were printed anonymously) from which most of the chapters in *Auld Licht Idylls* were compiled. This explains why in *Auld Licht Idylls* the narrator does not refer to himself by name and, indeed, in two chapters mentions Gavin Ogilvy as another, quite different, person from himself. By the time of *A Window in Thrums* and *The Little Minister* the narrator has acquired the name Gavin Ogilvy. He performs much the same function as the narrator in *Auld Licht Idylls* but he also acquires some of the attributes of the *character* Gavin Ogilvy in the earlier book, particularly his love of literature. The narrator's literary leanings are important because whilst Barrie's qualities as a prose stylist have been overlooked they are an important dynamic within the text. In each of his works of fiction Barrie's narrators are self-conscious literary artists. Even in *Auld Licht Idylls* we can see elements of the preoccupation with artistic creativity that would became central to his longer novels.

The rich texture of the writing in which the narrator introduces himself in the first chapter of *Auld Licht Idylls* serves to mark him off from his surroundings. Approaching the self-conscious opulence of that other snowed-up narrator, Adam Yestreen, in the later novella *Farewell Miss Julie Logan* (1931), the narrator's style places him apart from the community he goes on to describe, not just spatially and temporally but emotionally and intellectually as well. His schoolhouse is in the nearby glen which in winter becomes snowed-up leaving him cut off from the outside world and all humanity. But he is already cut off from his outside world in his cultural interests. Without human contact to temper him, he notes how the animals and the birds "have begun to regard me as one of themselves"; in contrast to the Christian certainty of the Auld Lichts, he is the observer of scenes in "natural history", writing of the Darwinist "doctrine of the survival of the fittest" in the "fierce struggle among the hungry animals for existence" (Barrie 1888: 5–6). The references to Darwin destabilise the later chapters on Church and community life, and Barrie's decision to place this chapter at the beginning of the volume, and the chapter on literature at the end, presents the reader with a modern, cultured frame within which to view this puritanical world of yesterday. The values which this past community embody are being challenged by a modern frame of mind.

The most significant alteration that Barrie made when revising the newspaper articles was to use his recently invented idea of "Thrums" as an organising principle for the book. "Thrums" is mentioned in only one of the newspaper articles from which *Auld*

Licht Idylls derives – the final one Barrie wrote before publishing the book. Elsewhere, whenever Barrie names his village it is usually "Wheens", and on other occasions the narrator will talk simply about "Scotland" – a word that, conspicuously, is used sparingly in *Auld Licht Idylls*. The fictional village "Thrums" is outlined in chapter 2 of the book and actually incorporates much of the language Barrie had used to describe Thrums in the serialised version of *When a Man's Single*, his novel which ran in the *British Weekly* from October 1887 to March 1888. When he came to publish *When a Man's Single* as a book, Barrie omitted all the descriptions he had by now lifted from the serialised version into *Auld Licht Idylls* just a few months before. These additions mean that in *Auld Licht Idylls*, in contrast to the factual idiom of the newspaper articles, the fictionality of the picture is stressed. Although the narrator is precise in his description of the town, he nevertheless draws attention to his own act of describing – "Thrums is the name I give here to the handful of houses jumbled together in a cup" (Barrie 1888: 9). We can see in this deliberate attention to the act of imagining the germ of the interest in the construction of reality by the artistic mind that will come to structure *A Window in Thrums* and *The Little Minister*, and be taken to the centre of the *Tommy* novels and *The Little White Bird*.

III

Unlike *Auld Licht Idylls*, *A Window in Thrums* was substantially composed from original material and planned as a book from the outset. The few chapters that are based on previously published material are interpolated into the main story of Jess and her family, creating a rather disparate structure. The tone is markedly different from *Auld Licht Idylls*. With the exception of the interpolated chapters, humour gives way to sentiment and the book has an overwhelming mood of sadness. Thomas Knowles notes a corresponding shift in perspective from the public to the private sphere (Knowles 1983: 111). This brings about a consequent shift in emphasis from the social to the emotional. Barrie has been much criticised for an excessive emphasis on emotion and the indiscriminate way in which he plays for the feelings of his readers. This, together with the emphasis on death and grief, has resulted in *A Window in Thrums* being held up as the apotheosis of the Kailyard.

After reading *A Window in Thrums*, Robert Louis Stevenson wrote to Barrie stating that he had "the glamour of twilight" on his pen (Stevenson 1995, VII, 447). Writing as one artist to another, what Stevenson probably meant by this seemingly contradictory phrase was Barrie's method of painting a picture through the faint, subtle lines of twilight rather than boldness of day. It indicates a characteristically late-Victorian taste for nostalgia – for the emotional tug and glamour of a metaphorical twilight – and offers a more appropriate context than Kailyard within which to understand Barrie's most maligned work. The "glamour of twilight" should not be seen as constituting Barrie's outlook on the social fabric of the world; if Thrums is a twilight society in *Auld Licht Idylls*, in *A Window in Thrums* it is only the backdrop to the story of the more intimate twilight world of Jess and her family. The OED defines glamour as: "magic, enchantment, spell" and "a magical or fictitious beauty [...] a delusive or alluring charm". Stevenson's insightful phrase indicates Barrie's ability to enchant the reader with the seemingly disenchanting scenes of death and decay and the consequent emotions of grief, loss and regret.

A Window in Thrums is characteristic of the *fin de siècle* in its emphasis on decline and its anticipation of the sense of an ending. It is also characterised by a pictorial method of presentation. A number of contemporary reviews linked the work to the Dutch school of painting: "The work is wrought with the finish, the precision, and the truth of excellent Dutch painting" (unsigned 1893: 75). Dutch genre painting, typified by the work of Teniers (1610–1690), was greatly admired by the Victorians and several novelists took the form as a model for their fictional construction of rural, peasant life. Thomas Hardy subtitled *Under the Greenwood Tree* (1872) "A Rural Painting of the Dutch School", and in *Adam Bede* George Eliot spoke of her delight in the "rare, precious quality of truthfulness" in Dutch paintings. (Eliot [1859] 1980: 223). The pictorial qualities of Barrie's work also link it to the genre of idyllic fiction, of which *Adam Bede* can be considered an example. Much recent criticism of the Victorian novel has looked to stress the formal diversity of fiction of the period and to break out of the narrow conception of the Victorian novel as predominantly concerned with social realism. One of the many sub-genres which has been re-identified is idyllic fiction. In her study of the form, Shelagh Hunter argues that the pastoral idyll has been relegated from its rightful place as a leading genre in mid- and late-nineteenth century fiction (Hunter 1984). Her discussion of the techniques and conventions of idyllic fiction enables us to see *A Window in Thrums* as a classic example of the form.

As I have stated, one of the main criticisms of Barrie's work is that it ignores, or downplays, social change. In his study of Kailyard, Ian Campbell judges that whilst change is always in the background in Kailyard fiction, George Douglas Brown brings it mercilessly to the foreground in *The House with the Green Shutters* (Campbell 1981: 92). As we have already seen, this judgement cannot really apply to *Auld Licht Idylls* and in a later article Campbell does admit that "unlike parts of Crockett's kailyard Scotland, Barrie's is not content to stand on a preservationist platform and watch the nineteenth century go by" (Campbell 1988b: 24). In the case of *A Window in Thrums*, however, treatment of social change might not be the most appropriate way of approaching the text; rather, as a work of idyllic fiction, stasis is a necessary component of the fictional design. This explains why plot is a subordinate concern in *A Window in Thrums*. F.R. Hart's comments of Maclaren apply, in the case of this text, to Barrie as well: "it is irrelevant to charge the author of the Victorian prose idyll with having no plot [...]. The idyll has formal unity of other kinds" (Hart 1978: 121). Reading *A Window in Thrums* as a work of idyllic fiction demands an approach that concentrates less on what is being described and more on how it is being described.[5]

As with *Auld Licht Idylls*, Barrie loosened the historical framework as he shaped the book. When composing *A Window in Thrums* he considered using historical dates in his text. In the first chapter we are told that "the sun had sunk on a fine day in June, early

---

[5] Cairns Craig also observes Thrums as "a town in stasis" but relates this to an "underlying pattern" in Scottish fiction where a static community is opposed to "a world beyond whose essential meanings are defined by history" (Craig 1979: 18). Craig sees Barrie's later novella, *Farewell Miss Julie Logan* (1931) as an important example of this pattern.

in the century, when Hendry and Jess, newly married [...] walked to the house on the brae that was to be their home" (Barrie 1889a: 9). In the margins of the manuscript Barrie scribbled "1813" next to this section but eventually decided against making specific reference to a historical date.[6] Instead, *A Window in Thrums* achieves its effects by adopting the "play of the timeless against the here and now" which Hunter identifies as characteristic of the idyll (Hunter 1984: 5). Change is pointed out on the very first page as we are told that the picture we are about to see is set in the past:

In the old days a stiff ascent left Thrums behind, and where is now the making of a suburb was only a poor row of dwellings and a manse, with Hendry's cot to watch the brae. (Barrie 1889a: 1)

Barrie's narrator goes on to describe in close detail what the picture would have looked like:

The house stood bare, without a shrub, in a garden whose paling did not go all the way round, the potato pit being only kept out of the road, that here sets off southward, by a broken dyke of stones and earth. On each side of the slate-coloured door was a window of knotted glass. Ropes were flung over the thatch to keep the roof on in wind.

Such detail is pictorial in technique and Barrie's style is similar to many passages in *Adam Bede*. Consider, for instance, the opening of chapter 4 of Eliot's novel:

A green valley with a brook running through it, full almost to overflowing with the late rains; overhung by low stooping willows. Across this brook a plank is thrown, and over this plank Adam Bede is passing with his undoubting step. (Eliot 1980: 83)

The prose here reads almost like stage directions, demanding its readers to paint a picture in the mind. Hunter argues that "a particular kind of interplay between picture and narrative is [...] a defining characteristic of the Victorian idyll" (Hunter 1984: 32). An obvious effect of this interplay is the suspension of narrative in order to

---

[6] Beinecke Library, Yale University (Uncatalogued).

achieve a stasis from which a picture of "idyllic balance" can be viewed:

> The idyllic novel must seek ways to halt progress in order to show permanent or potential relationships from a static point of view […] the static condition of a picture in which all the relationships can be seen at once. (Hunter 1984: 48–9)

A Window in Thrums is similar to *Adam Bede* also in being explicit about its own fictionality. Barrie's opening chapter can be compared to the famous interlude of Eliot's novel, "In Which the Story Pauses a Little." The narrators in both works demand a particular kind of reader-response to the story that follows. Hunter stresses that "the idyllic is conscious of and explicit about its own artistry, and makes its statements frequently by drawing attention to the presentation" (Hunter 1984: 40). In the description of the interior of the house on the brae, Barrie's narrator makes clear that he is imagining not describing the contents:

> I speak of the chairs, but if we go together into the "room" they will not be visible to you […]. Worn boards and ragged walls, and the rusty ribs fallen from the fireplace, are all that meet your eyes, but I see a round, unsteady, waxcloth-covered table, with four books lying at equal distances on it. (Barrie 1889a: 2)

The narrator is trying to paint a picture that no longer exists, and he must get his readers to cast off their social trimmings and see that picture in a certain way:

> Into this humble abode I would take any one who cares to accompany me. But you must not come in a contemptuous mood, thinking that the poor are but a stage removed from beasts of burden, as some cruel writers of these days say. (Barrie 1889a: 1–2)

As well as offering an attack on French naturalism, this passage contains a rejection of the Arnoldian denigration of the provincial, as the narrator demands a balanced view of the picture free from condescension. In idyllic fiction "the reader is meant to respond with a suspension of completed judgement and a recognition of potentially conflicting emotion" (Hunter 1984: 48). The narrator's role is crucial to the creation of this effect:

he speaks in all of them as a sophisticated observer of a simpler life; as one who understands, if he does not share, the assumed views of an assumed reader, and at the same time as one who understands but *cannot* share the life he depicts [...] he lays no claim to omniscience, but he does lay claim, implicitly, to being in possession of a vantage-point from which comparisons can be made. (Hunter 1984: 56–7)

In *A Window in Thrums* the narrator operates in precisely this way. As in *Auld Licht Idylls* he presents himself as both insider and outsider, balancing himself between an engagement with the sentiments of the people he is describing and a refusal to allow the reader to get too close to them. He is always present in the story that he is "trying to bring back" (Barrie 1889a: 3) from his memory but hardly ever involved in its action, always slipping in before the door swings to or retiring to the attic when the McQumphas are having an intimate, family moment.

The narrator's role is one of mediation, and he makes a point of saying that, whilst "to those who dwell in great cities Thrums is only a small place", to him, cut off in his lonely schoolhouse, it contains "a clatter of life" (Barrie 1889a: 6). His mediating role defends the right for Thrums to contain life, for the brae to have the "history of tragic little Thrums [...] sunk into it" (Barrie 1889a: 4). The oxymoron "tragic little" is a vindication of the right for Thrums to contain tragedy and profundity, however small and remote a place it might be. The strategy is similar to that of Hardy who at the beginning of *The Woodlanders* anticipates the "dramas of a grandeur and unity truly Sophoclean" that will take place in the sleepy "sequestered spots" of Little Hintock (Hardy [1887] 1998: 8). Both writers are reflexively aware of audience taste and incorporate an explicit defence of the provincial inside the rhetoric of the text.

The choice of Jamie as the name for the son has prompted some critics to reduce the text to a purely autobiographical statement. Harry M. Geduld sees in all of Barrie's novels and plays a "prototypic story" based on his relationship with his mother (Geduld 1971: 25). Parallels with Barrie's life can certainly be drawn but there as many distortions as parallels and a rigid autobiographical framework does nothing to elucidate the *art* of Barrie's fiction. The story is structured so as to invoke an emotional response to a particular set of themes and values: loyalty, separation and the threat of loss and grief. Jamie had left

Thrums for Tilliedrum to become a barber and, as the narrator explains, "Tilliedrum was his introduction to the world, and for a little it took his head" (Barrie 1889a: 177); he refuses to go to Church and eventually leaves Thrums for London. The use of prolepsis throughout the text forewarns us of the unhappy ending and colours our responses to the scenes between Jamie and his family. At first Jamie is a dutiful son, sending home money and returning home every summer. *A Window in Thrums* was written during a period when Barrie was dividing his time between Kirriemuir and London, and dramatises his own ambivalent feelings towards his inevitable separation from his family. But Barrie departs from autobiography by making the mother, father and sister all die and having Jamie return from London too late to witness their departure. For this he is roundly condemned by the narrator and the town. Barrie uses each death as a means of drawing an emotional response from his readers and the proliferation of deaths at the end of the book has helped to establish the association between Kailyard fiction and death-bed scenes. To F.R. Hart this makes the text "elegiac pastoral" (Hart 1978: 130) but to others the elegy was too much. Writing in the *Illustrated London News*, the novelist James Payn asked: "we cannot help asking ourselves whether we have not been made unnecessarily miserable. If village life is really so wretched as is here depicted what liars are the poets" (18 January 1890).

Throughout the text, Barrie eulogises the family sphere and the London woman who steals Jamie's affections away from Jess is described as "her who played the devil with his life" (Barrie 1889a: 203). The book undoubtedly did much to fuel the theory that Barrie had a mother fixation which drove and impaired his art. In the chapter "A Tale of a Glove", Jess and Jamie play out a silent power struggle over a lady's glove, both refusing to openly acknowledge the inevitable truth that it carries – that Jamie's affections will soon turn elsewhere and that mother and son will separate. Yet Robert Louis Stevenson told Barrie: "The glove is a great page; it is startlingly original, and as true as death and judgement" (Stevenson 1995: VII: 446). Shortly after, Stevenson wrote to Henry James: "what a page is the glove business [...] knocks a man flat; that's guts, if you please" (Stevenson 1995: VII: 451). Perhaps he admired Barrie's achievement in tackling a scene which could easily become coy or embarrassing.

Certainly his response is different from that of most twentieth-century critics, and it is significant that one contemporary reviewer absolved Barrie from two particular charges that would later be levelled against his work. Augustine Birrell in the *Speaker* argued that Barrie had "conceded nothing to the public taste [...] and of sentiment, that odious onion, not a trace is to be found in these sweet-smelling pages" (Brown 1952: 140). In the twentieth century Barrie would be judged harshly on precisely these issues.

In defending the art of *A Window in Thrums* one should not fail to point out elements that can justly be seen as faults, whether in construction or attitude. Some critics have detected voyeurism and cynicism in Barrie's presentation of his characters. Roderick Watson argues that he "miniaturises" the society (Watson 1984: 317) and David Craig complains that he "cocks snooks at the old village for its small-minded obsession with gossip but at the same time uses it as a pretext for appealing pathos" (Craig 1961: 291). Certainly the early chapters concentrating on Jess and her daughter Leeby present the characters in a very small world, "On the Track of the Minister", "Preparing to Receive Company" and keeping up with local gossip all conducted from behind the window in Thrums. George Blake concludes that "Barrie was consciously guying his own people" and was "incapable of pity for his fictional victims" (Blake 1951: 72). The charge has some weight and it is strengthened by the awkward structure of the book. The chapters interpolated into the story of Jess and Jamie, all drawn from previously published articles, suggest that Barrie was content to pad out the central story of the son from London with material which, following the success of *Auld Licht Idylls*, he knew appealed to the public. Blake refers to the book as "an 'aggregation' of sketches" (Blake 1951: 72) and Geduld – always Barrie's harshest critic – sees it as "a collection of journalistic sketches struggling to become a novel and failing miserably in the attempt" (Geduld 1971: 36).

Whilst *A Window in Thrums* clearly lacks overall unity of shape, the introduction of an element of plot can be seen as a step in a new direction. The novel marks the beginning of a rejection of whatever interest Barrie had shown in *Auld Licht Idylls* with representing social reality, and in it we can see a major development of the theme that will come to dominate his later novels. One of the effects of the rhetorical strategy of inducing emotion through the mediating role of the narrator is that Barrie represents inside the novel the dilemma of the writer of fiction – the difficulty of creating an illusion of reality in which his readers will believe. It is this dilemma that becomes central to Barrie's artistic concerns in his later work. At this stage of his career, he uses his narrator to try and convince the reader of the realism and veracity of the story of Jess and her family and the emotions involved in it. As his fictional career progressed, however, he became more interested in the role of the narrator and in the act of creating illusions of reality. His later novels are characterised by an intense interest in the creative mind; with storytelling and illusory realities. In *The Little Minister* he was to present a narrator who continually drew attention to himself as a writer. In *A Window in Thrums* the narrator is equally self-conscious but less explicit at this stage about the actual act of writing:

Away up in the glen, my lonely schoolhouse lying deep, as one might say, in a sea of snow, I had many hours in the years long by for thinking of my friends in Thrums and mapping out the future of Leeby and Jamie. I saw Hendry and Jess taken to the churchyard and Leeby left alone in the house. I saw Jamie fulfil his promise to his mother, and take Leeby, that stainless young woman far away to London, where they had a home together. Ah! but these were only the idle dreams of a Dominie. The Lord willed it otherwise. (Barrie 1889a: 181)

This passage is in keeping with the use of prolepsis in the text and serves to dramatise inside the novel the act of wish-fulfilment – the desire for the happy ending that will not come. But whereas a comparable passage in *The Little White Bird* (1902) would be used as a starting point for a metafictional analysis of the narrator's desire for illusory consolation, here the concerns of the narrator remain subordinate to the story of Jess itself. Though we can detect the roots of Barrie's proto-modernist concern with the construction of fictional reality, at this stage in his career it is a secondary issue and the novel proceeds to relate the story of Jamie's failure to return home before his family die.

Unfortunately, because of the implicit criteria contained within the critical term Kailyard, assessment of Barrie's fiction has focused too heavily – almost exclusively – on the way it represents social reality and projects an image of Scottish national life. Knowles discusses "the degree of factual 'distortion'" and charges Barrie with "avoiding a more penetrating account of the conflict of life styles and values involved in migration and social change" (Knowles 1983: 134. 119). Similarly, J.B. Caird complains of the suppression of "the authentic voice of the north-east" in favour of "that unreal caricature of a community he calls Thrums" (Caird 1977: 27). Caricature is an overstatement, but the chief problem with Caird's comment is its implicit rejection of fiction itself. It is assumed that Barrie is trying to depict Scottish reality. This is an assumption that continues to infect criticism of Barrie's fiction. In a recent essay, Richard Cook argues that the Kailyard texts are "national narratives" which imagine the Highland community as "the home of the nation" (Cook 1999: 1055, 1063). Cook's generalised – and error-laden – account assumes that all Kailyard villages are set in the Highlands and that Kailyard texts set out to construct a politically-motivated vision of the Highlands as authentically Scottish:

In Barrie's narrative, Highlanders hold the racial distinction of being organic holders of pure Scottishness, as affect becomes the way of reading the body's relationship to the nation. (Cook 1999: 1067)

The problem with this statement – apart from its confusion over what constitutes the Highlands – is its assumption that Barrie's rhetoric sets out to construct a type of Scottishness or a vision of the nation. As I have argued, this is the dilemma for the writer of regional and/or national fiction; but with the distance of more than a century it is surely time to recognise that in *A Window in Thrums* Barrie does not set out a vision of Scotland. Instead, it is possible to detect the beginnings of a vision of art and its relationship with reality. That vision becomes central to the themes and concerns of Barrie's later and longer novels which have been marginalised by the Kailyard context.

IV

Barrie's growing interest in the workings of the creative mind transformed the structure of his next major work, *The Little Minister*, about which I have written at length elsewhere (Nash 1999a). This has often been cited as the least defensible of Barrie's books, and on one level is simply a work of popular romance. Gavin Dishart, a pious, timid, young minister becomes bewitched by a gypsy woman who, after she has successfully won his love, drops her disguise and emerges as really an aristocratic lady. The story nevertheless operates on a number of levels mixing realism with romance in a manner that disconcerted contemporary reviewers. The early chapters use a real life historical event – the 1839 chartist uprising in Kirriemuir – through which to introduce the reader to the community and the minister's role in it. In his working notebook Barrie recorded historical details of life in the 1830s, and when he wrote to Donald Macleod – the editor of *Good Words* where the novel was serialised – he outlined the details of local colour that he intended introducing into his tale (Nash 1999a: 79). But whilst the setting might lean towards realism, the course of the novel moves away from it, because it is against this realist setting that Gavin Dishart is plunged into the fairy-tale world of Caddam Wood, where lives a gypsy family reputed to be "a race of giants", who "threatened the farmers by day and danced devilishly, it was said, at night" (Barrie 1891: 34). Gavin's adventures in this wood, where he meets and falls in love with the gypsy girl Babbie, are explicitly framed within myth and legend, allowing Barrie to set up as one of the main themes of the novel the interplay between romance and what is perceived as reality (Nash 1999a: 79–80).

Whilst the story of Gavin and Babbie is very much about understanding reality, the novel is also concerned with the construction of fictional reality. The narrator of *The Little Minister* was a relatively late idea in Barrie's composition of the work (Nash 1999a: 82). As the novel was finally structured he plays an important role in the plot and his prejudices and vested interests affect the way that he presents the story of Gavin and Babbie. Furthermore, his preoccupation with creating a fictional illusion comes to dominate the story. He identifies himself as a creative artist throughout and continually draws attention to his struggle to persuade the reader to believe in the story he is telling. The novel that was first conceived as a popular romance thus turned into something more ambitious – an analysis of the creative process itself. By introducing the artist-narrator into his design Barrie altered the impression of the whole book. *The Little Minister* was no longer a simple love story; instead it became an analysis of a mind that tries to create a love story.

With the publication of *Sentimental Tommy* (1896) and *Tommy and Grizel* (1900) – two novels that had an important effect on D.H. Lawrence – Barrie took the creative mind to the centre of his work. The *Tommy* novels are rich and wide-ranging in themes and ideas and full discussion of these neglected and undervalued works is beyond the scope of the present study. Having considered *Tommy and Grizel* at length elsewhere (Nash 1999b) I want to focus here on two aspects of *Sentimental Tommy* that point up the differences between this work and Barrie's earlier fiction: the relationship between fantasy and place and the treatment of education.[7]

J.A. Hammerton considers *Sentimental Tommy* to be:

a break-away from his earlier fiction in so far as it substitutes for the Thrums of Margaret Ogilvy the Kirriemuir of little Jamie Barrie. He is no longer seeing the town and its "queer folk" through the eyes of his mother, he is telling us of the days he knew himself, of his own boyhood, his own fantasies. (Hammerton 1929: 198)

But in this novel Barrie is not concerned with "seeing" the town so much as imagining it. He is not writing factually about an actual place or remembering the true incidents of a childhood in Kirriemuir. If in *A Window in Thrums* Barrie drew attention to the fictional construction of an imaginative place, in the *Tommy* novels Thrums becomes even more of a self-conscious construction. As F.R. Hart notes: "All sense of place in Barrie is deflected by multiple subjectivities in vision" (Hart 1978: 126). In *Sentimental Tommy* the relation between language, place and identity is deliberately complicated. Barrie transforms Thrums to fit in with his now central preoccupation with the workings of the creative mind.

---

[7] For a discussion of *Sentimental* Tommy as a whole, see Ormond 1987 (chapter 5).

Study of the draft of the story that survives in manuscript reveals that Barrie added large sections to the early chapters that expound on Tommy's relationship to the idea of Thrums. The novel had a long gestation. Barrie began planning it in 1891 and agreed to publish it in *Scribner's Magazine* in 1893. A series of changes in direction, together with bouts of illness, prevented his completion of it until 1895 and it was not serialised in the magazine until 1896.[8] In the intervening period Crockett and Maclaren had arrived on the literary scene, hastening the invention of the critical context of Kailyard and affecting forever Barrie's place within literary history. It is, therefore, surely not coincidental that he should have decided at a late date to alter the way that Thrums is presented as an imaginative community. *Sentimental Tommy* is, in part, a refutation of the kind of regional fiction with which he had become associated. It is clear that Barrie wanted to break free from his association with Thrums. In September 1894, he asked Thomas Weymss Reid, general manager of Cassells, "not to take one of the Scotch pieces" for his magazine as "I don't want [it] to be th[ough]t I must be Scotch even in short articles."[9]

The first part of the novel is set in London where Tommy constructs a picture of Thrums that is real in a storytelling environment:

Of the tales told by Tommy that day in words Scotch and cockney, of Thrums, home of heroes and the arts, where the lamps are lit by a magician called Leerie-leerie-licht-the-lamps [...] and the stairs are so fine that the houses wear them outside for show, and you drop a pail at the end of a rope down a hole, and sometimes it comes up full of water, and sometimes full of fairies – of these and other wonders, if you would know, ask not a dull historian, nor even go to Thrums, but to those rather who have been boys and girls there and now are exiles. (Barrie 1896a: 10)

Barrie incorporates in his novel a reflexive awareness of the way that his imagined place has been romanticised beyond its true, dull history. As R.D.S. Jack comments: "Those who evaluate Thrums with the realistic eye of the chronicler or social worker do so after having been eliminated explicitly by the author" (Jack 1992: 160). And it is

---

[8] For a full account of the genesis of the text, see Nash 1999c.

[9] Unpublished ALS, 24 September 1894 (Beinecke Library).

important to note that this passage was added to the manuscript draft;
the instruction not to go to Thrums reads like a warning against
pilgrimages to Kirriemuir, which by this date were becoming popular.
Another early passage in the novel, focusing on Tommy's mother, was
also a late insertion. Jean Myles is exiled from Thrums having made
an unwise marriage to Tommy's father, who is now dead. Alone with
her son in her house in London, she recreates the Thrums life:

> In the great world without, she used few Thrums words now; you would have known
> she was Scotch by her accent only, but when she and Tommy were together in that
> room, with the door shut, she always spoke as if her window still looked out on the
> bonny Marywellbrae. It is not really bonny, it is gey an' mean an' bleak, and you must
> not come to see it. It is just a steep wind-swept street, old and wrinkled, like your
> mother's face. (Barrie 1896a: 17)

That Barrie was interested in the issue of fact and fiction in relation to
regionalism is evident in his plan in 1890 to write "a story about a
man who falls in love with Emily Bronte after reading *Wuthering
Heights*. He travels to Haworth, only to arrive for the funeral"
(Ormond 1987: 13).

For Tommy himself, Thrums becomes a fantasy world where
there is a different linguistic system that he lives out with his mother
and where he imagines a different reality from the grubby world of
London poverty in which he lives. Tommy's created Thrums is a copy
of a copy, drawn, as it was for Barrie, from the second-hand source of
his mother's stories. And, again like his creator, Tommy fleshes out
the details of the stories with his own imagination. When he stumbles
upon a street in London where the inhabitants all speak with the same
accent as his mother, he thinks he has entered fairyland and at last
found Thrums. It is through his visits to this "enchanted street" –
where the London Thrums folk have formed a little colony – that
Tommy gradually pieces together his dream: "'That's it', Tommy
cried. 'I tell yer, everybody dreams on it!' and Tommy was right;
everybody dreams of it, though not all call it Thrums" (Barrie 1896a:
26).

Before she dies, Tommy's mother writes to Thrums to Aaron
Latta – the man she rejected when she ran off with Tommy's father –
asking him to look after Tommy and his sister Elspeth. By the time

Tommy gets to see Thrums and finds everything a bit of a disappointment the situation is reversed; London, from which he is now an exile, has become the fantasy world he uses in his stories:

His great topic [of story] was his birthplace, and whatever happened in Thrums, he instantly made contemptible by citing something of the same kind but on a larger scale that had happened in London […] Snow! why they didn't know what snow was in Thrums. (Barrie 1896a: 160)

By making Tommy a Thrums boy only by adoption Barrie is able to unsettle the entire notion of regional identity and locate it as something that the mind creates for its own convenience. Tommy's identity is complicated because of his ability to speak Scots and London words:

When Tommy was among his new friends [in Thrums street] a Scotch word or phrase often escaped his lips, but old Petey and the others thought he had picked it up from them, and would have been content to accept him as a London waif who lived somewhere round the corner. (Barrie 1896a: 63)

The irony is that that is exactly what he is. His Scots may not have been picked up from them but it is nevertheless picked up and is not his "natural" language. Whereas he is fluent in London, Tommy "picks out Scotch words carefully" in Thrums, and retains his London vocabulary – "It was the arrival of ain't in Thrums" (Barrie 1896a: 140, 146).[10]

Place is only one of many important components in the presentation of Tommy as a fantasist. Tommy is sentimental because the "most conspicuous of his traits was the faculty of stepping into other people's shoes and remaining there until he becomes someone else" (Barrie 1896a: 187). His identity consists entirely in role-playing. He is able to believe so completely in any imaginary situation that he loses the boundary between reality and pretence and has no concrete self. He takes on other people's emotions and lives in them as if they were his own. On one occasion Tommy swaps clothes with another boy who is in mourning for his father and agrees to do the

---

[10] For a sympathetic account of the presentation of Scots in this novel, see Letley 1988: 233–44.

mourning for him so that the boy can join in the street games. When in Thrums he writes letters for those members of the community who are unable to write themselves and, forced to take on the emotional conditions of others, he revels in the opportunity to express powerful sentiments which do not really belong to him. In one instance he has to write as a woman who wishes to tell her mother about the death of a friend; not only do his words induce tears in the eyes of both the person he is writing for and writing to, but they move him to tears also.

In both *Tommy* novels, the protagonist is presented as the archetypal artist, substituting reality for a world of his own making: "He and the saying about art for art's sake were in the streets that night, looking for each other" (Barrie 1896a: 83). We are constantly reminded of this artistic temperament but it is not until *Tommy and Grizel* that Tommy becomes a best-selling author. In *Sentimental Tommy: The Story of his Boyhood* he is, like Stephen Dedalus in Joyce's *A Portrait of the Artist as a Young Man*, an artist in the way he lives. The reviewer for the *Nation* thought that the work would herald a "new dawn" in literature dealing with the mind of the artist (28 January 1897). In this context, the novel can be seen as a precursor to modernist fiction, with its preoccupation with artists and the creative mind.

In contrast to the nostalgia of *A Window in Thrums*, in *Sentimental Tommy* Barrie is more ambivalent in his evocation of home. Tommy's mother warmly reminisces of Thrums to her son whilst affecting an attitude of contempt for "the old hole" and "the vulgar Thrums words" in her dishonest letters to the community (Barrie 1896a: 37, 73). Similarly, the inhabitants of London's Thrums Street "pulled down the blinds on London and talked of Thrums in their mother tongue" though "few of them wanted to return to it" (Barrie 1896a: 61). Again it is tempting to trace this alteration in attitude to the impact of the fiction of Crockett and Maclaren. Certainly this can be hazarded in respect of Barrie's attitude towards education in this novel. Barrie's treatment of the "lad o' pairts" theme is markedly different from what readers had encountered in the years between *The Little Minister* and *Sentimental Tommy*. In Maclaren's fiction, talented boys study Latin and Greek and excel at university;

those that live become ministers. The ending of *Sentimental Tommy*, by contrast, explores the incompatibility between this same education system and the artistic temperament.

Barrie had touched on the theme of education in *Auld Licht Idylls*. The dominant tone of humour in that text affects the presentation of a school system where "In his scholastic barn the dominie had thumped the Latin grammar into his scholars till they became university bursars to escape him" (Barrie 1896a: 131). In *Sentimental Tommy*, the chief school of Thrums is characterised in terms that would have been familiar to readers of Maclaren: "It was a famous school, from which a band of three or four or even six marched every autumn to the universities as determined after bursaries as ever were Highlandmen to lift cattle" (Barrie 1896a: 151). At first, however, Tommy attends the Hanky School run by Miss Ailie who finds "something wonderful about Tommy, you felt it, but you could not quite give it a name" (Barrie 1896a: 222). At a loss to define Tommy's special qualities she identifies him, quite inappropriately, as a "lad o' pairts": "I think, I really think [...] that he has got great gifts for the ministry" (Barrie 1896a: 223). Tommy, however, is everything that a potential minister is not: irresponsible, reckless and without faith in any moral system outside his own imagination. As George Douglas Brown does with young John Gourlay in *The House with the Green Shutters*, Barrie makes us aware of the inappropriateness of the path of education that lies before Tommy. Under his new tutor, Mr Cathro, Tommy undergoes the "cramming" and "stuffing" of his mind (Barrie 1896a: 224, 228). This is a crucial moment in the book because it is at this point that Tommy first reads *Waverley* and launches his own Jacobite uprising. At the very time when the forces of education would have him being crammed and stuffed with Latin, Tommy's mind is turned to literature and to creating and playing out his own work of imaginative fiction: "'Waverley' revealed to him that he was born neither for the ministry nor the herding, but to restore to his country its rightful king" (Barrie 1896: 234). Succeeding chapters illustrate Tommy's masterly imagination – and hint at Barrie's still-to-develop theatrical skills – in his stage-managing of "The Last Jacobite Rising", a fantasy which he lives out to the very full whilst his Latin lies unstudied.

Thomas Knowles misreads the ending of *Sentimental Tommy*. He argues: "as in other of Barrie's works, the way out of the simple life of Thrums is via the social mobility of education" (Knowles 1983: 93). But education is a dead end for Tommy who has to find an alternative escape route. At the examination Tommy fails to win a bursary when, instead of translating his English into Latin, he sits marvelling at the truth of the words set before him. His final chance to get to university is to compete for the Blackadder prise, a scholarship given to the writer of the best essay in the Scots tongue. Easily more imaginative than his methodical rival, Lauchlan McLauchlan, Tommy soars into his essay only to come unstuck in search for a single word he proves unable to locate. He wastes half of the allotted time searching for the *mot juste* and is so clearly beaten that the judges don't even deem it necessary to read the scripts. "Hantle" was the word Tommy was looking for to describe how many people were in the church in his story, and "puckle", "manzy", "mask", "flow" or "curran" would not do. This was the value to the writer of Scots recognised by Grassic Gibbon – the ability to "adorn his meaning with a richness, a clarity and a conciseness impossible in orthodox English" (Gibbon 1934: 165). Tommy is the sort of artist of whom Gibbon would have been proud.

Tommy and Grizel, published four years after *Sentimental Tommy*, dramatises the debilitating effects of Tommy's fantasies on other people, particularly the woman who loves him, Grizel. In this novel, the relationship between the artist's creative potency and his sexual impotence becomes the central issue and the work was clearly written out of the complexities of Barrie's own marriage. The themes of regionalism and the writer in the marketplace are, however, again revisited and incorporated into the fiction itself. At the end of the novel, Barrie focuses on the commercial misrepresentation of the artist. After the publication of Tommy's bestselling book, tourists flock to Thrums wrongly believing it to be the birthplace of "celebrated Tommy", whose portrait, we are told, is "now in America" (Barrie 1900: 425). At the end of this novel we are given a series of judgements on Tommy made by reviewers and commentators that fly in the face of the story we have been reading. The narrator's corrective rhetoric that "what he was we know" (Barrie 1900: 423) is ironic, as we realise that Barrie is questioning the whole idea of whether an artist's reputation has anything to do with the person he is. And significantly it is Tommy's Scottishness (which is only an adopted identity) that London critics seize upon as being the "individuality behind the work" (Barrie 1900: 424) – exactly as they did Barrie himself. In 1900, Barrie is shutting the door on his past career and gently refuting the way his work had become pigeon-holed.

V

In spite of the fact that *The Little Minister* and the *Tommy* novels sold better than the earlier titles, Barrie's fictional identity became fixed to Thrums and his earlier Scottish regional writing, largely as a result of the success of Crockett and Maclaren. A further contributory factor was the unexpected (at least to Barrie) success of *Margaret Ogilvy*. Originally planned as a preface to *Sentimental Tommy*, it was published separately in the same year and quickly became a best-seller. Of all Barrie's works, *Margaret Ogilvy* has had the most damning press. George Blake complained that "Barrie threw the portrait of his mother into the whirlpool of commerce" (Blake 1951: 73); Maurice Lindsay sees the book as an act of avenging on the parent (Lindsay 1977: 353) – an eccentric conclusion to say the least – whilst Ian Campbell considers it a "deplorable lapse of taste" (Campbell 1981: 105). Most critics have agreed that the book is central to understanding Barrie's life and it has also often been read – perversely – as part of Barrie's social vision of a Scottish community. Thomas Knowles devotes considerable space to the work in his analysis of the sociological credibility of Barrie's presentation of Thrums. Discussing Barrie's construction of his relationship with his mother, Knowles considers "the implied representativeness of their relationships for the community as a whole", concluding that Barrie "avoids describing the conflict of values entailed in migration and changed employment" (Knowles 1983: 123, 133). Such an approach seems entirely inappropriate to a text where Barrie is attempting to evoke in art the complex emotions attendant upon grief. Furthermore, much of the style and content of the text would seem positively to counter such an approach. Like *Sentimental Tommy*, *Margaret Ogilvy* is, among other things, Barrie's refutation of the way his earlier books had been critically received.

The rhetoric of *Margaret Ogilvy* is everywhere concerned with deception.[11] Barrie begins with his birth:

> On the day I was born we bought six hair-bottomed chairs, and in our little house it was an event, the first great victory in a woman's long campaign [...] I so often heard the tale afterwards, and shared as boy and man in so many similar triumphs, that the coming of the chairs seems to be something I remember, as if I had jumped out of bed on that first day, and run ben to see how they looked. (Barrie 1896b: 1–2)

The decision to begin at his birth, like David Copperfield, rather than with his earliest memory, like Pip in *Great Expectations*, means that Barrie can only *seem* to remember – it "is all guess-work for six years" (Barrie 1896b: 4). But Barrie is not just guessing in *Margaret Ogilvy*, he is imagining; and imagining all the time about deceiving:

> Neighbours came in to see the boy and the chairs. I wonder if she deceived me when she affected to think that there were others like us, or whether I saw through her from the first, she was so easily seen through. When she seemed to agree with them that it would be impossible to give me a college education, was I so easily taken in, or did I know already what ambitions burned behind that dear face? (Barrie 1896b: 3)

This early obsession with deception and affectation is developed throughout the text, nowhere more obviously than in the famous scene where Barrie recalls how, in an attempt to lift his mother from her grief, he dressed in the clothes of his dead brother and attempted to mimic his whistle in front of her.

Knowles's discussion of the sociological credibility of *Margaret Ogilvy* takes its point of departure from the early chapters where Barrie focuses on details of social change in Kirriemuir. In chapter 2, he recalls the impact of machines on the weaving industry:

> Before I reached my tenth year a giant entered my native place, and we woke to find him in possession [...]. Where had been formerly but the click of the shuttle was soon the roar of "power", handlooms were pushed into a corner as a room is cleared for a

---

[11] For a detailed discussion of deception in this text, see Cuthbertson 1997.

dance. [...] Another era had dawned, new customs, new fashions, sprang into life, all as lusty as if they had been born at twenty-one. (Barrie 1896b: 21)

Shortly after this section, however, he pauses in his account of the changes that gripped Kirriemuir in his childhood to consider the effects of these on family life:

So much of what is great in Scotland has sprung from family ties; it is there I sometimes fear that my country is being struck. That we are all being reduced to one dead level, that "character" abounds no more and life itself is less interesting, such things I have read, but I do not believe them. I have even seen them given as my reason for writing of a past time, and in that at least there is no truth. (Barrie 1896b: 23)

At first sight this passage seems no different from the numerous books of reminiscences that I discussed in the previous chapter. But Barrie quickly places a distance between those earlier books and his own work:

The reason my books deal with the past instead of with the life I myself have known is simply this, that I soon grow tired of writing tales unless I can see a little girl, of whom my mother has told me, wandering confidently through the pages. (Barrie 1896b: 24)

This reads like a defence of criticisms that would be put most fully several decades later by writers such as George Blake. The past is a source for Barrie's fiction but he openly takes up a position where he is *imagining* that past. He spends the rest of the chapter constructing new stories from those that had been told to him by his mother. He imagines days in the life of his mother's father, who died nine years before Barrie was born, and writes: "I have seen many weary on-dings of snow, but the one I seem to recollect best occurred nearly twenty years before I was born" (Barrie 1896b: 31).

Barrie was fascinated by how reality was constructed through stories and throughout *Margaret Ogilvy* he is explicit about his imaginative relationship with his native town in a way that must be seen as a response to the critical reception of his work:

But though the new town is to me a glass through which I look at the old, the people I see passing up and down these wynds, sitting, nightcapped, on their barrow-shafts, hobbling in their blacks to church on Sunday are less those I saw in my childhood than their fathers and mothers who did these things in the same way when my mother was young (Barrie 1896b: 41).

It is not Kirriemuir that he sees, but the Kirriemuir of his mother's stories.

Alert readers would have noticed that *Margaret Ogilvy* was not a straightforward (auto)biographical account of Barrie's or Margaret Ogilvy's life. Straightforward (auto)biography was impossible for a writer obsessed by the workings of the imagination and the construction of fictional reality. *Margaret Ogilvy* is always open to the constructed nature of autobiography:

The horror of my boyhood was that I knew a time would come when I also must give up the games, and how it was to be done I saw not (this agony still returns to me in dreams, when I catch myself playing marbles, and look on with cold displeasure). (Barrie 1896b: 29)

The germ of *Peter Pan* lies here, but to say that *Peter Pan* lies uncomplicatedly in Barrie's autobiography is to miss the way that Barrie observes an awareness of the constructed and multiple nature of the self.[12] The adult Barrie gazing on the boy Barrie in his dreams mirrors the way the adult Barrie is writing the boy Barrie, with an awareness of how that boy is inevitably a construction of the adult writer.

The chapters that follow, of Barrie's pursuit of the profession of authorship, his success with his early Auld Licht articles and his move to London, follow the events of his life closely. The chapter on Robert Louis Stevenson, however, raises the question of Barrie's identity in literary history and includes one of the few references – or near references – he ever made to the term Kailyard. The chapter celebrates Margaret Ogilvy's secret love for Stevenson's stories. Fearful of offending Barrie with her taste for a rival author, Margaret reads *The Master of Ballantrae* in private, playing out a game with her son who replaces the book on the shelf as swiftly as she can remove it. The

---

[12] Geduld (1971) is the fullest (and most inflexible) literary critical exposition of Barrie's work from an autobiographical basis.

game leads Barrie to imagine the voice of James Durie, Stevenson's hero, speaking from his lonely place on the shelf:

"Am I to be a wall-flower?" asked James Durie reproachfully. (It must have been leap-year.)
    "Speak lower," replied my mother, with an uneasy look at me.
    "Pooh!" said James contemptuously, "that kail-runtle!"
    "I winna have him miscalled," said my mother, frowning.
    "I am done with him," said James (wiping his cane with his cambric handkerchief), and his sword clattered deliciously (I cannot think this was accidental), which made my mother sigh. Like the man he was, he followed up his advantage with a comparison that made me dip viciously.
    "A prettier sound that," said he, clanking his sword again, "than the clack-clack of your young friend's shuttle." (Barrie 1896b: 136–7)

Barrie originally planned to use "kailyarder" rather than "kail-runtle", the change being made after he had completed a manuscript draft of the work on 11 July 1896.[13] Had he been reading the article by "Rix" discussed in my introduction entitled "The Slump in Kail-Runts"? The line shows that Barrie was aware of the context within which his work was being placed and *Margaret Ogilvy* seems to be at once a defence of, and a closure on, his earlier work.

VI

If Barrie had hoped that *Margaret Ogilvy* might encourage readers to view his writing differently, and that the new direction taken in *Sentimental Tommy* would be duly recognised, he was to be disappointed. In spite of his attempts to discourage a realist response to his fiction, reviewers seized on the representation of Scottish regional life in a way that only tightened his association with regional fiction and the newly created genre of Kailyard.

    To return to the context of regionalism outlined at the beginning of this chapter, it is clear that whilst the regional setting of a work of fiction did not restrict novelists from working within established fictional genres, the sociological status of fiction – the way in which it

---

[13] Beinecke Library MS, M36.

was used as a resource for tourism and historical study – meant that
novelists could easily be received as historians of their native place. In
Barrie's case, the boundaries between fiction and history were blurred
from the start. *Auld Licht Idylls* was seen by the *Athenaeum* as a
"successful attempt to preserve the features of one locality" (5 May
1888). Articles and letters appeared in journals debating the history of
the Auld Lichts in Kirriemuir and the genealogy of the sect.[14] *The
Little Minister* was identified as a straightforward act of memory:
"The fact is, Mr. Barrie has just taken the common people with whom
he was acquainted in his boyhood, and has set them down in print"
(McK 1891: 141). In spite of its conspicuously artificial rhetoric,
Margaret Ogilvy was identified as "the key to his life and writings"
and Auld Licht Presbyterianism (almost completely died out in
Scotland by the 1890s) "the essential fibre of his nature" (Ritson
1897: 579, 581). The *Athenaeum* wrote of *Margaret Ogilvy*:

Mr. Barrie and his followers have blown the embers of a dying fire – the tide has
turned and is sweeping away old landmarks. It is at such time that the need of
Conservators has arisen, and they have succeeded in rescuing some of the wreckage
from the flood; they have reconstructed for new generations the fragments still
remaining of bygone days and scenes. (30 January 1897).

As late as 1910 commentators were still seeing Barrie's early work in
terms of history:

The "Auld Licht Idylls" especially depicts a rugged tract of country manners which is
rapidly being smoothed away, and its minute delicate realism makes it invaluable to
the student of Scottish morals and religion during the middle of the nineteenth
century. (Moffat 1910: 21)

The success of *Auld Licht Idylls* and *A Window in Thrums* thrust
an identity upon Barrie and the success of Crockett and Maclaren
made it difficult for developments and alterations in his work to be
seen from an objective angle. Understanding of his fiction got trapped
in the Kailyard. The publication of *My Lady Nicotine* in 1890 led the
Spectator to worry that "the photographer of Thrums" was forgetting

---

[14] See Nicoll 1892a and 1892b and several other letters in the pages of the *British
Weekly*.

that his "heart is in Scottish life and character" (7 June 1890). "Mr Barrie's muse has crossed the border", announced the *Glasgow Herald*, "we can only hope [...] she has not forgotten to provide herself with a return ticket" (1 May 1890). When *Sentimental Tommy* was published in 1896, the *Catholic World* bemoaned that "Thrums does not thrive in a London atmosphere" (December 1896) and the *Times* wrote of the story's sequel that "Antaeus lifted from earth was not weaker than Mr. Barrie once outside Thrums. The story of Tommy and Grizel in Thrums is the real story, and it is told as only Mr. Barrie can tell it, because it is felt as only he can feel it" (17 October 1900).

Like Hardy and others writers of the age, Barrie was a victim of the publicity machine that constructed a regional image around his work.[15] But whereas Hardy was complicit in the construction of Wessex, Barrie left Thrums behind once the literary and tourist industry started to take grip. The numerous accounts of literary tours that appeared in magazines and periodicals were only the start of the process by which Barrie's work became indelibly associated with his home region. The earliest literary tour is a deliberately fictional account by William Robertson Nicoll, the man who played a crucial editorial role in the success of the Kailyard vogue. Writing in the *British Weekly* under his transparent *nom de plume*, Claudius Clear, Nicoll told his readers how he took the train to Thrums and met Gavin Ogilvy:

I had hardly stepped out of my carriage when I perceived the familiar form of the historian of Thrums descending the Brae. [...] Mr Gavin Ogilvy has retired from the onerous and responsible positions occupied by him as schoolmaster of Glen Quharity and precentor in the Free Church, and has taken up his abode in Thrums. His house may easily be discovered [...] from this he still accurately and extensively surveys the district. (Nicoll 1889: 231)

Nicoll concluded his imaginary meeting by stating that "I have simply to certify the veracity of the chronicler". In so doing, he propagated the idea that the Barrie's fiction was an accurate document of real life in regional Scotland.

Other tour articles were more explicitly factual. John Geddie

---

[15] For a discussion of Hardy in this context, see Gatrell (2003).

wrote and illustrated two essays for the magazine *Ludgate*, pointing out the landmarks to be found in the fiction (Geddie 1897, 1898). Illustrative material tightened the identification between author and place. A publication in the American journal *Dial* printed seventy pictures of Thrums accompanied by no literary criticism or comment at all (1 December 1896). Some tour articles admitted that Barrie's region was an artistic one. Margaretta Byrde commented:

Illusions certainly get dispelled in Thrums [...] if the eyes of the English-speaking race are turned upon Kirriemuir it is not with the expectation of finding it the real Thrums, but the ideal one [...]. The pen that drew the place and people did not merely transcribe life, it created it. [...] It is like tearing the pictures from a volume, this loss of the actual. The story often reads the better without them [...] the actual is not the real. (Byrde 1898: 325)

It is noticeable that these articles only begin to proliferate after the success of Crockett and Maclaren and at a time when Barrie was moving away from Thrums as the focus for his fiction.[16] Nevertheless, the extensive interest in Thrums penetrated historical and geographical accounts of Kirriemuir. In 1900 M.E. Leicester Addis published an article on the social history of the town entitled "A Harvest Home in Thrums" and four years earlier, in his *Thrums and its Glens: Historical Relics and Recollections*, James Stirton called Thrums "quite a geographical term" (Stirton 1896). Stirton's book includes etchings of the Auld Licht Manse, the Dominie's schoolhouse and Barrie's birthplace, and takes the reader on a tour of the town pointing out the locations in Barrie's books. A similar publication that appeared in the same year and which was aimed more explicitly at tourists was John Mills's *Through Thrums: A Handbook for Visitors to Kirriemuir and the District*. Pilgrimages to Kirriemuir became commonplace. The American journal *Outlook* recorded that Thrums was visited "in the summer of 1890 by 3,500 pilgrims" (Cunningham 1896: 552). Mills had written to Barrie enquiring about the location of his stories and had received the reply: "I sometimes purposely take

---

[16] In addition to those articles quoted from above, see Bremner (1894), Jackson (1894), Mullett (1900).

liberties with localities."[17] In his guidebook he takes his readers on a fiction-based tour of the town and also includes pencil sketches of "Typical Thrumsians", presumably genuine Kirriemuir people. Trade advertisements at the back of the book show how Thrums was taken up as an alternative name for Kirriemuir. Tourists were encouraged to sample the "Celebrated Rock," which bore a "True picture of the 'Window in Thrums' and the Residence of Mr. Barrie," or to visit the Thrums lending library or purchase a pair of Thrums boots with the special "A Window in Thrums" trademark.

Given the historical precedents of Burns and Scott, and the parallel interest in Hardy and Blackmore – the fictional Doone valley was actually recorded on Ordnance Survey maps – this spectacle of literary tourism should not surprise us. Yet two book-length studies written over thirty years later, J.A. Hammerton's *Barrieland: A Thrums Pilgrimage* (1929) and John Kennedy's *Thrums and the Barrie Country* (1930), show the extent to which understanding of Barrie's work remained closely associated with the social and geographical setting of his early books. Maps and photographs enable both books to provide an anecdotal history of Kirriemuir seen through the window of Barrie's early fiction, and other contemporary studies adopt the same approach even when there is no pretence to a focal interest in Thrums. James A. Roy's book, which on the dust wrapper claims to be "the first genuine critical appreciation" of Barrie's work, nevertheless opens with a chapter on the history of Kirriemuir (Roy 1937). Similarly, Patrick Chalmers' book, *The Barrie Inspiration* (1938), locates that inspiration in the region by giving an extensive account of Kirriemuir's social history.

These book-length studies show that, although Barrie had severed his links with Thrums at the turn of the century and became the most famous playwright of his age, in the twilight of his career, and in the wake of his immediate death in 1937, Kirriemuir and its social history was still indelibly wound up with his literary identity. The assimilation of Barrie's work into the context of regionalism helped create the concept Kailyard because it made central the critical emphasis on authenticity of national picture that has dominated

---

[17] Unpublished ALS, 13 October 1895 (Beinecke)

criticism. It is because his literary-critical identity was forged in this way that Scottish critics became eager to castigate his work on the criterion of failed social realism.

Chapter Three

S.R. Crockett: Romancing Galloway

I

If J.M. Barrie's career in fiction represents a movement away from realist techniques and a corresponding shift in the presentation of an identifiable geographical place in fiction, something similar might be said of S.R. Crockett, who achieved overnight success with *The Stickit Minister* in 1893. Like Barrie, and unlike Ian Maclaren, Crockett was a writer by vocation. As a student in Edinburgh he wrote poetry and supplemented his meagre scholarship with journalism. His early journalism appeared in the *Edinburgh Daily News* and he also wrote for the *Daily Chronicle* – where he was briefly art critic – and for *Lloyd's Weekly Newspaper* – a penny weekly with a large circulation aimed at the working-classes. In 1878 he spent six months in London living by the pen and it is reported that once "whilst on a visit to London, with a literary career in view, he was employed, for a short time, as a reporter of debates in parliament" (Harper 1907: 74, 125).

It was not unusual for writers of this period to combine literature with journalism and it was typical for Scottish writers to write for both the Scottish and the wider British markets. In this respect Crockett can be compared to Barrie, Andrew Lang, William Sharp and George Douglas Brown, among others, all of whom straddled the local and national markets in their journalism. Nor was Crockett's journalism restricted to religious topics and publications. Although he wrote "editorials on theological subjects for religious periodicals" (Donaldson 1989: 35) he contributed work on other subjects as well, and from 1890 he reportedly edited and wrote almost the entire contents of the Christian Socialist publication, *The Workers' Monthly* (Harper 1907: 35).

In his early career Crockett aspired to be a poet. His early verse appeared in the Dumfries and Castle Douglas weekly papers (Harper 1907: 61) and was later collected in a volume entitled *Dulce Cor*, published by Kegan Paul in 1886. In the same year the Edinburgh

printer David Douglas issued a volume "by the author of *Dulce Cor*"
entitled *Valete, Frates!*, dedicated to his fellow university students.
Neither volume made any impact and Robert Louis Stevenson advised
Crockett not to write any more verse "but use good Galloway Scots
for your stomach's sake – and for mine" (Stevenson 1995: VI: 175).
He was not alone in his opinion. Edward Garnett, the reader for the
publishing firm of T. Fisher Unwin, told his employers to advise
Crockett he should "never write another line of poetry" (Cited in
Collin 1991: 92–3).

    In terms of the Kailyard debate, the central Crockett text is *The
Stickit Minister*, his first published work of prose. Like *Auld Licht
Idylls* and Maclaren's *Beside the Bonnie Brier Bush*, it has its origins
in newspaper sketches but in Crockett's case the paper was a Glasgow
publication, *The Christian Leader*, a penny weekly. It is uncertain if
The Christian Leader was ever published in England and Crockett's
stories probably first circulated among a predominantly Scottish – as
opposed to British – readership. Compared to both Barrie and
Maclaren, he would have been less inclined to tailor his stories to an
audience predominantly – if not exclusively – outside Scotland. If this
fact discounts William Donaldson's charge that the Kailyard stories
were written for an exclusively Anglo-American audience (Donaldson
1986: 145), there remain two main accusations against *The Stickit
Minister*; one concerns the literary quality of the stories and the other
the alleged narrowness of vision. As with Maclaren, Crockett's
ministerial background has often been invoked in order to explain his
work. The emphasis of *The Christian Leader* was obviously religious
but in this period the religious press was not exclusively concerned
with religious topics; it was more a matter of tone than explicit
content.

    Some of the stories in *The Christian Leader* were grouped into
series, and it is those published under the heading "Ministers of our
Countryside" that have come to be associated with Kailyard. George
Blake argues that "as with everything of the Kailyard School",
Crockett writes "about life as seen through the manse window" (Blake
1951: 45). But these are not always "sweet amusing little stories"
(Blake 1951: 13) and Crockett frequently presents his ministers as
victims. As in some of Barrie's stories, gossip and false conjecture are

salient issues in *The Stickit Minister*; several chapters are concerned
with false judgement and opinion, often in the wake of impending
death. In the title story, Robert Fraser, who has sacrificed his own
career for that of his brother, is wrongly seen in the eyes of the world
as a failure and as a man consumed by jealousy. "Boanerges
Simpson's Encumbrance" is in a more comic vein. The encumbrance
is the minister's wife, who "was not at all the woman to dispense
afternoon tea to the session's spouses between the hours of three and
six" and whose lack of attention to her husband's brilliant sermons is
attributed to "a nature averse to the message of grace which so
strongly affected others" (Crockett 1893: 159, 167). Again, the
judgement is false. It emerges that the minister's wife is the author of
all his sermons and after she dies her husband bids a hasty retreat into
retirement.

Crockett invariably sides with his ministers and it is known that
his own experiences as Free Church minister in Penicuik were often
difficult. Unlike Maclaren's fiction, where the views of Elders and
parishioners are sacrosanct, several of the stories attack the way
ministers are treated by their people. In "The Courtship of Allan
Fairley", a minister refuses to turn his mother out of his house because
the ladies from the "big colony of dreadfu' respectable gentry in oor
pairish" feel unable to call upon her (Crockett 1893: 129). Similarly,
in "The Probationer", Thomas Todd is poorly treated by an
unwelcoming parish, and in "The Candid Friend" a sycophant reports
the gossip in the parish and unsettles the minister's confidence before
being roundly rebuked by the minister's wife. In each of these stories
the minister's position is reasserted at the end of the sketch. In
"Accepted of the Beasts", however, Hugh Hamilton becomes the
subject of gossip so malicious that it leads to an early death:

murderous whispers, indefinite, disquieting, suggesting vague possibilities of all
things evil, brought with them the foul reek of the pit where they were forged,
paralysing his work and killing his best usefulness. (Crockett 1893: 21)

Hamilton is presented as a paragon, whose nature is so good that he
remains oblivious to all the bad feeling around him. He is brought to
trial by the Presbytery and suspended but his conscience remains

clear. He dies with the words of Issiah 53:3 – "He was despised and rejected by men ..." – engraved on his tombstone.

Not all the ministers are victims. "The Lammas Preaching" comically exposes a minister who foolishly takes on the Galloway elements in a determination to carry through the sentiments of his sermon "Whatsoever thy hand findeth to do, do it with thy might". Comedy is also the watchword in "The Three Maister Peter Slees", where the third in a generation of ministers makes the mistake of digging into his ancestor's store of past sermons and preaching about the Duke of Wellington's triumph at Waterloo. As he was to do throughout his career, Crockett alternates in these stories between comedy, tragedy, realism, romance and pathos. Inevitably, as a collection, *The Stickit Minister* lacks shape.

As in Maclaren's fiction, local pride in Galloway is everything and outsiders are treated with suspicion. In "Trials for Licence" a scholarly Edinburgh laddie, with a mastery of Hebrew and Latin "an' ither langwidges that naebody speaks noo", is asked to read one of his Latin "discoorses in English" (Crockett 1893: 32). As soon as the substance of the doctrine is revealed, the young man is sorely judged by the presbytery and in the end is glad to be passed over by the parish. "Why David Oliphant Remained a Presbyterian" taps the emotions of history and family values. David, one of the "brilliant young Northmen" who yearly triumph in Oxford, resists the invitation to join the Anglican Church when his memories turn to his Cameronian background and his childhood in Galloway. Speaking "with the steady voice and eye that had come to him from his grandfather", David resolves he "must cleave to my own church and my own people!" (Crockett 1893: 113).

"The Heather Lintie" raises the issue of sentimentality and also Crockett's relationship to his material. It was one of the stories that Robert Louis Stevenson considered "*drowned* in Scotland" (Stevenson 1995: VIII: 153). Janet Balchrystie is a hard-working young woman whose mother died young and whose father – like several men in Crockett's fiction – is a drunkard. Gavin Balchrystie's afflictions and his ultimate death are lightly treated in Crockett's characteristically taught prose:

So it came to pass that one night Gavin Balchrystie did not come home at all, at least not till he was brought lying comfortably on the door of a disused third-class carriage, which was now seeing out its career, anchored under the bank at Loch Merrick, where Gavin had used it as a shelter. (Crockett 1893: 41)

The comic presentation of the tragic figure of Gavin contrasts sharply with the sentimental presentation of the pious Janet. An orphan, who as a young woman had kept her father's home spotless, Janet is plain, Church-going, and admired of the neighbourhood, so much so that the laird allows her to keep her house after the death of her father together with "a cow's grass, and thirty pound sterling in the year as a charge on the estate" (Crockett 1893: 43). The main plot, however, follows Janet's ambition to be a poet. Having published several verses in the local paper, and having had to endure the corrections of the senior office-boy, who had been instructed by the editor to "cut down, tinker the rhymes, and lop any superfluity of feet", Janet resolves to have the unexpurgated version of her poems printed as a book (Crockett 1893: 44). It falls to a "clever young reporter" on a paper that was making itself known for "exposures" to review the volume, and he duly turns out two columns of patronising cynicism disguised as praise – a "triumph of the New Journalism" (Crockett 1893: 48).

Although Crockett clearly positions himself against the clever young reporter, he nevertheless adopts a position of cynicism towards Janet. He mocks her provincialism and her misplaced confidence in her own abilities. Janet has no way of indicating corrections on the proof sheet but by writing out the whole poem again. She thinks initially of withholding her name but decides against it because "she felt she was not justified in bringing about such a controversy as divided Scotland concerning that 'Great Unknown' who wrote the Waverley Novels" (Crockett 1893: 46). Worse still, Crockett actually prints a stanza from one of Janet's poems so that the young reporter can mockingly laud the imagery by which Janet captures the death of two young lambs. The attitude of condescension thus jars with the overt sentimentality of the story's ending. Exhausted by her exploits as poet and orphan, Janet becomes ill and takes to her deathbed where one evening she is delivered the issue of the paper that contains the review of "The Heather Lintie". Nervously she reads the first line of the review: "A genuine source of pride to every native of the ancient province" (Crockett 1893: 51). With tears falling on the "precious paper", she collapses "in a rapture of devout thankfulness" resolving to read the rest in the morning, which she never sees:

> They found Janet on the morning of the second day after, with a look so glad on her face and so natural an expectation in the unclosed eye, that Rob Affleck spoke to her and expected an answer. *The Night Hawk* was clasped to her breast with a hand that they could not loosen. It went to the grave with her body. The ink had run a little here and there, where the tears had fallen thickest.
>   God is more merciful than man. (Crockett 1893: 52)

The piety of that last sentence would not be so irksome had Crockett not spent so many of the preceding pages mocking Janet himself.

One of the more impressive aspects of *The Stickit Minister* is the handling of dialect. Islay Donaldson notes Crockett's "keen ear for Scots" and discusses the gradations of Scots in the title story (Donaldson 1989: 60–2). In addition, several of the stories are narrated in a form of Scots by the character Saunders M'Quhirr, a farmer. Sometimes Saunders narrates in English but with a Scots inflection, as in the opening to "The Courtship of Allan Fairley, of Earlswood":

> This is no carried tale, but just as the minister himself told it to me. He was pleased like when he told me, an' I am giving you what is not to be told to everybody. Not that Allan Fairley need be ashamed, but proud the rather if every soul from here to Maidenkirk had the outs and the ins of the story at their fingers' end. (Crockett 1893: 124)

None of the words here need glossing for the outside reader, but the choice of language and the syntax are characteristic of regional speech and achieve the effect at which Lewis Grassic Gibbon aimed in *A Scots Quair* of "moulding the English language into the rhythms and cadences of Scots spoken speech" (Gibbon 1934: 173). In other stories, however, Saunders' narration contains words that are spelled phonetically:

> Rob Adair cam' in baith wat an' dry, an' to help baith, got a change o' claes an' his tea oot o' oor best cheena. Then when the pipes were gaun weel, they baith looked ower at me. Brawly kenned I that they were hotchin' for me to gie them the presbytery; but I gaed on askin' Rob aboot the price o' beasts, an' hoo mony lambs

had been selled on the hill that day, till my wife could stand it no longer. (Crockett 1893: 22)

Some of the spellings here, such as "cheena", merely indicate Saunders' accent, but the use of unglossed words such as "claes" and "hotchin'" suggest a different artistic strategy, one that anticipates James Kelman's refusal to draw a distinction between the language of narration and the language of dialogue. Although several of the Scots words in the book are glossed with parenthetical translations, the experience of reading these chapters is different from the other sections of the book where Scots is the domain only of dialogue.

William Donaldson has shown how Scottish newspapers of this period regularly printed discursive prose – fiction and non-fiction – in Scots. What he notes of such papers as *The People's Journal* and the *Glasgow Weekly Mail*, appears to apply to *The Christian Leader* as well. But Crockett's decision to retain his Scots narration for the book publication of *The Stickit Minister* to some extent challenges Donaldson's judgement that writers like Crockett tailored their stories to suit the demands of the middle-class, "Anglo-American" (or rather British) book trade. Crockett's handling of Scots is not his least achievement in these stories. In "The Probationer", where Saunders is entertaining his friend Thomas Todd, the narrator comments on writing in Scots:

Tammas can speak the English as weel as onybody, but when he gets among his own folk he prides himself on relapsing, so to speak, into the broadest Gallowa'. He laughs at me for being fond of writing in proper English. He says that I need not try it, for when I do my best, every sentence has got the "Gallowa' lug-mark" plain on it. But this is his nonsense. (Crockett 1893: 68)

Despite Saunders' caveat, his writing does have the mark of Galloway on it.

With the success of *The Stickit Minister* Crockett began to find his literary identity as the author of Galloway. It was the regional setting that captured the attention of reviewers. *The Athenaeum* saw Crockett as following MacDonald and Barrie in "recording the peculiar modes of speech and thought" in his "district" (6 May 1893) and *The Saturday Review* described the book as "Scotch stories, racy of the soil, told with a masterly command of dialect and national characteristics" (29 April 1893). At least two reviewers questioned whether the book wasn't too realistic. The *Saturday Review* judged that Crockett's stories seemed "powerfully realistic, almost too powerful for their tiny dimensions" and George Douglas in the *Bookman* echoed the sentiment:

> that blow from a poker which falls on a boy's head in "Duncan Duncanson"; that incident with the powder flask in "The Split in the Marrow-Kirk" – do they not savour somewhat too strongly of Mr. Kipling's manner to be perfectly in place among quiet tales of a Scottish parish? (August 1893)

Thanks in part to the success of Barrie's fiction, there was an established convention that tales of Scottish parishes, with their tiny dimensions, should be "quiet". Crockett's contribution to the genre challenged expectations.

As I discussed in Chapter 2, it was not unusual for reviewers, such as the *Saturday* reviewer quoted above, to collapse region into nation. In accounts of Crockett's works this became common. The *Athenaeum* considered *Little Anna Mark* (1900) to show "a great mastery of the finer and minuter differentiae of Scottish Character" (14 July 1900) whilst *The Bookman* considered *Cinderella* to contain "valuable additions" to the gallery of "disappearing Scottish 'types'" (July 1901). It became easy for reviewers to conclude that Crockett "understands his countrymen", as the *Athenaeum* wrote of *The Firebrand* (7 December 1901), and the national value of a piece of work became a quality in itself. Writing in the *Bookman*, William Wallace judged that whilst Crockett's treatment of love in *Lad's Love* (1897) was "vulgar", the novel was "true to Scotland and to Galloway rural life, and that is all that concerns me" (April 1897). This tendency to dissolve region into nation helps explain the anxiety over national representation expressed by the early Kailyard critics discussed in Chapter 1.

As with Barrie, Crockett's identity as a writer was quickly established as that of a regional novelist aiming to describe life and manners in his chosen locality. By and large his efforts outside this mode were treated with disapproval and any return to Galloway sparked remarks of reassurance. In its reviews of *The Banner of Blue*

(1903) and *Love Idylls* (1901), the *Athenaeum* concluded that "Mr. Crockett is always readable when he is on familiar ground" and that "he is never quite happy except in Galloway" (28 March 1903, 28 September 1901). Similarly, *The Spectator* announced of *The Standard Bearer*: "his foot is once more on his native hearth, and the atmosphere is thick with magnificent Kailyardisms" (4 June 1898). Few readers who have perused Crockett's historical romances set in Germany or elsewhere would argue that these works are superior to those set in Galloway, but it is clear that contemporary critics valued his work as a contribution to Scottish regional fiction above all else.

Unlike Barrie, however, Crockett did not find his identification with Galloway inhibiting and was prepared to make the most of the popular and critical interest that his fiction inspired. Two years after *The Stickit Minister* appeared he issued *Bog-Myrtle and Peat*, a second compilation of sketches from *The Christian Leader*. The sub-title – *Tales Chiefly of Galloway Gathered from the years 1889 to 1895* – makes explicit the regional focus and the volume announces itself as another dose of *Stickit Minister* stories. *The Stickit Minister's Wooing and other Galloway stories*, published much later in 1900, after Crockett had achieved success in different fictional modes, does so even more.

Crockett published *Bog-Myrtle and Peat* primarily for financial reasons and against the advice of his publishers. Edward Garnett, of Fisher Unwin, thought the sketches "pot-boilers" with "no original matter" (Cited in Collin 1991: 113). He advised his employers that "TFU can sell an edition, mostly to the semi-emancipated Scotch readers of the *Christian Leader*", but Unwin declined the volume and it was published instead by the minor firm of Bliss, Sands and Foster. For his part, Crockett told his publisher:

I had thought of all you say about "Bog-Myrtle & Peat" and there is truth in it, but I have been refurnishing and need money. So I have just one way of getting it, selling my wares, just the same as if I were a publisher. (Cited in Collin 1991: 113).

Throughout his career, Crockett retained this commercial view of his literary work and there can be no doubt that the hasty publication of *Bog-Myrtle and Peat* damaged his reputation, especially as that reputation had only recently been enhanced by the triumphant publication of *The Raiders* (1894).

In *Bog Myrtle and Peat*, there is no attempt to signal a fictional construction of place in the manner of Thrums or Wessex, and in spite of the emphasis on Galloway in the sub-title, the stories have a range of different settings and deal with a variety of subjects and different historical periods. Divided into five sections, "Adventures", "Intimacies", "Histories", "Idylls" and "Tales of the Kirk", the collection concludes with an epilogue "In Praise of Galloway". The quality of the stories is very uneven. The "Adventures" section includes a love story with a supernatural theme and a tale of smuggling set in the eighteenth century. "The Case of John Arniston's Conscience" is a story of a London-Scot who covets another man's wife and struggles with the ninth commandment but whose conscience is relieved by the fortunate death of the husband. "Histories" is oddly titled since it focuses mainly on the theme of education. The character of Kit Kennedy is given his first airing and "The Colleging of Simeon Gleg" is another humorous story about a "lad o' pairts". "Intimacies" are mostly centred around figures of the Kirk. "A Scottish Sabbath Day" looks back on the youth of Walter Carmichael in the Cameronian Kirk; "The Prodigal Daughter" is also set in the "latest years of last-century" (Crockett 1895: 235), and tells the story of the daughters of the Cameronian minister.

Once again some of the stories are narrated by Saunders M'Quhirr and "The Last Anderson of Deeside" was almost certainly the story that prompted "T. Duncan" to pen the satire in the *Glasgow Herald* discussed in Chapter 1. In Duncan's sketch, Saunders McWhannel from Drumwhinnie becomes a successful Kailyard novelist in London; in Crockett's story, Saunders M'Quhirr, the farmer of Drumquhat, tells to his friend the story of Walter Anderson, the minister's son, who had won prizes at college but who had succumbed to sin in London. The story, told in thick dialect, reduces Saunders' friend to tears and is in almost every way characteristic of the kind of storyline that became associated with "Kailyard". The son who leaves the sanctuary of the home comes to grief in the city and returns home too late to make amends with his family. The narrative is one that Barrie had explored artfully in *A Window in Thrums* and which Maclaren would later use more than once.

Bog Myrtle and Peat did nothing to enhance Crockett's reputation, as Duncan's sketch proves. The *Saturday Review* was especially condemning suggesting that Crockett "has still to learn not to snivel at his own essays in pathos, nor to be alarmed at his own bogle stories", and wryly commenting: "one cannot help admiring the sturdy patriotism that makes this kind of book a commercial success" (20 April 1895). If *Bog-Myrtle and Peat* and *The Stickit Minister's Wooing* showed that Crockett was happy to plough the fertile soil tilled by the success of *The Stickit Minister*, the publication of *Raiderland* (1904) reveals a different attitude towards regionalism. Subtitled *All About Grey Galloway, its Stories, Characters, Humours*, this text combines fiction with history to the extent of blurring them. As the reviewer for the *Academy* remarked: "Mr Crockett is not making a guide book, but rather a garrulous literary companion to the guide-books which already exist" (12 November 1904). In addition to imaginative stories, *Raiderland* contains an explicitly factual account of the region and the same reviewer considered "The Diary of an Eighteenth-Century Galloway Laird" to be "a really important contribution to our knowledge of the social life of Scotland just before the dawn of the nineteenth century".

Fiction and history existed in close relation for Crockett. As an historical romancer he was obliged to be accurate with facts. In an article he explained that he preferred "at the very least three years of prolonged residence" in a place "before I begin even to draw up chapter-headings". At the time of writing he claimed that he had built up "over two hundred volumes of indexed cuttings [and] over a thousand notebooks" (Crockett 1900: 6). His determination to be authentic in his treatment of the past led him to research his stories seriously, but in his early career he was accused of plagiarising from his sources. In his review of *The Lilac Sunbonnet* in the *Academy* (3 November 1894), William Wallace called for Crockett "to deal with the serious charge of plagiarism which has been made against him in Scotland" and recorded how a section from the chapter "The Cuif before the Session" had been "lifted without acknowledgement" from "Jockey and Maggy's Courtship", a chapbook by Dugald Graham (d.1779) whose works had been reprinted in 1883. The comparisons are indeed striking. Wallace quoted a section from the chapbook:

Mither, I hae been three or four times through the Bible and the New Testament, and I never saw a repenting stool in't a' [...]. But a daft history book tells me that the first o' them was used about Rome among the Papists [...].

And compared this to a section from Crockett's chapter:

Mother I've been through the Testaments mair nor yince – the New Testament mair nor twice – an' I never saw naethin about stools o' repentance in the house o' God. But my son Saunders was readin' to me the ither nicht in a fule history buik, and there it said that amang the Papists [...].

Crockett replied in a letter to the *Academy* defending his use of this source and adding (somewhat naively) that the same accusation had already been made by both the *Glasgow Herald* and the *Literary World*. Two weeks later, in the same paper, he again defended himself, arguing that the chapbooks were "pure gold to the romancer" (28 November 1894). To be fair to Crockett, he did sometimes acknowledge his sources in print. At one point in *The Stickit Minister* he quotes directly, in a footnote, from *Harper's Rambles in Galloway* (Crockett 1893: 275) and in a preface to *The Men of the Moss Hags* (1895) he notes that the story was based on research undertaken in Edinburgh University Library. He also made a special request to the *Bookman* to declare in its notice of *The Raiders* that "Few books are less original [...] in so far that almost every prominent incident has been taken from contemporary sources" (April 1894). Whilst all historical fiction depends upon historical research, Crockett was surely unwise to lift complete chunks of material from his sources, although he denied actually copying anything.

In spite of his willingness to identify himself with the context of regional fiction, Crockett experimented with different forms and genres in the novels that followed immediately after *The Stickit Minister*. It is on these works that his place in literary history rest.

II

In 1894 Crockett published four books. In addition to *The Raiders* and *The Lilac Sunbonnet*, two shorter novels, *Mad Sir Uchtred of the Hills* and *The Play Actress*, appeared in Unwin's *Autonym Library*, a series of books published at the cheap price of 1s 6d. 1894 was the year that the libraries all but destroyed the three-volume novel and Crockett's fiction appeared at a time when publishers like Unwin were experimenting with issuing fiction at much lower prices than was customary – titles in the *Autonym Library* were sold at one quarter of the retail price of *The Lilac Sunbonnet*. Nevertheless, it was the two longer novels that received the most attention. If some of the stories in *The Stickit Minister* support George Blake's view of Crockett's fiction as narrowly concerned with religion, examination of his novels challenges that conclusion. In several works Crockett is openly critical of institutional religion, nowhere more so than in *The Lilac Sunbonnet* where he attacks the narrowness of both religion and education, challenging it with the power of nature and the landscape to arouse feelings of love.

Like a typical "lad o' pairts", Ralph Peden has been "colleged by the shillings and sixpences of the poor hill folk" (Crockett 1894: 267) but he finds the life set out before him to be inhibiting. Ralph's father belongs to the Marrow Kirk, a rigidly narrow sect which Crockett invented and which he had introduced into *The Stickit Minister*. Ralph is a student in Edinburgh and is sent to Galloway to train to be a minister of the Marrow with his father's friend Allan Welsh, the only other minister of the sect. But "the lad's bent was really towards literature" (Crockett 1894: 220) and Ralph manages to leave his Latin and the teachings of the Church behind, embrace the love of Winsome Charteris, and emerge at the end of the novel as a happily married and successful poet. Abandoning the pulpit for the pen was something that Crockett was himself to do shortly after the publication of *The Lilac Sunbonnet*. As Islay Donaldson states: "the parallel is obvious" (Donaldson 1985: 292) and there are elements of Crockett in Ralph Peden. Far from preaching a Free Church message through his fiction, the treatment of religion in the novel shows a writer adopting a much more critical and individual position concerning ecclesiastical and doctrinal issues.

Throughout the novel, the Marrow Kirk is treated humorously and dismissively. It is introduced as "that sole treasure-house of orthodox truth in Scotland, which is as good as saying in the wide world – perhaps even in the universe" (Crockett 1894: 14). The break-up of the Marrow Kirk at the end of the novel is presented comically as the two ministers each depose the other for sins against the Church. Like Maclaren, Crockett rejects the narrowness of doctrinal religion. When Ralph finally renounces the Marrow Kirk to his teacher, he is described as stepping "into the clear, sobering midnight" (Crockett 1894: 269) – night is more clear than the doctrine of the Church. As Ralph tells his father at the end of the novel, if he were to join the Marrow Kirk he "must forget my humanity in order worthily to serve it!" (Crockett 1894: 326).

As noted by Islay Donaldson, the comic treatment of religion disappointed William Robertson Nicoll. Writing in the *British Weekly*, Nicoll advised: "Better leave religion alone than use it merely for comic effect" (18 October 1894). But Crockett's view of religion in *The Lilac Sunbonnet* has its serious side. For him religion comes not from doctrine but from love: "All true and pure love is an extension of God" (Crockett 1894: 283). The Marrow Kirk forbids Ralph from marrying Winsome because she is "the daughter of an unblest marriage" (Crockett 1894: 266); the irony is that her unknown father is none other than Allan Welsh, the Marrow Kirk minister himself. But Crockett's deification of love is not abstract, it is rooted in the treatment of nature and the description of landscape which is an essential part of the text. What Ralph Peden finds in Galloway is not only love for Winsome but love for Nature, and it is in his appreciation of the Galloway landscape that his character develops. We are told that "Ralph loved Nature instinctively, and saw it as a town-bred lad rarely does" (Crockett 1894: 106). In his time as a minister, Crockett regularly gave sermons on the love of nature as the love of God, and the rich natural descriptions found in so many of his novels give some indication of why Ruskin found them appealing.

The natural description in *The Lilac Sunbonnet* is most effective when presented from the perspective of the central character. It is

Nature that distracts Ralph away from his studies and the Marrow Kirk. In chapter 1, his reading is interrupted by a "humble-bee", whose flight is then described from Ralph's perspective:

The humble-bee buzzed a little more, discontentedly, thought of going back, crept out at last from beneath the Hebrew Lexicon, and appeared to comb his hair with his feeler. Then he slowly mounted along the broad blade of a meadow fox-tail grass, which bent under him as if to afford him an elastic send-off upon his flight. With a spring he lumbered up, taking his way over the single field which separated his house from the edge of the Grannoch water – where on the other side, above the glistening sickle-sweep of sand which looked so inviting, yet untouched under the pines by the morning sun, the hyacinths lay like a blue wreath of peat smoke in the hollows of the wood. (Crockett 1894: 15)

We follow the flight of the bee over the Galloway landscape with Ralph's eyes, and as Donaldson points out, "if Ralph is to be so deeply moved by the richness of summer, the reader must be made to feel it too" (Donaldson 1989: 76). Here "location" is far from being "flat, featureless, and vague" as one critic has written of Kailyard fiction (Shepherd 1988: 311).

F.R. Hart notes that *The Lilac Sunbonnet* is "drenched in the imagery of Eden" (Hart 1978: 118) and at one point the landscape is explicitly termed "a later Eden" (Crockett 1894: 298). But Crockett's treatment of Nature makes his world closer to pantheism than the "neo-paganism" identified by Hart.[1] God is identified as part of the universe:

It was a marvellous dawning, this one that Winsome waited for. Dawn is the secret of the universe. It thrills us somehow with a far-off prophecy of that eternal dawning when the God That Is shall reveal himself – the dawning which shall brighten into the more perfect day. (Crockett 1894: 89)

The interplay between light and darkness is further developed in a later section where twilight is deified:

both light and darkness, night and day, are but the accidents of a little time. It is twilight – the twilight of the morning and of the gods – that is the true normal of the

---

[1] Donaldson notes this and suggests comparisons with George MacDonald (1985: 302–3).

universe. Night is but the shadow of the earth, light the nearness of the central sun. But when the soul of man goeth its way beyond the confines of the little multiplied circles of the system of the sun, it passes at once into the dim twilight of space, where for myriads of myriad miles there is only the grey of the earliest God's gloaming, which existed just so or ever the world was, and shall be when the world is not. Light and dark, day and night, are but as the lights of a station at which the train does not stop. They whisk past, gleaming bright but for a moment, and the world which came out of great twilight plunges again into it, perhaps to be remade and reillumined on some eternal morning. (Crockett 1894: 270–1)

The presentation of a twilight world on the edge of dissolution yet carrying the anticipation of creation is characteristic of the *fin de siècle*. The Wagnerian reference to the twilight of the Gods places the description within a particular cultural context and the word "perhaps" puts any Christian certainty at a distance. In his final sermon at Penicuik Crockett had assured his congregation that he would teach the "same vital truths" in his fiction: "Literature has need of believing men to hold aloft the banner of belief" (Donaldson 1989: 49). But that belief was not to be espoused in any simplistic worldview. Crockett was to revisit this preoccupation with twilight and apocalypse in *The Raiders*.

Ralph and Winsome's love is frequently presented in apocalyptic terms:

Winsome Charteris had come so suddenly into his life that the universe seemed newborn in a day [...]. It was not the same world as it had been a week ago [...]. There was the light of a new life in their eyes [...] a brand-new world was in the making". (Crockett 1894: 51, 257, 282, 360)

In the chapter "Midsummer Dawn", Nature is described as "suddenly dissolv[ing] into confused meaninglessness" as Ralph and Winsome meet, and when they part the breaking of day is associated with the breaking of a new world:

As Winsome and Ralph turned towards the east, the sun set his face over the great Scotch firs on the ridge, whose tops stood out like poised irregular blots on the fire centred ocean of light.

It was the new day, and if the new world had not come with it, of a surety it was well on the way. (Crockett 1894: 110–11)

It was Crockett's presentation of love that offended J.H. Millar, who argued that Crockett "opens the sluices to an irresistible flood of nauseous and nasty philandering" (Millar 1895: 391). His objection is to Crockett's style of displacing the physicality of sexuality onto external objects and other parts of the body. As in George Du Maurier's *Trilby*, published the year after *The Lilac Sunbonnet*, the forbidden sight of a naked foot figures as a displaced object for sexual desire. When he observes Winsome and Meg Kissock barefoot at the blanket washing, we are told "The hot blood surged in responsive shame to Ralph Peden's cheeks and temples" (Crockett 1894: 24). Later on, he and Winsome "daringly" think of running barefoot over the grass (Crockett 1894: 201). Crockett constantly stresses the effect of sexual attraction on the nerves, pulses and blood of his hero and heroine: A "ripple of girl's laughter" sends "a strange stirring of excitement along the nerves" of Ralph; when a breeze blows down "a flossy tendril of Winsome's golden hair", "his hand tingled with the desire to touch it" (Crockett 1894: 17, 115). Similarly, Winsome's awakening love for Ralph is described as a "bursting bud"; Ralph's poems quicken her "pulse"; his wooing generates "Little ticking impulses [which] drummed in her head" (Crockett 1894: 109, 91, 211). In the exultant chapter "The Dark of the Moon", the actions of the nerves and the blood are strongly stated: "Time and again the blood rushed to his temples […] the thrill electric of the contact […] she looked up throbbing and palpitating […] the dammed-back blood-surge drave thundering in his ears" (Crockett 1894: 238–41).

For George Blake, these sorts of descriptions make it "hard for any reasonably literate adult of the mid-twentieth century to read *The Lilac Sunbonnet* without nausea" (Blake 1951: 47–8). Islay Donaldson counters, suggesting that Crockett's "method of illustrating through external objects the tension between the sexes" approaches that of D.H. Lawrence (Donaldson 1989: 79–81). As Donaldson notes, the lilac sunbonnet itself is the strongest of the sexual symbols and the scene where Winsome swings it provocatively leading Ralph to snatch it out of her hands and tear it is strongly suggestive in its sexual symbolism. The sunbonnet serves much the same function as the minister's hat in Barrie's *The Little Minister*, and William Wallace, in his review in *the Academy*, noted other parallels:

There is a suspicion of Mr Barrie's Egyptian in Winsome Charteris [and] the confession of Mr Welsh, the Marrow minister, that he is the father of Winsome Charteris, at once recalls the confession of the Dominie in *The Little Minister*, that he is Mr Dishart's father. (3 November 1894)

Crockett was not averse to borrowing ideas from other writers and he must have been conscious of the comparison. If so, the borrowing points up the distinction between the two writers in the treatment of sexuality. Whereas Barrie's characters play out a game of wits in the mind, Crockett's focus is on the physical sensuality of his lovers.

The book has several other points of interest, not least the presentation of life on a Galloway farm, which, as Donaldson states, "is no pastoral idyll but a real unidealised rural society" (Donaldson 1985: 295). The humorous sub-plot, featuring the trials and tribulations of the gravedigger, Saunders Mowdiewort, shadows the main love-plot and allows Crockett to include large sections of dialogue in Scots. Most of the lower-class characters, including Winsome's grandmother and the maid Meg Kissock, speak in dialect. Parenthetical translations are provided for some of the words and, like Maclaren, Crockett sometimes provides a lengthy definition for those words that cannot adequately be translated into English:

It may be well to explain that there is a latent meaning, apparent only to Galloway folk of the ancient time, in the word "cuif". It conveys at once the ideas of inefficiency and folly, of simplicity and the ignorance of it. The Cuif is a feckless person of the male sex, who is a recognised butt for a whole neighbourhood to sharpen its wits upon. (Crockett 1894: 72)

A further example of this comes in a later chapter where the word "henchin" is glossed as "jerking from the side" (Crockett 1894: 310). Emma Letley finds in *The Lilac Sunbonnet* "an overt and self-conscious display of the foreign" and considers the parenthetical glosses "part of a commercial effort to market Scotland as a foreign place" (Letley 1987: 245, 247). In later editions of Crockett's works publishers appended glossaries to the novels.

The Lilac Sunbonnet has not worn as well as *The Raiders*, chiefly because of the intrusive narrative preaching. The novel is littered with aphorisms that frequently jar, not least when the observations are about women. In the chapter where Ralph and Winsome declare their unbounded love for each other the narrative is frequently interrupted by such comments as:

Winsome knew even better than Ralph that he must go, yet the most accurate knowledge of necessity does not prevent the resentful feeling in a woman's heart when one she loves goes before his time. [...] It was hardly fair. Winsome acknowledges as much herself; but then a woman has no weapons but her wit and her beauty – which is, seeing the use she can make of these two, on the whole rather fortunate than otherwise. (Crockett 1894: 293, 295)

Whilst this preaching never takes the form of sermonising, Crockett is always looking to drive home his points. It is the method of direct statement that makes the representation of women both pious and stereoptypical. We are constantly being told that Winsome embodies ideal womanly virtues: "A woman ever longs to be giving herself [...] it is the heritage of the woman to be stronger in the crises which inevitably wait upon love" (Crockett 1894: 247; 302).

Blake considered that "Crockett's jaunty air of realism conveys the impression that he really believed this mass of sludge to be pretty good and almost possible" (Blake 1951: 51). His criticism is a reaction to the blending – or collision – of realism and romance. Crockett's use of a real identifiable place gives his fictional world more than just an air of reality; real place names are mentioned and the descriptions of Galloway farms and landscape are an essential part of the text. The criticism, therefore, turns on form and genre. As I argued in relation to Barrie, the choice of an identifiable genre such as idyllic fiction – or in Crockett's case idyllic romance – demands an appropriate critical approach. But whilst it is demonstrably wrong to castigate Crockett on grounds of realism, the indeterminate form of *The Lilac Sunbonnet* is something of a weakness. Indeed Crockett was himself uncertain about what form best suited his story. In a letter to Thomas Fraser, he revealed how his plans for the novel changed as he became more clear of his chosen form:

I began Meg Kissock and Jess with the idea of making them real and of the soil. But I had to go back and heighten them – writing the first chapter – Jess meeting Ralph – last of all. I am a romancer, and not a Zola, and instinctively felt that in a story which was meant not to be an exposure nor a photograph, but a love idyll, I could not make the real article go. (Cited in Collin 1991: 109)

Documentary realism was not Crockett's intention but the handling of narration shows him struggling to work out how best to balance realism and romance. The narrator occasionally uses the first person pronoun and on one occasion indicates that he is compiling the story from manuscript sources: "We have often tried to recover Ralph's reply, but the text is corrupt at this place, the context entirely lost. Experts suspect a palimpsest" (Crockett 1894: 296). On another occasion Crockett breaks off from his narrative and addresses an imagined reader whom, he suggests, might consider the story "plainly impossible" (Crockett 1894: 289). This uncertainty about how to articulate the realism of his story reveals a writer still struggling to find the form that best suited his artistic interests. In this respect, *The Raiders* – written after *The Lilac Sunbonnet* but published before it – was a notable advance.

III

The Lilac Sunbonnet was immediately popular. The large first impression of 10,000 copies was sold out on the day of publication. Much of the demand had to do with the triumphant success of *The Raiders*, published six months earlier in April 1894, which became one of the best-selling novels of the year. When the manuscript of was submitted to the publishers in October 1893, Edward Garnett thought it "decidedly clever & better than we thought Crockett could do" (Cited in Collin 1991: 105). Six months earlier, Garnett had rejected "A Galloway Herd", Crockett's first serial story published in *The Christian Leader* from October 1891 to July 1892, finding it no more than "a bundle of sketches hastily tied together" (Cited in Collin 1991: 97). *The Raiders* was an altogether different proposition, and Garnett made many suggestions for alterations and amendments to the style and substance of Crockett's manuscript, which the author followed.

Crockett's debts to previous writers in *The Raiders*, especially Hogg, Scott and Stevenson, are clear, and much was made of them by reviewers. William Wallace in the *Academy* considered that the echoes of Stevenson and R.D. Blackmore meant that Crockett could not be considered "a great, in the sense of an original, romancist" (3

November 1894). Certainly the abduction plot is very similar to that in *Lorna Doone* (1869) whilst the presentation of a young man thrust into events beyond his control, carried along powerless by the drift of history, follows the formula perfected by Scott and later exploited by Stevenson. In its review, the *Daily Chronicle* said of Crockett: "The new Barrie of yesterday is today a second Stevenson."[2] The parallels with Stevenson are inescapable. As in *Kidnapped* the retrospective narration offers two contrasting voices. The cautious, contemplative, mature Patrick recounting the adventures of his younger self, is plunged into an alien world beyond his control and forced into impulsive acts of spontaneity as he struggles to interpret what is going on around him. There are other similarities: Patrick's father, like David Balfour's, dies early in the story leaving him alone in the world, and the whole relationship between Patrick and Silver Sand recalls that of David and Alan Breck. Silver Sand has his own unique qualities as a fictional character, but he performs much the same function as Alan, with one notable difference. Like Alan he flits in and out of the narrative, and of Patrick's adventures, as if he inhabits another world from the hero, and Patrick is never completely certain of his loyalty, just as David is never certain of Alan's. The difference is that Silver Sand acts out of moral choice, having turned his back on the Cameronian stock, appalled at the atrocities of the killing times.

   The Raiders is similar to *Kidnapped* also in the way that Patrick responds to his adventures by recalling those he has heard in stories. Tales and traditions come true for Patrick as he discovers the Murder Hole:

There had long been a tradition of such a place in the stories that went about the countryside, and made our flesh creep as we told tales by the fire in the winter forenights. I had never been a believer in such like, accounting it foolish clatter; but now it seemed likely that I should learn something very definite concerning it. (Crockett [1894] 2001: 190)

This dynamic is a staple component of adventure romance and Crockett exploits another tried and tested convention of the form when, in the foreword to the novel, he sets up a realistic, domestic

---

[2] Quoted in an advertisement in the Bookman, April 1894.

scene which acts as a contrast to the ensuing adventures. The works of Stevenson, Rider Haggard, and later John Buchan, follow this pattern. The shift to the first chapter, where Patrick recounts an experience when he is caught up in the crossfire of the raiders, plunges us directly into a world that is as disorienting for the reader as it is for Patrick. The early chapters describing Patrick's domestic life on Isle Rathan, dismissed as rambling by Donaldson, add further to the presentation of a domestic scene of contentment that is soon invaded by destructive forces as Patrick is uprooted from his comfortable position as "captain" and usurped from his land by the smugglers and gypsies.

Patrick's domesticity makes him a reluctant hero. He reflects on his adventures with more tears than pride and is constantly reminding himself of the world of comfort he has left behind. But there is ambivalence to his feelings. In recounting his adventures Patrick emphasises the conflicting feelings of fear and relish that he has for the threatening situations in which he finds himself. As with his feelings for May Maxwell, however, the novel charts his change from illusions of certainty to admissions of confusion: "truth to tell I believed not in my own unshakeable logic [...]" (Crockett [1894] 2001: 170–1). Patrick is also a reluctant lover and he repeatedly tries to convince himself that he does not care for the betwitching May. By the end his resolve is broken and just as he is forced to reconsider his outlook on life in general he openly acknowledges his romantic feelings for her. May herself is no stereotypical romance heroine and, again like Babbie in *The Little Minister*, is an imposing, dominant force over the hero. She saves Patrick from his early encounters with the smugglers and does so again by killing the bloodthirsty dogs of the gypsies when Patrick is feebly incapacitated with an injured foot.

Compared to *The Lilac Sunbonnet*, religion plays little part in *The Raiders*. As Donaldson notes, Patrick's father "is not a deeply religious man" and the advice he gives to his son on his deathbed is to avoid extremes and embrace freedom (Crockett [1894] 2001: 105–6). *The Raiders* is less a Free Church novel than a typical *fin de siécle* novel, suffused with the sense of fear of a changing world and the anticipation of apocalypse. The sense of another world, unknown, but invading the present is characteristic of fiction in the 1890s. The mysterious figure of Silver Sand, and his oversized, beastlike dog provide that in *The Raiders*, but it is in the presentation of the ever-changing Galloway landscape that Crockett manages best of all to present a world where the boundaries between the known and the unknown are constantly shifting and unclear to character and reader alike. As John Burns has noted, the image Patrick presents of himself at the beginning of the story when he is caught up in the smugglers' raid, of being "a fly on a sheet of white paper" is emblematic of the text, with "the human figure seen as small and defenceless within a greater frame" (Burns 2001: viii). Early in the novel Patrick declares he cannot think of anything "bonnier or sweeter in this world than a May morning on the Isle of Rathan by the Solway shore" (Crockett [1894] 2001: 13). By the end of his adventures this world has given way to one of apocalyptic desolation as Patrick's narrow life of subsistence on the Solway firth is taken over by more powerful forces of fear, evil and suffering.

Deprived of his life of comfort, Patrick is forced to reinterpret the boundaries of his understanding of morality, human motives, and even the physical status of the world. Donaldson notes Crockett's use of movement in description and his achievement in capturing the visual, aural and spatial sensations of landscape (Donaldson 1989: 134). Light is offset against dark, movement against stillness, sound against silence; and the Galloway landscape becomes charged with supernatural overtones. This is a world where dead men seem to rise of their own accord; horrible beasts "monstrous and not of the earth" run loose at night; stars shine "with a strange green the like of which I had never seen" (Crockett [1894] 2001: 253, 283). The land itself is seen as preying on humanity, as in the Murder Hole with its "open mouth [...] waiting like an insatiable beast for its tribute of human life" (Crockett [1894] 2001: 271).

Patrick finds his sense of the boundaries of imagination and reality shifting and comes to look upon the world not in terms of a divine pattern but as one of chaos where opportunity is everything. At one point, when he is struggling to cross the terrifying terrain of the Wolf's Slock, he discovers a staff that he fears might belong to one of his enemies. His conclusion is indicative of the attitude towards religion in the novel: "it was a good kent, and served me well, so why all this bother about who made it? So it is also with the making of this world" (Crockett [1894] 2001: 172). In Patrick's world, one makes use of what one can find for there is no time to bother about who made things. The world that he encounters is one in constant threat of dissolution: "suddenly we heard before and above us a tremendous roaring noise, as though the bowels of creation were gushing out in a great convulsion" (Crockett [1894] 2001: 263). After Patrick escapes over the icy cliffs from his stranded position in the waters of Loch Valley, the vision he has from the ledge of the cliff of the enemy camp near Loch Enoch is one of a "desolate waste" charged with apocalyptic overtones:

I saw a weird wide world, new and strange, not yet out of chaos – not yet approven by God; but such a scene as there may be on the farther side of the moon, which no man hath seen nor can see. I thought with some woe and pity on the poor souls condemned, though it were by their own crimes, to sojourn there. (Crockett [1894] 2001: 273–4)

It is no coincidence that when Silver Sand reads to Patrick out of the Bible, he reads "oftenest from the Apocalypse, which somehow appealed strongly to him" (Crockett [1894] 2001: 301). When the two men emerge from the cave in which they have sought refuge from "The Sixteen Drifty Days" they emerge to a world of brightness "like the Kingdom of Heaven". The landscape has altered: "The night before we had seen only a whirling chaos of hurrying flakes of infinite deepness. The morning showed us the great valley almost levelled up with snow." But this is no simple allegory: "The same frost-bound whiteness had covered all. The old world was drowned in snow and there was no Bow of Promise to be seen. Perhaps because we had offered no sacrifice" (Crockett [1894] 2001: 309). Crockett's new world is not the simple projection of the comfortable Christian world offered by Genesis.

IV

William Wallace was surely right when he wrote in his review in the *Academy* that "*The Raiders* is conspicuously superior to *The Lilac Sunbonnet* in style, in flow of narrative, and in plot" (3 November

1894). Nevertheless, in his final assessment of both works Wallace concluded that Crockett's "achievements prove nothing as to the future. They may be but the preliminary canters of genius; or they may be the best work of a second rate writer who has struck oil." Crockett had certainly struck oil, in so far as he had discovered a talent for a mode of writing that was popular. In the wake of the success of *The Raiders* and *The Lilac Sunbonnet*, he took the decision to give up his position as minister of the Free Church at Penicuik and become a professional author.

The success of his early books soon made Crockett a writer in demand. He received invitations to give speeches and attend dinners and in 1895 was asked to write introductions to a new edition of Galt's works, which had been edited by David Storrar Meldrum with the assistance of George Douglas Brown. It would be interesting to know what Brown made of Crockett's feeble prefaces, which are full of windy eulogies and empty of any analysis or shrewdness of observation. Periodicals and publishers besieged him with offers and as many as eleven volumes of fiction were written and published in the years 1895–1899 alone. Most of these, including *The Men of the Moss Hags* (1895), are set in Galloway but from 1900 onwards Crockett published several historical romances set in Europe which, as noted, were not especially well received. Crockett worked in a variety of genres. As Islay Donaldson has stated, "far from being a practitioner of what had come to be called 'Kailyard' fiction, he was almost obsessionally willing to tackle any new fashion that came along" (Donaldson 1989: 146). These included several children's books and, at the very end of his career, a detective story.

In terms of the Kailyard debate, two novels from Crockett's early period are especially significant – *Cleg Kelly* (1896), set in part in the slums of Edinburgh, and *Kit Kennedy* (1899), which deals with the Scottish education system. The character of Cleg had featured in two of the stories in *The Stickit Minister*. Expanded into a full-length novel, *Cleg Kelly: Arab of the City* was serialised in both the *Cornhill* – "the premier fiction-carrying magazine of the century" (Sutherland 1988: 150) – and the *Sunday School*. It was thus circulating to two audiences, one used to reading fiction with a religious emphasis, the other being readers of the highest quality fiction of the day. Readers of the *Sunday School* would have had to cope with the striking first sentence: "'It's all a dumb lie! – God's dead!'" Cleg's defiant words remind us that Crockett was writing at a time when scientists and philosophers were discrediting the literal truths of Christianity and pronouncing the twilight of the Gods. Crockett did not believe that God was dead, of course. The underlying message of *Cleg Kelly* is that Cleg has more natural Christian impulses than the missionaries who preach at him. Like Maclaren, Crockett was an advocate of a form of Christian Socialism but in *Cleg Kelly* he treats religion in a strikingly different way from Maclaren, favouring realism over idealism. Whereas Maclaren's fiction celebrates a Christian community working for each other, the events of Cleg Kelly's life take place once he is cast out from the mission and made an "outcast and alien from the commonwealth" (Crockett 1896: 2).

Crockett was not a stranger to the Edinburgh slums; his time as a theology student enabled him to experience at first hand the plight of the poor and the false piety of some of the missionaries. His is not the view of an outsider. The Christian community of missionary Edinburgh is at the opposite end of the spectrum from Maclaren's Drumtochty. Rather than seeing in Cleg's behaviour the resourcefulness of a boy struggling to survive and battle against the state of poverty in which he finds himself, the missionaries see in his mischievousness, his swearing, his outspokenness and his blasphemy only signs of a sinful nature that will not listen to religious instruction. Cleg is victim of the society that has failed him. His mother died when he was young; his father is a drunkard and a burglar. Although he is presented as the voice of real Christian values, he is not in any way the pious boy of conventional Sunday School literature. For all his "natural" Christianity, he is fundamentally rebellious, and the narrative tone constantly asks us to approve of the way he fights against the forces of authority. There is also humour in the way he is presented, as in his mocking imitation of the "Track Woman":

"Good day, poor people," he said, "I have called to leave you a little tract. I don't know how you can live in such a place. Why don't you move away? And the stair is so dirty and sticky. It is really not fit for a lady to come up. (Crockett 1896: 313–4)

Cleg goes through many different adventures during the course of this novel and manages to escape the city ending up in Galloway. Crockett treats the city/country contrast in a more straightforward way than Maclaren, who uses it to reinforce his presentation of Drumtochty as a place that embodies ideal moral and Christian values. Cleg certainly finds more freedom in Galloway and is treated more kindly, but the landscape is used mainly as a backdrop for the principal attraction which is the adventures themselves. Nevertheless, F.R. Hart is surely right when he argues that Crockett's urban realism is taken over by "the values of romance and idyll" (Hart 1978: 119).

Donaldson considers the episodic nature of *Cleg Kelly* a weakness and narrative structure was not one of Crockett's strengths. Nevertheless, the concentration on a series of loosely related incidents is not untypical of the "gamin" genre and it perhaps shows Crockett working with the serial audience uppermost in his mind. The value of the novel lies principally in the characterisation of Cleg and the realistic portrayal of slum life in Edinburgh. Compared to the fiction of Robina F. Hardy, who wrote a number of books drawing on her experiences as a missionary worker in the Grassmarket, it is brutally realistic. There is nothing spared in the description of the tenement in which lives Cleg's friend, Vara Kavanagh, whose mother is a prostitute and a drunkard. The following description is not untypical of scenes throughout the novel:

In the corner lay Sal Kavannah, with a pair of empty bottles tossed at her side, her heavy black hair over her face. She lay all drawn together in a heap. Tied to the bed was Vara, bleeding from a cut on the head, and trying to cover her arms and hands from his sight. But Hugh and the baby remained in the bunk together, sleeping peacefully. It was upon poor Vara that the brunt of the woman's maniac fury had fallen. (Crockett 1896: 96)

It is hard to reconcile this writing – in which the novel abounds – with the criticism that Crockett wholly neglected to deal with Scottish urban life and the darker side of life in general. Everywhere he goes in Edinburgh Cleg meets dirt, squalor and insect-ridden homes. As F.R. Hart states, the early chapters are "urban realism for any taste" and the scenes of drunken violence are *"Oliver Twist* without Dickensian sentimentality" (Hart 1978: 120).

Cleg Kelly represents the critical highpoint of Crockett's career. William Wallace of the *Academy* had his opinion raised by the story, which he considered "by far the best work Mr Crockett has yet produced" and "out of sight the ablest and richest story of gamin life that has appeared in our time – the story that recalls most readily *Oliver Twist* and *The Hunchback of Notre Dame*" (9 May 1896). Publication in the *Cornhill* indicates Crockett's standing in the literary world in the mid-1890s. In his early career he was not viewed simply as a popular author whose stories appealed only to a lowbrow literary audience. His serials appeared in a variety of periodicals and magazines, including some of the most prestigious publications of the era – *Little Anna Mark* also appeared in the *Cornhill* and *The Firebrand* was serialised in *Temple Bar*, another established shilling monthly. Equally, it is wrong to suggest that the forum (and readership) for his work was primarily that of religious journals and newspapers. It is true that some novels appeared in religious magazines. *The Men of the Moss Haggs* was serialised in *Good Words*, a magazine set up in 1860 by the Scottish publisher Strahan but later owned by Isbister. It is important to note, however, that religious magazines were among the most important outlets for serial fiction. *Good Words* attracted leading novelists such as Thomas Hardy (*The Trumpet Major*, 1879) and Anthony Trollope (*Kept in the Dark*, 1881). Nevertheless, it did have a reputation for piety and prudery. Hardy was asked to change a lovers' meeting from a Sunday to a Saturday and informed by the editor that his serial should avoid "anything – direct or indirect – which a healthy parson like myself would not care to read to his bairns at the fireside" (Wright 2003: 15). *The Men of the Moss Haggs* would have been acceptable not because it articulated a specific religious message – it doesn't – but because it was safe in morals and attitude.

Crockett's attitude towards the serial market was greatly affected by his employment in 1893 of the literary agent A.P. Watt. Almost immediately Watt found ways of increasing Crockett's literary earnings. In September, Crockett informed Unwin that whilst he had earned over £250 a year from *The Christian Leader*, and £150 from "Nicoll's work" and theological papers, "Watt had enabled him to escape and 'to write more fiction' by trebling his income in six months" (Cited in Collin 1991: 101). Watt's chief input was to secure large payments for the serialisation of Crockett's novels. The serial rights in *The Lilac Sunbonnet* had been sold to *The Christian Leader* for a mere £60, a fraction of the price Crockett would command for later serials. Crockett learned quickly that most of the money in the fiction market in this period was in serialisation. As he told Unwin: "serial publication at first, is so much more valuable" (Cited in Collin 1991: 102).

Whilst magazines like the *Cornhill* represented the canonical face of serial fiction, the expanding market meant that more lucrative financial opportunities lay elsewhere. As Peter Keating notes, there was a "proliferation of magazines, newspapers and periodicals directed at very clearly defined groups of readers" which contributed to the "relentless fragmentation and categorisation of fiction" at the end of the century (Keating 1989: 340). One such group was the woman reader, and Crockett's serials appeared in some of the new women's magazines. *Lad's Love* (1897) was serialised in *The Lady's Realm* whilst *Ione March* (1899) appeared in *The Woman at Home*, one of William Robertson Nicoll's publishing ventures. Crockett also profited from two other developments in the serial market. The first was the newly remunerative American market, brought about by the harmonisation of UK and US copyright in 1891. Hitherto, works by British authors could be published in America without the author receiving any payment. With the introduction of new copyright legislation, however, money could be made on both serial and volume publication. An American firm such as Harper was able to pay far larger sums for serials in its weekly and monthly magazines than could British publishers. Both *The Grey Man* and *The Red Axe* were serialised in *Harper's Weekly* and the *Bookman* reported that the payment made by *Harper's* for *The Grey Man* was "one of the largest paid during recent years to any British author" (November 1894: 38). Thomas Knowles notes how Crockett also leapt on the superior financial rewards of the American book market (Knowles 1983: 71).

The second development was the expansion of newspaper syndication, where firms would buy up serial rights to novels and then lease them out to provincial newspapers. The largest syndicating operation in America was McClure's, who purchased the serial rights

to *The Men of the Moss Haggs*. In the final third of the century, fiction
syndication expanded in Britain as well, chiefly through the enterprise
of Tillotson & Son (Law 2000). Scotland had led the way in the
practice of serialising full-length novels in newspapers from the mid-
1850s and the Glasgow newspapers in particular remained important
sites of serialisation in the 1890s. In this period it was not uncommon
for novels to be serialised in both metropolitan magazines and
provincial newspapers. *The Grey Man* is a case in point. Serialised in
the metropolitan magazine *The Graphic*, it was also published in the
Newcastle Weekly Chronicle and the *Glasgow Weekly News*. *The Red
Axe* was also published in *Glasgow Weekly News* – further evidence
that there was a Scottish market for Crockett's work.

In this context, the publication of *Kit Kennedy* in the *People's
Friend* is significant. A Dundee penny weekly, the *Friend* is one of
the papers that William Donaldson singles out as supporting a
tradition of vernacular Scottish fiction that he sees as separate from,
and opposed to, the Kailyard (Donaldson 1986). The location of serial
publication shows that *Kit Kennedy* was a novel with a Scottish
audience, and in terms of the Kailyard debate this is important because
of its treatment of the "lad o' pairts" theme. As I discuss in Chapter 4,
the "lad o' pairts" is often invoked as a defining characteristic of
Kailyard fiction. Crockett was himself a "lad o' pairts" who won a
place at university through a bursary competition but his attitude
towards education was not always positive. In "The Biography of an
Inefficient", a story in *Bog-Myrtle and Peat*, Ebenezer Skinner is
presented as an archetypal "lad o' pairts", "born of poor but honest
parents" who have only one ambition: to see their son "wag his head
in a pulpit" (Crockett 1895: 382). Ebenezer goes to Edinburgh and
shuns the social activities of other students, concentrating on his
Greek and Latin:

He studied all that he was told to study. He read every book that by the regulations he
was compelled to read. But he read nothing besides. […] His college learning acted
like an unventilated mackintosh, keeping all the unwholesome, morbid personality
within, and shutting out the free ozone and healthy buffeting of the outer world. Many
college-bred men enter life with their minds carefully mackintoshed. Generally they
go into the Church. (Crockett 1895: 384–5)

Coming from a college-bred man who himself entered the Church, that final statement is blunt in its honesty. Ebenezer proves a failure as a minister because his flawless knowledge of Latin and Greek has impeded his acquiring any knowledge of life.

Although it is Maclaren's story "Domsie" that has become the most famous representation of the "lad o' pairts", it is in fact *Kit Kennedy* which presents the most sustained treatment of the theme. A later Crockett novel, *The Loves of Miss Anne* (1904), features a herd boy who goes to university when he has saved enough money; Kit, by contrast proceeds through a bursary competition, and this makes him a more typical "lad o" pairts" in the tradition of Scottish education. Crockett's picture of the parish school is in sharp contrast to Maclaren's. Kit's village dominie is Duncan Duncanson, whose own story is told in *The Stickit Minister*. Though an able teacher, Duncan is a victim of drink. *The Stickit Minister* story follows him to the grave and in Kit Kennedy we again hear of his "three trips to the 'Red Lion' every day" (Crockett 1899: 86). Nor is there anything idealist in Crockett's presentation of the parish school, which can offer imaginative boys like Kit very little. He ends up correcting his teacher in one of his lessons and spends most of his schooldays playing truant because there is nothing to learn. Symbolically, he hides his unthumbed books under a hearthstone in a disused saw-mill where they eventually perish in a storm; schoolbooks are just too mundane for a boy who "had always known that he would be a great man one day, and already begun to be anxious about the writing of his biography" (Crockett 1899: 184).

As Harper notes, the novel contains some autobiographical content (Harper 1907: 55–7). Like Crockett, Kit does not know who his father is. Christopher Kennedy senior ran away from Kit's pregnant mother and, having been sacked from his job as a classics master, this "scholar and gentleman" spends most of the novel disguised as a drunken tramp. When Kit is forced to go to work on a farm he is befriended by Christopher, who offers to teach him the classics without revealing his identity to the boy. Eager to learn, Kit accepts, because Latin is "the language, a knowledge of which is universally believed in Scotland to unlock the doors of success in every profession" (Crockett 1899: 216).

Kit's schooling by his father is contrasted to the education of Jock MacWalter, the son of the farmer for whom Kit works. Jock's mother is eager for her boy to become a minister but whereas in Maclaren's stories the mother of the "lad o' pairts" emerges as a paragon of Godliness, Crockett treats the theme of education comically. Mrs. MacWalter's faith in her boy is misplaced:

He sits there and learns a' the day through. Aye that's a Greek buik or a Hebrew; I dinna ken what yin o' the twa. Jock is a fair neeger at baith languages, and as for Laitin, Dominie MacFayden says that he canna learn him ony mair. (Crockett 1899: 234)

Both John and Kit are put forward for the bursary competition even though, as his mother freely admits, John doesn't need the bursary to get him through college. Catching a chance glimpse one day at John's edition of Virgil, Kit is amazed to find a volume full of "helps and aids and informations":

He could never hope to obtain from his poor barren dictionaries, and by the slow process of looking up every word, such a wealth of classical lore as lay open to the possessor of this volume. (Crockett 1899: 235)

This is in no way celebrating equality of opportunity. At the bursary competition Kit is presented as unusual because outside the system: "All the other entrants came from well known burgh or famous parish schools, long celebrated for "sendin' up lads to the college" (Crockett 1899: 238). The examiners coolly predict a "downcome" for the poor lad battling against "all these academy fellows." But Kit sails through the paper and is awarded the premier bursary; John MacWalter comes last.

Crockett's presentation of the bursary competition reinforces the myth of the meritocracy of Scottish education as the best candidate wins out in the end, but he is more than critical about the actual conditions in which the competition is played out. He is also critical of university life. At Edinburgh Kit falls into decadent company and wastes his time at lavish restaurants and the theatre. Guided by Christopher – who eventually reveals his identity – and by a Free Church Minister who takes him round the slums of Edinburgh, Kit is gradually brought to an awareness of his Christian responsibilities. In spite of the somewhat pious ending, the novel is exuberant and humorous. In a work that, in its serial form, was read by a predominantly Scottish audience, Crockett cannot be accused of perpetuating myths of Scottish education.

V

Crockett's readiness to embrace the financial riches of the serial market contributed to the decline in his reputation and the criticisms that he wrote to a formula. Reviewing *Kit Kennedy* the *Athenaeum* found the book enjoyable but detected "an undue proportion of 'cauld kail het again'" (16 September 1899). Such criticisms became common. *Literature* wrote of *Little Anna Mark* that "there is, above all, a sense of what the public wants" (18 August 1900) and the *Academy*, in an unsigned review, wrote disparagingly of *The Grey Man*, judging that Crockett had "contented himself with the merest bookmaking" and that its claims to rank as literature were of the "very slightest. [...] To adopt one of his own Scotticisms, he just 'havers along' through the allotted number of pages" (21 November 1896). There can be no question that in a good number of his books Crockett was guilty of writing to a formula and supplying a ready-made market in a way that was almost relentless. In 1909 alone, four titles appeared under his name. Crockett's speed of production counted against him, not just because of the effect on the quality of his work, but also because it made it difficult for publishers to market his books successfully. George Macmillan told Crockett that *The Firebrand* (1900) would have had a better chance "if three other books by the same author had not appeared in the course of the year."[3]

Crockett's correspondence with Macmillan reveals his attitude to serial fiction and the financial rewards of scholarship. It shows how his determination to put serial rights before book publication affected the way his works were preserved for posterity. Macmillan repeatedly chased Crockett over the years 1895–1902. With a large and profitable

---

[3] 23 December 1901, BL Add. MS. 55468, fol. 306.

line in religious and educational books, the firm's small literary list was built on distinction rather than anticipated profits. It actively pursued only those writers whose names might uphold the firm's reputation or in whom the partners had a special interest – Hardy, James, Tennyson and Kipling were the flagships. Crockett's attractiveness to Macmillan gives some indication of the high literary status that he acquired in his early career. In 1895 Macmillan New York captured the American rights to *The Men of the Moss Haggs* but, in spite of considerable effort, the firm was unable to secure Crockett for the UK market until 1901. The reason was that Crockett had made arrangements for serial publication of several novels well in advance, but as George Macmillan advised him, success in the serial market did not make for posterity:

what one may call the auction plan may lead to larger payments in the first instance but we very much doubt whether in the long run an author does not do better by sticking to one publisher when he has found one that believes in him and is prepared to do his best for him.[4]

Only two of Crockett's books were published by Macmillan: *The Firebrand* (1901) and *The Dark o' the Moon* (1902) – a sequel to *The Raiders*. The firm paid £1000 for *The Firebrand*, which was serialised in its own magazine, *Temple Bar*. The sum was considerably more than Macmillan usually paid for a serial, but as Frederick Macmillan put it to his colleague Mowbray Morris: "his books do very well (the novel just published by Smith, Elder [*The Red Axe*] is very well spoken of & has sold largely)."[5] Crockett's insistence on earning the largest possible sums for serial fiction eventually priced himself out of the market catered for by *Temple Bar*, the *Cornhill* and other prestigious monthlies.

Before *The Firebrand* was published, Macmillan opened the question of issuing a uniform edition of Crockett's works: "our experience shows that it is greatly to the advantage of an author's books that they should be, at any rate in assuming their permanent

---

[4] BL Add. MS. 55450, fol. 12.

[5] BL Add. MS. 55458, fol. 739. Crockett himself recorded that Smith Elder sold 25,000 copies of *The Red Axe* in ten days (Donaldson 1989: 183).

form, in the hands of one house."[6] It is significant that a publisher should think that Crockett's novels would reach a "permanent form". Far from seeing Crockett as a popular author whose work was ephemeral, Macmillan were offering him the chance to be placed alongside uniform editions of the firm's other leading writers such as those of Hardy and Kipling. Crockett referred the firm to Watt, but the agent made an offer that was conditional on Macmillan paying a large sum for the serial rights of Crockett's next available novel. This the firm turned down, explaining: "We have no magazine which can bear the burden".[7] Over a year later, Maurice Macmillan reopened the issue, asking Crockett:

Is it worthwhile to allow your books to be spread among half the publishers of fiction in London merely for the sake of the sums which your agent can get from two or three magazines? [...] the system of hawking round an author's MSS is [not] one which has anything to recommend it, especially in the case of writers who aspire to something more than ephemeral popularity. Dickens, Thackeray, Scott, George Eliot, Mr Gaskell, Trollope (to a great extent) found that it was to their advantage that their books should be kept together, and we cannot help thinking that those writers who adopt the same methods of publishing will in the end prove the most successful even from the financial standpoint.[8]

That Crockett should have been discussed in the same context as these giants of nineteenth-century fiction is revealing enough. His eye, however, was always on the immediate rewards of authorship.

J.M. Barrie's portrait of Crockett, preserved in a letter to Arthur Quiller-Couch of 23 March 1896, is that of a writer interested only in the financial aspects of authorship:

Crockett was with us for a week-end. "His terms are" – "he sells" – "Watt says" – "his publishers say" – "his terms" – "his sale" – But otherwise he is all right and kindly and oh, he is happy. (Meynell 1947: 10)

Crockett allowed these issues to dominate and contented himself with being a popular author. Islay Donaldson reminds us that Crockett

---

[6] 11 February 1901, BL Add. MS. 55465, fol. 151.

[7] 28 February 1901. BL Add. MS. 55465, fol. 357.

[8] 21 March, 1902. BL Add. MS. 55469, fol. 258

"was never a rich man and had many calls on what income he had" (Donaldson 1989: 276). The furious pace at which he wrote was obviously on one level a response to financial need. But it was also a recognition of the demands of the marketplace. In a speech given in Dalbeattie in 1907 he voiced his opinions on the matter:

> We authors cannot always do just exactly what we would like. The publisher tells you to cut down the dialect because the English public does not understand it. (It ought by this time). The editor must have a book on a certain subject because public interest calls for it. The land that holds the heather and the sheep does not hold the money for the man who has to live by his pen. So that to a certain extent the author is dependent upon a more distant public. (Harper 1907: 164–5).

All professional authors write for the market but not all keep the market as uppermost in their creative minds as did Crockett. That last sentence shows how he accepted that the main market for his fiction lay outside Scotland and that he was willing to compromise his work on that account. Consideration of the range of his fiction shows that at times – notably in his early novels – he was able to make that compromise without damaging his art or his representation of Galloway or Scotland. But in the end the market defeated him. In the twentieth century his reputation sank. Critics of his later novels were, as Donaldson notes, "either cursory in their references" or else "positively hostile" (Donaldson 1989: 266). His once significant sales dipped and in 1912 he had unearned advances on several novels, amounting in some instances to three figure sums (Donaldson 1989: 278).

In 1913, the year before Crockett died, Watt submitted *The Azure Hand* to Chatto & Windus. The firm's reader, Frank Swinnerton, was dismissive: "The dullest detective story I ever read. It is hard work to read, unconvincing in its very mathematical accuracy, and contains not the faintest, slightest, shadowiest thrill of any kind whatsoever."[9] Crockett's final experiment with a new form was an absolute failure. *The Azure Hand* was published posthumously, but at his death

---

[9] 16 April 1913. Chatto & Windus archive, Reading University Library. Uncatalogued. The book was published posthumously by Hodder & Stoughton in 1917.

Crockett's vogue was well and truly over. George Blake's final assessment is not without substance:

It is only fair to see a novelist like Crockett as one born in an unlucky hour. The Kailyard novel was a late flower of the Presbyterian predominance in Scottish life; that and memories of the Jacobites were shortly to prove unacceptable to twentieth-century citizens. No writer of unusual talent could continue to work in these terms, and the writer of insufficient talent must continue to deal in outmoded stuff. Barrie was in the former class and turned himself into the expert dramatist he was from the first obviously destined to be. Crockett, lacking that extra little bit of horse-power, could not create a bridge for himself and flogged himself, his talent and his material into the limbo (Blake 1951: 52–3).

Chapter Four

The Sentimental Art of Ian Maclaren

I

The question of realism, which is fundamental to the Kailyard debate, does not solely consist of issues of social realism and national representation. Whilst most of the reaction against the fiction of Barrie, Crockett and Maclaren turns on the allegedly unrealistic – or unrepresentative – portrayal of Scottish life, there is a related issue that concerns artistic method. Kailyard novelists have been criticised for failing to follow some of the trends in fictional realism at the end of the nineteenth century. The sentimental strategies of Maclaren, in particular, have been judged harshly by critics who lament the failure of Scottish novelists to be, in the words of George Blake, "what is nowadays called 'documentary' in character" (Blake 1951: 7).

In his study of Kailyard, Thomas Knowles discusses the work of Barrie and Maclaren in the context of debates over realism at the end of the century. He argues that Kailyard was "a commercial and ideological phenomenon designed to promote a moral ethos" and act as "a bastion against the ungodly aspects of literature in the nineties" (Knowles 1983: 47). Peter Keating shares this view, suggesting that popularity of Kailyard lay in public reaction to realism:

Barrie's stories [...] began to attract attention shortly after the Vizetelly trial, and the works of Crockett and Maclaren that followed were exactly contemporary with the bowlderisation of Zola's novels, the hysterical press attacks on Ibsen, Moore and Hardy, and Wilde's trial. (Keating 1989: 338)

These views are undoubtedly correct but it is easy to lose sight of the fact that responses to realism in this period were prompted by aesthetics as well as morals. Knowles argues that Barrie and Maclaren retreated from realism for moral reasons:

the choice of the rural alternative was a retreat, not only from the most typical and central social environment of the time, but also from a reality charged with images both powerful and threatening, conflicting and chaotic. (Knowles 1983: 9)

The extent to which an author retreats from "the most typical and central social environment of the time" will inevitably depend upon the range of his experience. Barrie's focus on a small town is entirely defensible in view of his upbringing. Maclaren, however, knew the city well, having ministered in Glasgow and Liverpool. Nevertheless, whilst his focus on rural life can be considered a retreat in this sense, his fiction should not be seen as a retreat from realism altogether. In fact, few contemporary reviewers identified the work of either Barrie or Maclaren as an "alternative" to realism, as Knowles suggests. The *Spectator* commented of Barrie: "Happily, there is more of Teniers than of Zola in his realism; more happily still, there is more of Wilkie than of Teniers" (21 September 1889). Similarly, William Wallace argued in the *Bookman* that Maclaren "has set himself deliberately to lay bare the recesses of simple Scottish tenderness and love, to oppose these realities to the so-called realism of the Rougon-Macquart horrors" (December 1895). In these reviews, and in many others, the realism of Barrie and Maclaren is contrasted to French naturalism and becomes part of a bid on the part of reviewers for what "realism" ought to be.

As Knowles notes, Maclaren and Barrie both contributed to the debate over realism in their own critical essays. In an essay first published in *Literature* in 1897, Maclaren wrote in complaint of the "slum school" of fiction:

One breathes throughout an atmosphere of filth, squalor, profanity, and indecency and is seized with moral nausea. There are such things as drains, and sometimes they may have to be opened, but one would not for choice have one opened in his library. (Maclaren 1897: 80)

Barrie's article on Thomas Hardy adopts a similar stance:

The professional realists of these times, who wear a giant's robe and stumble in it, see only the seamier side of life, reproducing it with merciless detail, holding the mirror up to the unnatural instead of to nature, and photographing by the light of a policeman's lantern. The difference between them and the man whose name they borrow is that they only see the crack in the cup, while he sees the cup with the crack in it. (Barrie 1889b: 59)

The difference here is that whereas Maclaren's attitude is predominantly moral Barrie is more concerned with artistic method. In opposing "realist" with "professional realist" Barrie does not advocate a rejection of realism but suggests how realism might be achieved. He makes the same point in his article on Kipling arguing that "the drawback of collecting dirt in one corner is that it gives a false notion of the filth of the room [...] we want to see the whole room lighted up that we may judge the dirty corner by comparison" (Barrie 1891b: 368–9). The idea of having a perspective of the whole was an aesthetic agenda that would soon be contested by the rationale of modernist fiction, with its claims for seeing reality in fragments and impressions. Barrie's ideas in these early critical articles are old-fashioned and at odds with the development of his own fiction. His comments nevertheless make clear that in this period "realism" was not an absolute term but one under constant interrogation. To Henry James, realism had "myriad forms" (James [1884] 1985: 201) and to Stevenson it regarded "not in the least degree the fundamental truth, but only the technical method of a work of art" (Stevenson [1883] 1950: 378).

Barrie's work was judged by most of his contemporaries to have fulfilled expectations of realism. Arthur Quiller-Couch considered *A Window in Thrums* to be "the true triumph of the realist" (Quiller-Couch 1892: 169) and Hardy also judged it "a faithful representation of reality" (Weber 1954: 90). It is clear from such assessments that in this period realism meant more than just social criticism. Maclaren's fiction was understood in similar terms. The *Daily News* commented on *The Days of Auld Langsyne*:

Realism of the most downright, absolute order, his work is, from first to last, but realism seen through one of the most sympathetic, most poetic temperaments of his day. [...] Writers of genius have presented to us certain phases of Scotch rural character, Mr. Watson is almost unique in his power of revealing that curiously complex character in all its completeness.[1]

The collation of "realism" and "poetic" typifies the critical reception of Maclaren's work and points up how realism could be understood in this period not in opposition to idealism but in relation to it. George Lewins wrote of Maclaren: "the fascination is intensely realistic and yet the conception which produces it is in the highest sense ideal" (Lewins 1896: 471). This is the same conception of realism that was expressed in mid-century by George Lewes, who argued that the opposite of realism was not idealism but "falsism" (Cited in Levine 1981: 10). For Lewes: "the true meaning of Idealism is precisely this vision of realities in their highest and most affecting forms, not in the vision of something removed from or opposed to realities" (Cited in Anderson 1988: 7). It is this understanding of realism that allows *The Speaker* to say without any intended oxymoron that Maclaren's "pictures are marvels of idealistic realism."[2]

Realism in this sense does not mean, as it did for the naturalists, the accuracy of sociological representation. Rather, it incorporates an understanding of mid-Victorian ideas of sympathy. When Barrie writes in his essay on Kipling that "Sympathy is the ink within which all fiction is written" his words echo those of George Eliot, who in *Adam Bede* describes "sympathy" as "the one poor word which includes all our best insight and our best love" (Eliot 1980: 531). In a letter to Charles Bray of 5 July 1859, Eliot makes clear the artist's obligation to sympathy:

If Art does not enlarge men's sympathies, it does nothing morally [...] the only effect I ardently long to produce by my writings, is that those who read them should be better able to imagine and to feel the pains and joys of those who differ from themselves in everything but the broad fact of being struggling erring human creatures. (Eliot 1954: III: 111)

---

[1] Quoted in advertisement in *Kate Carnegie and Those Ministers*, second edition (1896).

[2] Quoted in advertisement in *Kate* Carnegie *and Those Ministers*, second edition (1896).

To Eliot, the ability to arouse the reader into a sympathetic emotional response was the moral purpose of Art. The act of feeling, or expressing sympathy, was a sign that author and reader shared the same moral values. It is this sharing of moral values that is the key to understanding Victorian ideas of the sentimental.

Victorian sentimentalism has received a bad press. Oscar Wilde's famous remark that "one must have a heart of stone to read the death of Little Nell without laughing" (Cited by Ellmann 1987: 441) has come to be seen as indicative of the shift in attitude towards the sentimental. But Wilde stood apart from the common reader and it is clear from the impact of Maclaren's work that at the end of the century readers could still respond to sentimental scenes as they had to the deaths of Little Nell and Paul Dombey some fifty years before. In its review of *Beside the Bonnie Brier Bush*, the *Echo* defied "any right-minded person to read aloud certain passages [...] with dry eyes and unfaltering voice."[3] In an introduction to one of Maclaren's later works, Charles W. Gordon – better known as the author "Ralph Connor" – recorded his first experience of Maclaren's stories:

Twelve years ago, to while away the hour of a journey from Edinburgh to Glasgow, I bought the British Weekly and began to read, at first idly, then with interest, and at last with delight, a story entitled "A Lad o' Pairts." "Read that," I said, thrusting the paper into the hands of my Scotch professor friend in Glasgow. He stood up at the mantel, but had not gone far in his reading when "Jean," he called to his wife in the next room, "come in here and listen to this;" and read, till, unawares, his voice failed, broke, and I discovered him with shamed face looking at us through tears. (Maclaren 1907: v)

Maclaren judged from the correspondence he received that "the book seems to have produced a much stronger and more general emotional effect upon men than women" (Noble 1895: 515). Certainly his stories seem to have had an emotional appeal to educated, but not necessarily literary, men. William Gladstone is reported as saying that he found the story of the "Lad o' Pairts" "most touching, most true and beautiful" and thought there had "never been anything written finer than the sketch of that country doctor" (Nicoll 1908: 171).

---

[3] Quoted in advertisement in the *Bookman* (February 1895).

In the twentieth century, the idea of art arousing an emotion and moving its audience to tears came to be seen as suspicious and aesthetically inferior to art that alienates its readers through techniques of defamiliarisation. This pattern of assessment and evaluation underpins the attack on Kailyard in Ian Campbell's study. Analysing a short section from "Domsie", Campbell points up the idealism of Maclaren's depiction of a scholar's bedroom and concludes: "All is poverty and roses, pastoral beauty and present death. It is frozen in tableau for the sympathetic response, its serves its purpose, it is forgotten" (Campbell 1981: 70). Much of the rhetorical method of Victorian fiction, however, was concerned with encouraging the reader to adopt a specific response to the text – to be moved to tears, laughter or (Eliot's beloved term) sympathy. It was the successful deployment of an artistic strategy of arousal that many commentators considered to be most important about Maclaren's fiction.

For a variety of reasons, the significance of sentimentalism as a literary technique in the Victorian period has been under-represented. Fred Kaplan argues that sentimentalism underpins much of the output of many of the novelists of the period and that it "should not be evaluated in terms offered by the mimetic tradition [...] to which it is in fundamental, purposeful opposition" (Kaplan 1987: 5). Kaplan draws a distinction between sentimentality and sensibility:

Sentimentality is the possession of innate moral sentiments; sensibility is a state of psychological-physical responsiveness. [The Victorians] were attracted to sentimentality as a moral and communal ideal rather than to sensibility, which promoted separation and withdrawal.

This was precisely the taste for which Maclaren's fiction catered. Commenting on the characters in *Beside the Bonnie Brier Bush*, the *Times* stated: "out of the pages of Oliver Goldsmith we hardly know where to look for their equals in sheer unaffected warm-heartedness" (19 January 1895). Ian Campbell argues that the technique of Kailyard writers amounts to a failed attempt to replicate the model of literary sensibility espoused in Henry Mackenzie's *The Man of Feeling* (1771), but as Kaplan notes: "*The Man of Feeling* had lost most of its relevance by the Victorian years. In contrast, Goldsmith's *The Vicar of Wakefield* (1766) became for the Victorians the bible of moral sentiment" (Kaplan 1987: 33–4). Victorian Sentimentalists took as their philosophical base Adam Smith's *Theory of Moral Sentiments*, which they had inherited through such novelists as Fielding, Richardson and Goldsmith, and which argued for the existence of innate moral sentiments. As Eliot writes in "The Natural History of German Life":

a picture of human life, such as a great artist can give, surprises even the trivial and the selfish into that attention to what is apart from themselves, which may be called the raw material of moral sentiment. (Eliot [1856] 1992: 263)

This philosophical framework is what lies behind both the content and technique of Ian Maclaren's fiction and helps explains why his work appealed to the Victorian reading and reviewing public.

What follows is not an apologia for Maclaren's fiction but an explanation of how its rhetorical strategies work and how they are used to convey the author's moral and ideological principles, particularly in relation to the construction of Drumtochty as a fictional place and the themes of education, religion and rural life.

II

William Power has called Ian Maclaren "perhaps the only real Kailyarder" (Power 1935: 160). A perceptive remark, because most of the criticisms that have become embedded in the Kailyard term derive from characteristics of Maclaren's stories. The main characteristic of his fiction is its celebration of community values at all levels of society, frequently dramatising moments of reintegration following conflict or separation. In "Domsie", the first story in *Beside the Bonnie Brier Bush*, the communal ideal is extolled through the image of the local boy made good. This has become the most famous of all Maclaren's sketches and the story of the "lad o' pairts" is often invoked as a defining characteristic of Kailyard. Ian Campbell considers the *motif* a "necessary" and "familiar" part of the genre (Campbell 1981: 95, 9); Edwin Morgan also refers to the theme as "typical" (Morgan 1974: 169) and Thomas Knowles uses the "lad o' pairts" as part of his opening definition of the "'classic' form" of Kailyard:

typically thematic is the "lad o' pairts" the poor Scottish boy making good within the "democratic" Scottish system of education, and dying young as a graduated minister in his mother's arms with the assembled parish looking on. (Knowles 1983: 13–14)

Education is certainly a recurrent theme in much Kailyard fiction, but the formula described here is "typically thematic" only of "Domsie" and even then Geordie Howe doesn't actually live to be a minister. Nevertheless, the association between Kailyard and the "lad o' pairts" has become fixed and is not just restricted to literary criticism. The historian David Forrester uses this story to arrive at the conclusion that "the kailyard authors" offered their readers a selective reality of the conditions of schooling and university entrance in the 1890s (Forrester 1991: 162). Similarly, the sociologist David McCrone takes this one short sketch as the basis for his chapter "Getting on in Scotland", arguing that Kailyard gave cultural voice to the "lad o' pairts" which was the "personum" of the "virtues of Scottish education" (McCrone 1992: 95).

It may be more than coincidence that the very first story in *Beside the Bonnie Brier Bush* should have become the basis of so many definitions of Kailyard. Perhaps we need read no further. I have argued elsewhere that the use of this story as a definition has led to a distorting account not only of the treatment of education in this fiction but also of the characteristics of Kailyard (Nash 1996). Crockett and Barrie certainly treat education in a much different way, as I have shown in previous chapters. Furthermore, it is too easy to judge Maclaren's treatment of education solely from the perspective of social realism. His use of aspects of the socio-historical realities of the Scottish education system can be seen in the general context of the themes and values that pervade his fiction.

The "lad o' pairts" is the exemplum of the supposedly egalitarian nature of Scottish society. R.D. Anderson notes that from 1850 education became a recurrent topic in articles in Scottish magazines, where the egalitarian nature of schools and universities was celebrated. The "peer and peasant" theme of social diversity and the conditions of "open competition" typified by the bursary system, allowed the "lad o' pairts" to rise from a position of poverty to rub shoulders at university with the privileged and wealthy. (Anderson 1985: 87–90). The *motif* of the "lad o' pairts" had circulated in literary texts long before Maclaren first introduced the term to cultural discourse and made it almost synonymous with "Kailyard". The typical contents of the myth were laid out most cogently in Neil Maclean's *Life at a Northern University* (1874). This novel charts the progress of a youth from the intellectual clutches of the village dominie to university life at Aberdeen via a bursary competition. A preface records how Scottish universities "open their doors to the poor as well as to the rich" and are "the pride and boast of our country" (Maclean 1874: v, vi). It is proclaimed that a university education is the "*summum bonum* of every Scotchman" and stated that "it is principally from the lower or working classes that the best scholars are obtained" (Maclean 1874: 17, 19). The village dominie provides tuition free of charge for any clever boy whose parents cannot afford to pay him. It is the bursary system which is most strongly identified as evidence of the democratic structure; it is declared to have "done more for first-class education than any other system thought of" and is identified as the key to a Scotsman's aspirations of freedom: "As I walked home in drenching rain or biting sleet, I would cry out to the roaring winds, 'O for a bursary!'" (Maclean 1874: 103, 239).

The focus on the bursary competition is where Maclean's novel differs from Maclaren's treatment of the "lad o' pairts" in "Domsie". There is no mention of a bursary in Maclaren's story; instead his objective is to show how family and community come together to support their "lad o' pairts". As in Maclean's novel, a college education is presented as the aspiration of every Scottish family:

There was just a single ambition in those humble homes, to have one of its members at college, and if Domsie approved a lad, then his brothers and sister would give their wages, and the family would live on skim milk and oat cake, to let him have his chance. (Maclaren 1894: 13)

Domsie – who "could detect a scholar in the egg, and prophesied Latinity from a boy that seemed fit only to be a cowherd" (Maclaren 1894: 9) – is willing to forego his fees to teach Geordie Howe Latin and Greek. Geordie's family, however, cannot afford to send their son to university and Domsie has to persuade Drumsheugh, a local farmer, to pay the boy's college fees. David Forrester considers the plot an unrealistic portrayal of the actual conditions of university entrance, finding "farce in the description of how Domsie obtained financial sponsorship for Geordie Howe's progress to university". But Maclaren's intention is neither realism nor farce. Instead, his aim is to celebrate the way an individual undergoes sacrifice for the good of the community. In Maclaren's fiction, education is not seen in terms of individual aspirations or achievements. Instead, the "lad o' pairts" becomes a focus for the community; he is "their scholar", battling against the advantaged "High School lads", and his duty is to carry the name of his parish:

gin a laddie gaes up frae the Glen tae the University, an' comes oot at the tap o' his classes, bringin' hame three medals ilka spring, an' opens secret things in nature that naebody kent afore, an' is selected by Government tae foon places o' learnin ayont the sea, that laddie belangs tae Drumtochty. (Maclaren 1895: 169, 26, 218)

Geordie Howe doesn't enter university through a bursary system because Maclaren wants to show how a poor Drumtochty boy can go to university only because of the good heart of a local farmer and the community at large.

It is, nonetheless, useful to see Maclaren's treatment of education in relation to historical reality. The opening of "Domsie" establishes at once that the narrator is looking back fondly on a style of education now past: "The Revolution reached our parish years ago, and Drumtochty has a School Board, with a chairman and a clerk, besides a treasurer and an officer". (Maclaren 1894:3). The Education (Scotland) Act of 1872 formalised school provision and school management and had the effect of introducing "southern innovations which threatened to make education narrower in scope or more constrained by class distinctions"; as a consequence, the "parish school ideal of common education became part of the construction of a mythical history of Scottish education" (Anderson 1985: 83, 97). Maclaren's stories undoubtedly contributed to this construction. The grand word "Revolution" immediately reveals the author's attitude towards the changes. In an interview Maclaren commented: "I look back with great affection upon the old Scottish Parish Schools. They really fostered scholarship as the Board Schools certainly never will" (Blathwayt 1899: 288). His villagers are in agreement. As one avers: "it was the prospeck o' the Schule Board and its weary bit rules that feeneshed Domsie [...] he wud hae taen ill with thae new fikes, and nae college lad to warm his hert" (Maclaren 1894: 4).

Nevertheless, Maclaren's principal concern is with the power of community, as a later story, "The Passing of Domsie", makes clear. Domsie has decided to retire, and he and the minister reminisce over the past when the end of each University session "showered medals" on Drumtochty (Maclaren 1898: 417–8). "They have made it known in every university in Scotland" remarks the minister (Maclaren 1898: 422–3). To honour their dominie the parish resolves to establish a bursary in Domsie's name to help "puir scholars" (Maclaren 1898: 429). Everybody contributes: the poor, the lairds, even the "Drumtochty fouk in the Sooth". When a reception is held in the Kirk, scholars from abroad and from all walks of life return to pay homage to "the master who first opened us to the way of knowledge" (Maclaren 1898: 435).

Maclaren's other main story about education displays similar concerns. "His Crowning Day", included in the largely unknown collection *His Majesty Baby* (1902), focuses on the graduation day of a shepherd's son and celebrates the peer and peasant theme of Scottish education. The narrator imagines the shepherd's son entering the university:

The lad before him is a noble's son, and the one following is a merchant's, and so sons of the rich and of the poor, of the high and of the low, they go together, into the one Republic on the face of the earth, the Republic of Letters. (Maclaren 1902: 148–9)

Once again, however, what is given most attention is not the system of meritocracy but the selfless sacrifice of the shepherd boy's family:

I should have gone down into that hall, and held a special and unheard-of graduation ceremony, conferring a degree of a new kind altogether upon that shepherd and his wife, because without their unworldly ideals, and their hard sacrifices, and their holy prayers, John McPherson had never knelt there that day in his white silk glory, Master of Arts with the highest honours. (Maclaren 1902: 155)

One further example can help to show that Maclaren used the myths
and legends of Scottish education to suit his fictional and ideological
ends. *Young Barbarians*, a collection of stories for boys, is based on
Maclaren's own school experiences. Here, in a different genre, the
school is still presented as a place where peer and peasant meet and
where the dominie is a paragon, but the "lad o' pairts" is turned on his
head; there is no respect at all for the promising scholar:

> When Thomas John reached the university he did not altogether fulfil the expectations
> of his family, and by the time he reached the pulpit no one could endure his
> unredeemed dullness. (Maclaren [1901] 1985: 15)

Maclaren's ideological attitude to education is flexible enough to
adapt itself to different genres and reading markets.

The issue of education constitutes only a small portion of
Maclaren's fictional output. That it should have been seized upon as
so central to his writing, and as a defining characteristic of Kailyard, is
perhaps more indicative of the kind of demands and interests that have
motivated critics in their construction of "Kailyard" culture. Forrester
charges both Maclaren and George Douglas Brown for ignoring the
unions, clubs and societies which in the 1880s first established a sense
of community life in Scottish universities (Forrester 1992: 159–160).
But Maclaren didn't even write about life in universities except for the
one short story from *His Majesty Baby* discussed above. Certainly if
one measures Maclaren's stories against historical fact they can be
found wanting, but his aim was always to construct an ideal picture
and never slavishly to represent facts. That construction of an ideal
picture can be seen in the treatment of other topical issues in his
fiction.

III

More than anything else, Maclaren's fiction needs to be understood in
relation to the author's ministerial background. In a perceptive review
in the *Academy*, William Wallace identified the main differences
between the Rev. John Watson and Barrie: one was a layman, the
other a clergyman; Barrie was alive to the "comedy and tragedy" of

his fictional world, Maclaren was concerned for the "material and spiritual welfare of his" (24 November 1894). It has become a critical commonplace to accuse Maclaren of being out of touch with the social and cultural imperatives of his time but so far as the topics of Church and religion are concerned his fiction is fully engaged with contemporary issues. Callum G. Brown argues that the Kailyard novels "need to be relocated by modern critics" within a "religious popular culture" current at the time (Brown 2001: 155). Examination of the contexts and the treatment of the theme of religion reveals Maclaren's fiction as a vital part of the history of Scottish Presbyterianism.

Following his studies in Edinburgh, Maclaren became an assistant at Barclay Free Church.[4] In 1874 he was called to the parish of Logiealmond in Perthshire where he ministered for less than three years before moving to Free St Matthew's Church in Glasgow. His experiences in the Glasgow parish provided the basis for his final collection of stories *St Jude's* (1907). One of his congregation recorded that John Carmichael, the fictional minister, was just "John Watson altered and adapted" (Cited in Nicoll 1908: 83). In 1880 Maclaren took up the position of minister in the Presbyterian Church of England at Sefton Park, Liverpool. William Robertson Nicoll records that his congregation in Liverpool was "largely Scotch either by birth or by descent" (Nicoll 1908: 86). He resigned his charge in Liverpool in 1905 and died, aged 56, whilst on his second tour to America in 1907.

Maclaren was not predestined to be a minister. At university he had no association with religious circles and "not the remotest contact with Church work" (Nicoll 1908: 45). His love for rural life seemed to bode for a life in farming but under the instigation of his father he trained for the ministry. His choice of the Free Church was by no means obvious and his principals were not dogmatic. His father was an elder in the Free Church but his maternal ancestry was Catholic and Jacobite and it was from his Highland background that he found his *nom de plume*, taking his mother's maiden name and the Gaelic form of his Christian name. In his early years in Logiealmond he adopted in

---

[4] For convenience, I will refer to Watson by his penname of Ian Maclaren.

his private conduct much of the discipline of the Roman Catholic Church.

This background establishes two important aspects of Maclaren's religious attitude – his ecumenicalism and his moderate theology. This attitude must be understood in the wider context of debates in the Free Church, and religious life in general, at the end of the nineteenth century. In a short but valuable article, Christopher Harvie reminds us that Maclaren's fiction is set against the changes brought about by "the social and intellectual fluidity of the 1870's and 1880's" (Harvie 1982: 9). The impact of Darwinism and German Biblical scholarship tested the faith of all Victorians, not least George Eliot who later translated David Friedrich Strauss's scholarly account of the historical realities of the Gospels. In the Free Church, William Robertson Smith, a prominent proponent of Biblical scholarship, was expelled from his post as Professor of Hebrew and Old Testament exegesis at the Aberdeen Free Church College on charges of heresy. Together with the issue of Disestablishment – to which Maclaren was strongly opposed – the debates over the Bible contributed to what Harvie terms "an unsettled context" within which "there was a move towards a new, less dogmatic, more vital religion on the part of younger men in the churches". Maclaren was one of these younger men and in his fiction he celebrates what Knowles correctly identifies as themes of "consensus and reconciliation" between religious types (Knowles 1983, chapter 3). Maclaren builds a Godly Commonwealth around a structure of feeling that is conveyed through a deliberately sentimental strategy.

The phrase Godly Commonwealth is associated with Thomas Chalmers (1780–1847), whose portrait is the "chief glory" of the vestry of the Free Church in Drumtochty (Maclaren 1894: 122). Like Maclaren, Chalmers moved to Glasgow having previously ministered in a rural parish, and his experiences of the industrialising city led him to believe that the cause of urban deprivation was the breakdown of community spirit. He developed an innovative programme of social reform involving the revival of the parish system on a national level and the introduction of rural values into urban areas.[5] As we shall see,

---

[5] For a full account of Chalmers, see Brown 1982.

Maclaren's fiction embodies the principles behind Chalmers' methods and teachings, but Chalmers' more immediate influence on Maclaren's religious principles lies in his role in the 1843 Disruption in the Church of Scotland. The Disruption was the culmination of a prolonged dispute over patronage and concerned the spiritual independence of the Church, especially the right for parishoners to influence the appointment of ministers. In his fiction Maclaren celebrates that right and also the freedom of individual conscience. The congregation in *Beside the Bonnie Brier Bush* scrutinise young ministers strictly, none more so than Donald Menzies who "filled the hearts of nervous probationers with dismay" (Maclaren 1894: 58).

The duties and responsibilities of ministers is inevitably a central issue in Maclaren's fiction. Maclaren admitted to being a poor preacher in his early career and, as a consequence, in Edinburgh he was entrusted "with a large amount of pastoral visitation" (Nicoll 1908: 67). The first story in the *St Jude's* looks back on John Carmichael's apprenticeship in Drumtochty, showing how his congregation helped him to overcome a lack of confidence in his own preaching. In later life, however, Maclaren became noted for the power of his sermons. Matthew Arnold heard him preach on the day that he died and "remarked that he had rarely been so affected by any preacher as by Dr. Watson" (Nicoll 1908: 130).

The lectures on Practical Theology that Maclaren delivered to Yale University, published as *The Cure of Souls* (1896), give a full account of his opinions and reinforce the ideas that emerge from the fiction. Several of his stories are concerned with the practice of preaching. Maclaren was not an evangelist and he thought evangelical preaching "careless to a scandal, and almost squalid in style, with vain repetitions of hackneyed words by way of exhortation" (Nicoll 1908: 111). In Drumtochty "well-meaning evangelists who came with what they called 'a simple Gospel address' [...] lost heart in face of that judicial front, and afterwards described Drumtochty in the religious papers as 'dead'" (Maclaren 1894: 200). Equally, Hellfire preaching was at odds with Maclaren's sense of a benevolent God. In "Domsie", the old "Revival man" whose "preaching on hell" haunted Geordie Howe in his youth is contrasted to the comforting, motherly God who speaks through Geordie's mother.

Revivalism and evangelical preaching are both treated negatively in
Kate Carnegie and those Ministers (1896), Maclaren's most detailed
account of the different types of minister in Scotland.[6] Principal
amongst "those ministers", apart from Carmichael, is the "supra-
lapsarian" Jeremiah Saunderson, who embodies an extreme form of
Calvinism. Although Maclaren clearly rejects the old man's teaching,
he is treated sympathetically throughout. Saunderson, who was later to
become the subject of a book himself (*Rabbi Saunderson*, 1899)
quarrels with Carmichael when the young man gives a sermon that
attacks those "who still believed in the inflexible action of the moral
laws and the austere majesty of God" (Maclaren 1896: 307). The
Rabbi responds with a sermon that dwells on predestination, "the
absolute supremacy of God and the utter helplessness of man"
(Maclaren 1896: 315); as if by Divine response, the oil lights flicker
and go out.

    Maclaren's main criticism, however, is levelled at preaching
inspired by German Biblical scholarship. When one minister "being
still young, expounded a new theory of the atonement of German
manufacture" he is sorely judged by the glen for his "blindness of
heart" (Maclaren 1894: 57). The key word is "heart". Biblical
scholarship involved the intellect, but theology based upon the
intellect alone was, for Maclaren, inadequate. As Nicoll recorded:

He was wont to illustrate the reconciliation between dogma and religion by a
reference to a picture of the meeting of St Dominic representing dogma, and St
Francis representing religion. When they met they flung their arms around one
another and kissed each other; and so he was wont to say in the end would the religion
of the soul embrace the reverent dogma of the intellect. (Nicoll 1908: 71)

Maclaren did not object to the intellectual significance of Biblical
scholarship but he thought it had no place in the pulpit. In *The Cure of
Souls* he states: "For any teacher of the Bible to ignore or disparage
the reliable, or even probable results of criticism, and not to give them
to his people, is a serious neglect of duty". He believed that "careful
and systematic instruction in the literary and historical circumstances
of the Bible" was best delivered "in classes to be conducted by the

---

[6] For a fuller discussion, see Knowles 1983: 188–193.

minister, and where the pupils can have the full benefit of his knowledge" (Watson 1896: 78).

A story that address this issue directly is "His Mother's Sermon", which focuses on John Carmichael's arrival in Drumtochty. A young minister, fresh out of college, Carmichael is determined to "state the present position of theological thought" (Maclaren 1894: 85–6). His aunt, who accompanies him to Drumtochty, fears that the minister's "new views" will not be understood by the "plain country fouk" who "need a clear word tae comfort their herts and show them the way everlasting" (Maclaren 1894: 89–90). Again, we have the emphasis on the heart, and Carmichael's aunt, who is described as "a saint, with that firm grasp of truth, and tender mysticism, whose combination is the charm of Scottish piety", speaks for the author (Maclaren 1894: 86). At the beginning of the story, his aunt recalls how, five years earlier, Carmichael's mother had died with the parting hope that, should her son enter the ministry, she would be forever satisfied if, in his first sermon, he should "speak a gude word for Jesus Christ" (Maclaren 1894: 87). Maclaren based his ministerial teaching on the life, death and resurrection of Christ. As Nicoll recorded, "Christ was to him the centre of theology and preaching" and in his first sermon in Liverpool he affirmed his intention to "preach the Cross of Christ" (Nicoll 1908: 213, 92). In "His Mother's Sermon" he sets up a conflict between Biblical scholarship and Christ in terms that, characteristically, employ imagery from nature:

Black massy clouds had begun to gather in the evening, and threatened to obscure the sunset, which was the finest sight a Drumtochty man was ever likely to see, and a means of grace to every sensible heart in the glen. But the sun had beat back the clouds on either side, and shot them through with glory and now between piled billows of light he went along a shining pathway into the Gates of the West. The minister stood still before that spectacle, his face bathed in the golden glory, and then before his eyes the gold deepened into an awful red, and the red passed into shades of violet and green, beyond painter's hand or the imagination of man. It seemed to him as if a victorious saint had entered through the gates into the city, washed in the blood of the Lamb, and the after glow of his mother's life fell solemnly on his soul. (Maclaren 1894: 90–1)

God speaks to Carmichael not through his theological books but through the beauties of nature and a vision of his mother washed in the blood of Christ. The minister puts his books out of mind as he composes his sermon:

The brilliant opening, with its historical parallel, this review of modern thought reinforced by telling quotations, that trenchant criticism of old-fashioned views, would not deliver. For the audience had vanished, and left one careworn, but beautiful face, whose gentle eyes were waiting with a yearning look. (Maclaren 1894: 92)

The natural description, inducing in the minister the memory of his dead mother's words, works to encourage a similar act of identification in the reader. Maclaren's sermons on Christ obviously had a powerful appeal. Matthew Arnold was reported to have said after hearing Maclaren preach: "Yes […] the Cross remaineth, and in the straits of the soul makes its ancient appeal" (Nicoll 1908: 130). Given this response it is easy to see how others saw the appeal as well, and why many considered it more than ancient in its relevance.

The theme of Biblical scholarship is picked up again in "A Grand Inquisitor", the first story in the five-part sketch "The Transformation of Lachlan Campbell". In this sketch Maclaren combines his rebuttal of Biblical scholarship with an attack on theological and doctrinal conflict. Campbell, a Highlander, recently arrived from the parish of Auchindarroch, upholds the principles of the auld kirk – "his life business was theology" and his prayers full of hope that "the backslidings of Scotland might be healed" (Maclaren 1894: 103). As the parish inquisitor, Campbell soon finds fault with Carmichael, whose sermon "on the same parable of nature Jesus loved" (Maclaren 1894: 109) falls short in the old man's eyes:

"[…] I am not thinking that trees and leaves and stubble fields will save our souls, and I did not hear about sin and repentance and the work of Christ. It iss sound doctrine that we need, and a great peety you are not giving it." (Maclaren 1894: 110)

Carmichael takes immediate offence and the two men part in anger. Maclaren's purpose in this story is not to attack the doctrinal religion espoused by Campbell but to point out how arguments over doctrine erect barriers between men:

Perhaps the minister would have understood Lachlan better if he had known that the old man could not touch food when he got home, and spent the evening in a fir wood praying for the lad he had begun to love. And Lachlan would have had a lighter heart if he had heard the minister questioning himself whether he had denied the Evangel or sinned against one of Christ's disciples. They argued together; they prayed apart. (Maclaren 1894: 111).

Campbell's questioning of Carmichael's doctrine, and the young minister's own "fair idea of himself", lead Carmichael to make what the narrator terms "a great mistake". He embarks upon a course of sermons on Biblical criticism, designed "to place Drumtochty on a level with Germany". The narrator counsels caution, explaining that "Drumtochty was not anxious to be enlightened about the authors of the Pentateuch, being quite satisfied with Moses" and adopts a position that Maclaren held in his own professional life: "Why could he not read the subject for his own pleasure, and teach it quietly in classes? Why give himself away in the pulpit?" Carmichael stands firm:

Had he not been ordained to feed his people with truth, and was he not bound to tell them all he knew? We were living in an age of transition, and he must prepare Christ's folk that they be not taken unawares. (Maclaren 1894: 113)

The significance of this "age of transition" in Scottish religious life (and Scottish cultural life more generally) should not be underestimated. Maclaren was writing at a time when the impact of Darwinism, Biblical scholarship, and questions over doctrine and the relationship between Church and State were placing religious life in a state of transition. A modern critic suggests that the conflicts in Maclaren's fiction revolve around "relatively minor individual moral struggles" (Cook 1999: 1057) but religious doubt was hardly a minor struggle for the Victorians. Far from being out of touch with contemporary issues in the Church, Maclaren was actively involved in the debate. His article of 1905 on "The Church Crisis in Scotland" dissected the historical background behind the debate over disestablishment and the crisis that arose when a minority among the Free Church dissented from the union in 1900 of the United Presbyterian and Free Churches. (Watson 1905).

As the Rev. John Watson, Maclaren wrote several theological books, including a life of Christ, *The Life of the Master* (1901). Some

of his opinions brought accusations of heresy, especially on the
question of the authority of the Gospels (Nicoll 1908: 213–16).
Maclaren's aim was to draw attention to the words of Christ as the
very substance of the Gospel message and to downplay the doctrines
and dogmas that have arisen from interpretation of them. In a study of
The Theology of Modern Literature, the Rev. S. Law Wilson
summarised Maclaren's aim in his stories as "largely to convince us of
the uselessness of all theology" (Wilson 1899: 324). But in *The Cure
of Souls* Maclaren stated clearly that "theology is an absolute
intellectual necessity". Maclaren positions himself against two
extremes – the Rationalistic school, which sees the "Catholic creeds"
as "antiquarian documents, which are outside criticism", and the
Evangelistic school, which "bitterly resent[s] the application of
literary methods" to the Bible (Watson 1896: 82, 84). He rejects the
argument that the "great Christian doctrines" have "no more vitality
than a fossil of the carboniferous period" but he equally deplores the
"extreme simplicity" of the those who are "quite convinced that the
mystery of Christ's sacrifice is made luminous beyond desire by some
time-worn illustration of a person jumping into a boat or throwing
himself from a burning house" (Watson 1896: 84–5). Maclaren's
argument was not with theology but with "all this railing and girding
at doctrine" which he considered "one of innumerable forms of
modern cant" (Watson 1896: 87).

  The story of Lachlan Campbell makes this position clear.
Carmichael's lectures on Biblical criticism bring uproar: "The peace
of the Free Kirk had been broken and the minister was eating out his
heart" (Maclaren 1894: 115). The situation is resolved by the
intervention of Margaret Howe, the mother of Geordie, the "lad o'
pairts". Margaret reappears in several other stories in the two
collections and becomes a paragon of the community. As one old
woman declares: "Margaret Hoo is nearer the hert o' things than
onybody in the Glen" (Maclaren 1895: 275). And after she has
counselled him beside the bonnie brier bush, Carmichael realises that
the "the voice of God" is in Marget not Biblical scholarship. He
immediately seeks out Lachlan Campbell and the two men pray
together, respectful of each other's opinions, in a moment of

communality which strikes to the heart of Maclaren's social and religious vision:

They knelt together on the earthen floor of that Highland cottage, the old school and the new, before one Lord, and the only difference in their prayers was that the young man prayed they might keep the faith once delivered unto the saints, while the burden of the old man's prayer was that they might be led into all truth. (Maclaren 1894: 120)

As Christopher Harvie asks of another story: "In the 1860's would Free Church and Auld Kirk, probably glowering at one another from expensive and half-filled buildings, suspend hostilities with such alacrity?" (Harvie 1982: 8). It was part of the intention of Maclaren's fiction to make that happen by creating a unifying religious climate. Maclaren commanded a following in Liverpool precisely because of his lack of dogma. Nicoll considered that "there were very few congregations in England made up of recruits from so many armies as Sefton Park Church" and Maclaren himself attested to having members "every shade of Presbyterianism [...] of many nations [...] and as many creeds, high and low, narrow and broad, and no creed at all" (Nicoll 1908: 91). The division in the Church has been seen by nationalist historians as the "shattering" of a "great force for the cohesion of Scottish society" (Scott 1988: 19). Maclaren's ecumenical vision can be seen as an attempt at national cohesion. In his review in the *Bookman*, George Adam Smith judged of "Lachlan Campbell" that "A patriot could not to-day have served his country better than by such a story" (October 1894).

In another story, "For Conscience Sake", Maclaren presents Established Church and Free Church coming together over an issue of religious politics. When a factor refuses to renew a farmer's lease unless the farmer joins the established Church, everybody is outraged, including Doctor Davidson, the minister of the established Church. The whole glen comes out in favour of the farmer, Burnbrae, leading Drumsheugh to remark: "The Auld and the Frees shother tae shother for the first time since '43 – it'll be ground" (Maclaren 1895: 36). At the end of the story, when Burnbrae's farm holdings have been replenished, the glen assembles for a feast and a Bible reading. Dr Davidson motions to the Free Church Minister to take up his position at the head, but his compeer demands otherwise: "Doctor Davidson, there is neither Established nor Free Church here this night; we are all one in faith and love, and you were ordained before I was born" (Maclaren 1895: 113).

A vision of unity that accommodated a respect for individual conscience was at the heart of Maclaren's hopes for the Church in Scotland. As he wrote in his 1905 article on the crisis in the Church: "it was intolerable that there should be in a country parish three churches with not the slightest difference between them except a different theory about the relation of Church and state" (Watson 1905: 244). Harvie notices the same vision in the "ecumenicalism of the funeral" in "Domsie". The final part of that sketch focuses not on the theme of education but of religious unity. As Harvie shows, an ecumenical selection of Geordie's friends assemble for the funeral and Auld Kirk and Free Kirk come together in a religion that is "heterodox and humanistic" (Harvie 1982: 10). The established minister delivers a sermon which soon dispenses with any doctrinal or theological rhetoric in favour of simple, universal sentiment:

The Doctor's funeral prayer was one of the glories of the parish, compelling even the Free Kirk to reluctant admiration, although they hinted that its excellence was rather of the letter than the spirit, and regarded its indiscriminate charity with suspicion. [...] The doctor made a good start, and had already sighted Job, when he was carried out of his course by a sudden current, and began to speak to God about Marget and her son, after a very simple fashion that brought a lump to the throat, till at last, as I imagine, the sight of the laddie working at his Greek in the study of a winter night came up before him, and the remnants of the great prayer melted like an iceberg in the Gulf Stream.

"Lord, haw peety upon us, for we a' luved him, and we were a' prood o' him." (Maclaren 1894: 48).

Maclaren's fiction regularly centres on the power of sentiment to unlock human – and what he takes to be Christian – values and emotions. In *St Jude's*, Maclaren makes a joke at the way that the "elect" detect in Carmichael evidence of Arminianism, Morisonianism, Socinianism and Pelagianism. Carmichael mounts "the feelings of ordinary humanity" against "the pedantic arguments of theology" (Maclaren 1907: 41), and puts the case for worldly codes of love and sacrifice:

"[…] Will you say that a mother's love to her son, lasting through the sacrifices of life on to the tender farewell on her deathbed, is not altogether good? That a man toiling and striving to build a home for his wife and children and to keep them in peace and plenty, safe from the storms of life, is not acceptable unto God? That a man giving his life to save a little child from drowning, or to protect his country from her enemies, is not beautiful in the sight of Heaven? That even a heretic, standing by what he believes to be true and losing all his earthly goods for conscience' sake, has not done a holy thing[?]"

No man answered, and it was not needful, for the minister's human emotion had beaten upon their iron creed like spray upon the high sea cliffs.

Human emotion breaks through creeds, and it is exactly these values that Maclaren explores – and celebrates – in his fiction.

Maclaren has often been seen as representative of a narrow form of evangelical, Free Church Presbyterianism. But assessment of his theological position needs careful discrimination. It is wrong to conclude that in his stories "faith is all, works nothing" (Davies 1974: 161). In "Past Redemption", a story in *The Days of Auld Langsyne*, he implicitly advocates a belief in universal salvation. Posty, as he is affectionately known, is an unbeliever and a heavy drinker, who meets his death when heroically saving a young girl from drowning. When the Free Kirk minister is asked what has happened to Posty "on the ither side" he triumphantly acquits him and prophesies that he has been saved. The story landed Maclaren in hot water, so much so that he was led to defend his position in a sketch entitled "An Evangelist" published in *Afterwards*. The sketch dramatises a meeting between Maclaren and Elijah Higginbotham, an earnest evangelist "determined to do his duty, which was to hold back as many of his neighbours as he could from going to Hell" (Maclaren 1898: 304). Elijah objects to the suggestion of salvation by good works, arguing that Posty dies in sin "with no sign of repentance", and "is sent to Heaven as if he were a saint" (Maclaren 1898: 313). Maclaren reminds him of the story, and the simple tale of Posty's courage affects the evangelist to the point where "there was no Elijah Higginbotham anywhere to be found now, only an excited man, concerned about the saving of a little maid" (Maclaren 1898: 323–4). As well as defending his position on salvation by works, Maclaren uses this story to remind his readers of the affective, restorative power of story-telling.

Universal Salvation is also the subject of a story in *St Jude's*. Simeon MacQuittrick – the "inflexible and impenetrable subject of Lowland Calvinism" – subjects Carmichael to "A Local Inquisition" (the title of the sketch), which Maclaren treats ironically and dismissively. In contrast to Predestination, Carmichael preaches universal salvation:

When Carmichael boldly declared that the Divine love embraced the human race which God had called into being, and that Christ as the Incarnate Saviour of the world had laid down His life, not for a few, but for the race, and that therefore there was freeness of pardon and fulness of grace for all men, and when finally he called God by the name of Father, the inquisitors sighed in unison. They looked like men who had feared the worst, and were not disappointed. (Maclaren 1907: 35)

MacQuittrick challenges this position with his comment that "the end of this deceiving error, which pleases the silly heart, is Universalism – nae difference between the elect and the multitude." Maclaren would not have thought the heart "silly", however, and the story follows Carmichael's resistance to "a conscientious and thorough-going theology, against whose inhumanity and ungraciousness both his reason and his soul revolted" (Maclaren 1907: 37). Reason and soul – mind and heart – revolt against inhuman theology.

IV

An essential aspect of Maclaren's stories is his representation of farm life in rural Perthshire and, as Ian Carter has noted, his Drumtochty books deal in part with "the social consequences of agrarian capitalism" (Carter 1976: 2). Although Carter mixes up Maclaren's characters (confusing Hillocks with Drumsheugh), the points he raises about Maclaren's depiction of farming are important. Drumsheugh is alone among the farmers in Drumtochty in leasing a large farm and producing not for subsistence but for the market. This means he is not a peasant farmer, like all the others, but a capitalist farmer; and yet, as Carter notes, "we see him acting again and again in an oddly uncapitalist fashion" (Carter 1976: 7). Rather than reinvesting his profits he chooses to invest them in the community, supporting

Geordie Howe through university, attending to his fevered grieve, and putting up the money so that the Queen's doctor can save the life of the wife of a fellow farmer. It is not the market that is Drumsheugh's master but the community. As Carter states: "Maclaren's emphasis on harmony between peasants and large farmers in Drumtochty is so insistent precisely because he knows that the peasantry is a doomed class" (Carter 1976: 9). Writing in the 1890s about the 1860s and 70s, Maclaren hones in on the communal, mutually-supportive way of life that was being encroached upon by capitalist forms of farming. This is not so much a wilful distortion of reality as a nostalgic evocation of what is taken as an ideal form of existence.

The anti-capitalist portrayal of farm life is explored more fully in two other stories that Carter does not mention. In "A Triumph in Diplomacy" we learn about the special circumstances of farm life in Drumtochty:

Farms were held on lease in Drumtochty, and, according to a good old custom, descended from father to son, so that some of the farmers' forebears had been tenants as long as Lord Kilspindie's ancestors had been owners. If a family died out, then a successor from foreign parts had to be introduced. (Maclaren 1895: 3)

This unlikely custom invests the farmers' lives with an historical permanence, putting the tenant on a level with the landowner. It also lays emphasis – artificially – on continuity as an ideal of rural life. In this and other stories, it is the tradition of farming unchanged by time or technical development that is celebrated. When one of the leases is taken up by a "guileless tradesman from Muirtown" (Maclaren 1895: 3), his farm improvements soon fail.

More critical is the relationship between landowner, factor and tenant. As with the theme of education, Maclaren's purpose is to create a world where different sections of society, with different material interests, can come together in a shared, common humanity. In "A Triumph in Diplomacy" this is explored through the process of negotiation for the renewal of a lease. In Drumtochty, "Farms were not put in the *Advertiser* and thrown open to the public from Dan to Beersheba" (Maclaren 1895: 6); this is because there is an unspoken contract between tenant and factor that the lease will be renewed on terms that are satisfactory to both. "For Conscience Sake", the story of

Burnbrae mentioned above, explores what happens when this unspoken contract is challenged. A new factor – the cousin of an English lord – refuses to grant Burnbrae his lease unless he agrees to join the established Church. The story has an historical basis. After the Disruption of 1843, "in rural districts, especially the Highlands, Free Church adherents experienced persecution at the hand of landowners who viewed the new church as a challenge to the traditional social order" (Lynch 2001: 72). The community is outraged by the conditions imposed upon Burnbrae, not just because a man is being asked to put his work before his religion, but because the factor is meddling with a farmer's historical association with the land. The right for a tenant to farm his own piece of land – regardless of the fact that he does not own it – is presented as inalienable:

What richt hes ony man tae hand ower the families that hev been on his estate afore he wes born tae be harried an' insulted by some domineering upstart o' a factor, an' then tae spend the money wrung frae the land by honest fouks among strangers and foreigners? (Maclaren 1895: 28)

The explicit Marxist message here is easy to miss because we think of Maclaren as conservative and traditionalist; and, in fact, Hillocks' words are not the prelude to a radical claim of right for the working classes. Whilst Maclaren's ideal community endorses hierarchy, it projects the relationship between the landowning and the working classes as a mutually-beneficial contract. When Lord Kilspindie learns of the demands his new factor is putting upon his tenant, he intervenes and restores the lease to Burnbrae for long enough to ensure that the farmer's son will be able to take possession when Burnbrae dies. What moves Kilspindie to this action is the appeal Burnbrae makes to a common history between farmer and laird:

"For twa hundred years an' mair there's been a Baxter at Burnbrae and a Hay at Kilspindie; ane wes juist a workin' farmer, an' the ither a belted earl, but gude friends an' faithfu'; an' ma Lord, Burnbrae wes as dear tae oor fouk as the castle wes tae yours." (Maclaren 1895: 88–9)

This anti-capitalist dynamic pervades Maclaren's fiction and forms part of his presentation of a community that is self-sufficient and self-supporting. The system of medical provision is also free from capitalist structures. William Maclure, the selfless and industrious doctor is given a free house and fields by Lord Kilspindie. In return, he never demands payment from his patients – "His fees were pretty much what the folk chose to give him and he collected them once a year at Kildrummie fair" (Maclaren 1894: 245). To expect monetary reward would be to confuse materialism with spirituality and love. As Jamie Soutar puts it: "The doctor has never been burdened wit' fees, and a'm judgin' he coonted a wumman's gratitude that he saved fraw weedowhood the best he ever got" (Maclaren 1894: 281).

The doctor is more of a paragon than even the minister and the dominie, traversing the glen and the surrounding area through floods and snowdrifts at a moment's notice and without rest – "for such risks of life men get the Victoria Cross in other fields"; MacLure gets nothing but the secret affection of the Glen, which "knew that none had ever done one-tenth as much for it as this ungainly, twisted battered figure" (Maclaren 1894: 239). He is presented as one of the people, admired for his brotherliness and his lack of pretension. Like the Dominie, there are "no new-fangled wys" with the Doctor, whose simple, "barbarous" remedies are contrasted favourably with those of "the sooth" (Maclaren 1894: 244). And, again like the Dominie, he is presented as the very model of a type that no longer exists. He presents himself as "the last o' the auld schule", who did what he could to keep up with the new medicine but who had little time for reading (Maclaren 1894: 295).

In a letter to William Blackwood, Maclaren commented: "It seemed to me that Doctor Davidson could only be developed in the course of the serial which will show how opposite sides of faith and politics have some underlying harmony".[7] When he dies the Doctor is elevated to a Christ-like status: "Death after all was victor, for the man that saved them had not been able to save himself" (Maclaren 1894: 317). He receives the ultimate payment for his services in death when the community arranges for his funeral expenses and braves extreme weather to turn out for the service. It is thought appropriate that the Doctor dies during winter and people from neighbouring regions flock

---

[7] Unpublished ALS, 14 August 1895 (National Library of Scotland).

to join the locals. Lord Kilspindie comes up from Muirtown Castle in a display that temporarily dissolves class distinctions. Leaving his overcoat behind and dressing in his funeral blacks like the rest of the community, Kilspindie is one of the eight men who lowers the doctor's coffin into the earth.

This egalitarian impulse runs throughout Maclaren's stories, as human charity overcomes the inequities of class distinction. When Annie Mitchell is dying, the doctor avers that the only man who can save her is the Queen's own surgeon. As the Doctor explains:

"But it's hard, Jess, that money wull buy life after a', an' if Annie wes a duchess her man wudna lose her; but bein' only a puir cottar's wife, she maun dee afore the week's oot." (Maclaren 1894: 254)

Just as he had done for Geordie Howe's schooling, Drumsheugh digs deep into his savings and produces the money, explaining that his once bitter heart has disappeared since that day "beside the brier bush whaur George Hoo lay yon sad simmer time" (Maclaren 1894: 257). The Queen's Doctor is duly summoned and, after a death-defying journey through the flood, Annie's life is saved. Rather than accept payment, however, the surgeon is so moved by the Drumtochty spirit that he tears up Drumsheugh's cheque for one hundred guineas. The capitalist system of monetary payment for services is brushed aside when a shared ordeal brings out the common charity of man.

The stories of Burnbrae and Dr. Maclure both bring into focus the sentimental technique Maclaren employs in his writing. Maclaren's fiction quickly became notorious for its numerous death-bed scenes. The long protracted scene of Doctor's Maclure's death, "The Doctor's Last Journey", is hard for a modern reader to endure. As the doctor hovers in between life and death, his sleep is interrupted by dreams of his visits to the sick and memories of his childhood prayers. Alone with his friend Drumsheugh he dies with "peace" gathering "round his closed eyes" and the words of the twenty-third psalm on his lips (Maclaren 1894: 302). As Eric Anderson notes:

an age like ours, which approves frank description of the sexual act but finds the act of dying embarrassing in reality and in fiction, cannot quite respond as did Maclaren's original readers, whose taboos we have neatly reversed. (Anderson 1979: 138)

The reversal of taboos is what leads Maurice Lindsay to dismiss Maclaren's work as containing scenes of "the utmost triviality" (Lindsay 1977: 349), as if death and salvation were trivial to the Victorians. In one of his religious books, Maclaren writes:

Death is a very successful teacher of that faith we all long to possess; the conviction of the Unseen [...] a young child with Christ does more to illuminate the other world than all the books that ever have been written. (Watson 1897: 33)

Nevertheless, even William Robertson Nicoll is forced to admit that in Maclaren's fiction "a disproportionate space is given to descriptions of deathbeds" (Nicoll 1908: 180).

We can see how Maclaren's sentimental technique works in the depiction of Burnbrae and his wife in "For Conscience Sake". As they prepare to leave their farm, Maclaren presents the couple's feelings by focusing on the sentimental value of the objects which capture their attachment to the land and their home. An old chair by the fireside induces in Burnbrae memories of when he was a boy; the swing of the gate reminds him of his father; the rose bush reminds him of a flower he gave to his wife, the leaves of which now adorn the cover of her Bible; every object is charged with sentimental value so as to induce in the reader an identification with the character's feeling. Excessive sentimentality is one of the main charges against Maclaren's writings, and in this sketch it has considerable weight because the application of sentimental value to anything that can carry an association of feeling becomes indiscriminate. The main sentimental focus falls on Burnbrae's dead daughter and his wife's pain at having to leave her child. Jean is associated throughout with the organic image of flowers: "There was no 'beloved' nor any text" on her plain tombstone "but each spring the primroses came out below, and all summer a bunch of pinks touched the 'Jean' with the fragrant blossoms" (Maclaren 1895: 52). Maclaren's technique is to keep the figure of the dead child before the reader at every opportunity in the story so as to suck every last bit of sentiment out of the situation. Jean's mother sows a "patch of annuals" in the shape of her daughter's name and each year the blossom blooms on the apple tree planted when the young girl died. When the animals are gathered for the sale of Burnbrae's stock they are "penned in the field below the garden, where the dead lassie's

name bloomed in fragrant mignonette" (Maclaren 1895: 71); when
Burnbrae's wife gathers together her few remaining possession she
digs up the plants from the garden protesting:

"A' cudna leave them, John, an' they'll mak oor new gairden mair hame-like. The
pinks are cuttin's a' set mysel', an' the fuchsias tae, an' Jeannie carried the can and
watered them that simmer afore she dee'd." (Maclaren 1895: 82–3)

As Nicoll comments: "the feelings are deliberately and cruelly
harrowed by an accumulation of pathetic incidents and words" and
Maclaren himself admitted that his fiction did not wholly escape the
dangers of sentimentalism (Nicoll 1908: 180).

Maclaren frequently uses descriptions of nature to reflect human
conditions in an artistic technique that is akin to pastoral. One
example from "His Mother's Sermon" has already been mentioned. In
the first story in *St Jude's* there is what amounts to a reworking of
Hardy's "Darkling Thrush". Before his meeting with the elder, when
Carmichael is described as "a broken man" following his latest
sermon, we are told "there was not a sound except a thrush welcoming
spring with his cheerful note, and caring not that winter had settled
down upon a human soul" (Maclaren 1907: 8). The story closes with
the same image, only Carmichael can now feel the spiritual spring that
the speaker in Hardy's poem cannot:

When the minister passed the garden gate half an hour afterwards there was no man to
be seen, but the birds on every branch were in full song, and he marked that the
hawthorn had begun to bloom. (Maclaren 1907: 17)

The image of the bird is used in several other stories and the
technique of conveying human emotions through natural images is
employed again and again in a manner that becomes wearisome when
the stories are read one after another. But it is worth taking one further
example to illustrate this important aspect of Maclaren's style. In "A
Fight with Death", Saunders, Drumsheugh's grieve, lies ill having
caught a fever after "an adventurous visit to Glasgow" (Maclaren
1894: 267). As his employee battles with death, Drumsheugh seeks
consolation in the landscape. As he wanders through the fields at
dawn, the night is presented as insubstantial; the "shadowy forms" of

the sleeping cattle carrying a "suggestion of death" (Maclaren 1894: 275). There is a conspicuous appeal to the senses. The smell of ripe corn gives promise of the harvest soon to come but the sound of an owl evokes in Drumsheugh a childhood fear. Maclaren then makes a direct appeal to the reader's emotional identification with his character. Drumsheugh is a lonely man with no-one to love and "an indescribable sadness over his heart". The scene is made all the more effective for having Drumsheugh distanced from his house, "all dark and cold". As the day breaks, however, the tone shifts. The reddening of the sky that foretells the rising of the sun and the trembling of the air "as if one had whispered" are both presented as apocalyptic images. Once again the image of the bird is transformed, from the hooting owl that frightened Drumsheugh in his youth to the blackbird bursting into song at the break of day. Once again it is a God revealed in his own Creation that brings spirit to Drumsheugh's resolve.

V

Maclaren's idealism permeates all areas of his fiction and stretches realism to its furthest limits. The underlying emphasis on a selfless group of individuals working not for themselves but for each other without expectation of earthly reward, presents a picture that approaches utopia. But Maclaren's world is not utopia because it is demonstrably somewhere. It is easy to see why contemporary readers could respond to the sketches as representative of Scottish life because, however much Maclaren employs idyllic and pastoral modes, the close regional setting encourages a realist response on some level. Assessment of the sociological accuracy of Maclaren's picture, such as that undertaken by Knowles, inevitably reveals distortion and the question of whether Maclaren distorted reality has always been an issue for debate. In the sketch entitled "An Evangelist" mentioned above, Maclaren defended the realism of his stories. Speaking through his own voice and not that of a constructed narrator, he responds to criticism of his work:

I had been reading that morning an interesting and very caustic review, in which it was pointed out that no people had ever lived or ever would live so good as the inhabitants of Drumtochty: that I had confused together the (mythical) garden of Eden with a Scots village; that the places were really very different in morals and general environment; that it was a pity that the author did not know the limits of true art; that what was wanted was reality, not sentimental twaddle. (Maclaren 1898: 306)

Maclaren goes on to explain that the critic considered "A Servant Lass" – the story of a London doctor who had taken a servant girl into his house that she might die there in peace – was an extravagant unreality that "proved my unfitness to be an artist in life":

Up to this point I had been much humbled, and had been trying to profit by every word of wisdom; but now I laid down the paper and had a few moments of sinless enjoyment, for this incident had been lifted bodily out of life, with only some changes in names, and was the only fact in the book. A poor puling idealist! – yet even in my most foolish flights I had kept some hold on life.

Maclaren recognises his idealism but defends the actual basis of his story. Clearly he was writing from experience, but writing involved employment of artistic forms. As an unsigned article in the *Bookman* suggested, with his childhood experiences of farming communities Maclaren would have been well aware of the darker side of life:

He could tell of these things as plainly and remorselessly as any man. But he has chosen to be silent. Because he has confined himself to one aspect, it does not follow that this aspect is untrue. When we admit the lifelikeness of David Teniers the Younger's studies of vulgar Dutch life, we are surely not driven to conclude that the painter who omits such scenes is false to his art or to life. (April 1901)

As with Barrie, we have the comparison with Dutch painting, and in an interview Maclaren hints that he might easily have written a novel like *The House with the Green Shutters*: "I should like to write a story dealing with the darker side of Scottish life – and there is a darker side that I have not yet touched" (Noble 1895: 519). Given the associations that have been built up around Maclaren's fiction this is a surprising remark. It suggests, however, that the decision to write idylls was a choice of literary genre as much as moral conscience.

It is too easy to dismiss Maclaren's village as having nothing to do with the real Scotland. As I have shown, in its presentation of education, religion and farm life Maclaren draws on realities, even if he uses those realities for sentimental effects. Proper investigation of the social and religious context of Maclaren's writings does reveal an awareness of important changes in Scottish society. In a recent analysis, Richard Cook argues that Maclaren constructs Drumtochty as a "Highland community" and "an ideal national space [...] radically distinct from the lowland regions of Scotland and the southern lands of England" (Cook 1999: 1056). But Drumtochty lies on the Lowland/Highland divide and in stories such as "The Transformation of Lachlan Campbell" Maclaren engages with the collision between Highland and Lowland religious and cultural values.

Ian Carter makes an important observation when he notes that Barrie's and Maclaren's books are exactly contemporary with the growth in mass tourism and the "unprecedented production of guide books" in the last two decades of the century. Carter argues that Maclaren's novels draw on the "fervent Balmoralism" behind that mass tourism and reminds us that Drumtochty is in fact the name of a glen in Kincardineshire, an important tourist centre in the period (Carter 1976: 4). In this context the construction of Drumtochty as a fictional place is important, and as I discussed in relation to Barrie, the mode of idyllism promotes the construction of a place locked in time. Maclaren's presentation of Drumtochty can be seen as escapist, but it is inkeeping with the author's wider concerns.

As Knowles has discussed, the role of the narrator is central to the presentation of Drumtochty as an outside place. The narrator in *Beside the Bonnie Brier Bush* is inconsistent in characterisation. Like Barrie's narrator, he appears to adopt a middle ground between the reader and the community he is describing. He speaks in English throughout – except in one instance which is surely a slip of proof-reading – but it is not clear whether he is an insider or outsider. At one point he refers to his "London friends" and of Drumtochty as "my adopted home" (Maclaren 1894: 134). Elsewhere, however, he positions himself as a member of the community and regularly uses "we" and "our" when outlining the behaviour and characteristics of the glen. He also frequently uses the first-person pronoun and on occasions the comments are set in the present, e.g. "From the manse pew I watch keenly" (Maclaren 1894: 59). The voice is not intended as autobiographical because the narrator is a layman. Indeed, he facilitates Maclaren's vision by adopting a position on matters of theology that purports to be objective and disinterested but is in fact Maclaren's own. When he listens to one sermon he speaks for his author when he declares: "I was convinced, who am outside dogmas and churches, that Christ was present" (Maclaren 1894: 97).

Drumtochty is deliberately set out as a secluded place, on the borders of the Lowlands, and locked in the past: "The railway did not think it worth while to come to Drumtochty, and we were cut off from the lowlands by miles of forest, so our manners retained the fashion of the former age" (Maclaren 1894: 133). Ian Campbell rightly points to the "double vision" here. The Kailyard village ignores the changes wrought on the outside world by the coming of the railways but the reader is assumed to know of them. In another story Maclaren uses the issue of language to make the same point: "While Drumtochty was in its natural state, and the influence of Southern culture had scarcely begun to play on its simplicity, we had other forms of speech" (Maclaren 1895: 233). Drumtochty is presented as a self-sufficient world where outside influences are treated with suspicion; the residents always get the better of interfering outsiders who try and impose their way of life on the glen. The great world beyond is generally painted as a destructive environment. Those who leave the community for reasons of self-improvement carry with them "as a working capital, sound education, unflagging industry, absolute integrity, and an undying attachment to Drumtochty" (Maclaren 1894: 34); for some unfortunate characters, exposure to "foreign climates" brings illness or early death.

Throughout his work, Maclaren contrasts the country to the city, where anonymity and rootlessness is all:

a townsman may be born in one city and educated in a second, and married in a third, and work in a fourth. His houses are but inns, which he uses and forgets; he has no roots, and is a vagrant on the face of the earth. But the countryman is born and bred, and marries and toils and dies on one farm, and the scene he looks at in his old age is the same he saw in his boyhood. His roots are stuck deep in the soil, and if you tear them up, his heart withers and dies. (Maclaren 1895: 55)

Two stories dramatise the relationship between country and city. In "A Servant Lass", Lily Robertson goes to London to work as a maid, with a bag of dried rose-leaves to remind her of the scents of the glen. She soon falls victim to the "dangers that beset a young girl's path in the great Babylon" (Maclaren 1895: 74). Her fellow workgirls squeeze her wages out of her and no-one in her house can tell her the way to the Kirk until she finds a Perthshire man, who turns out to be "conneckit wi' Drumtochty" (Maclaren 1895: 76). Before long, report comes that "Lily's deein', and it's London 'at hes killed her" (Maclaren 1895: 79). Jamie Soutar rushes south where he finds that Lily's upper-class employers have washed their hands of her. Fortunately, she has been taken in by a kindly Scottish doctor, who, in a typically egalitarian impulse, treats her "as if a' wes a leddy, an' his ain bluid" (Maclaren 1895: 83). The story concludes, inevitably, with a death-bed scene and Jamie arranging for Lily to be brought home in her coffin, her dying wish being "tae lie in Drumtochty kirkyaird wi' ma mither an' grannie" (Maclaren 1895: 87).

Another variation on this theme is the story of Flora Campbell. We are never told why Flora deserts her home, moves to London and becomes, in her own words, not worthy to cross her father's door. Flora's sin is obviously unmentionable and her father scores out her name from the family Bible, though only with "wavering strokes" and with the "ink run as if it had been mingled with tears." (Maclaren 1894: 136). In London Flora feels the absence of community:

it iss weary to be in London and no one to speak a kind word to you, and I will be looking at the crowd that is always passing, and I will not see one kent face, and when I looked in at the lighted windows the people were all sitting round the table, but there wass no place for me. Millions and millions of people, and not one to say "Flora" and not one sore heart if I died that night. (Maclaren 1894: 151–2)

The effects of life in the city are explored most fully in *St Jude's*. In this collection, Carmichael's experiences of a Glasgow parish are contrasted to the demands of ministering to the glen. In the city Carmichael has to struggle to bring light out of darkness:

When he rose to preach, with the heavy pall of the city's smoke and the city fog encompassing the church, and the glare of the evil-smelling gas lighting up its Gothic recesses, his heart sank and for the moment he lost courage. Was it for this dreary gloom and packed mass of strange people he had left the sunlight of the glen and the warm atmosphere of true hearts? […] for an instant, as he faced his new environment and before he gave out his text, he wished that by some touch of that fairy want which we are ever desiring to set our mistakes right, or to give us our impossible desires, he could be spirited away from the city which as a countryman he always hated, back to the glen which he would ever carry in his heart. (Maclaren 1907: 23)

The city does not prove to be "evil", however. Carmichael quickly learns that "there was an opportunity of spiritual power in this city pulpit which the green wilderness could not give" (Maclaren 1907: 24). Maclaren's intention in these stories is not, however, to explore the social conditions of these city dwellers. In another story, "The Power of the Child", Carmichael develops a plan to send the poor children of the parish on an annual holiday into the country.

"[…] It is the contrast between the slum of the city and the joy of the country which, I confess, has touched my heart, for I am a countryman; I love its hills and glens, and fields and flowers, and running burns and hedgerows, with the honeysuckle and the roses in the middle of the hawthorn. With that vision before my eyes, and the sweet smell of the country in my nostrils, I go into a court of the city and I see a child living, or rather dying, in a house of a single room, without air and sun, and playing in a dirty court instead of on the grass, and beside a gutter instead of a stream of clean water." (Maclaren 1907: 176)

That Maclaren was aware of the problems of the city is evident; that he should, in a passage like this, turn his back on them in favour of exploiting a nostalgic reverence for the country can unquestionably be seen as an abnegation of responsibility. Yet there is considerable evidence that Maclaren did anything but abnegate his responsibilities to the poor in Glasgow and Liverpool in his actual ministerial life. A socially and ideologically derived criticism can judge him unfavourably for adopting a particular focus in his stories but Maclaren would not have thought it unacceptable to devote his energies as a minister rather than as a writer to addressing the conditions of the poor. In "The Power of the Child" Maclaren nevertheless uses his sentimental strategy to make a particular social comment. The focus of the story is not the children but a rich member of the congregation whose meanness is lifted by the minister's plans. John Murchieson – "the model and standard of parsimony" (Maclaren

1907: 164) – embodies a materialism that comes in the way of sentiment:

an old man who had come to seventy years of age and never had known the sweetness of love, who was out of touch with children and a stranger to kindness, to whom life was nothing else than a weary grind and purposeless money-making. (Maclaren 1907: 170)

The barrier of materialism is broken down by Carmichael's description of the countryside, quoted above. Murchieson is so moved that he not only finances the children's holidays but increases the salaries of his office staff and gives a thousand pounds to the building of a children's infirmary. The story concludes with Carmichael's words: "This is the real Murchison, only we didn't know him before, and he didn't know himself" (Maclaren 1907: 186). Maclaren's aesthetic of emotion has a social function, because the moral of the story is that worldly values of materialism can obscure the universal human heart that, to Maclaren, embodies Godliness. By allowing the heart to rule the purse men like Murchison can act to relieve poverty, social inequity and the consequences of a modern, materially-driven business environment of the city.

The regenerative virtues of the country feature in "Oor Lang Hame", the final story of *The Days of Auld Langsyne*, one of his more successful idylls and, in spite of Maclaren's many subsequent stories, something of a closing statement on Drumtochty. The story operates on a number of levels and shows clearly how Maclaren achieves his sentimental effects. It is another variation on the theme of the prodigal son and some reviewers wondered if the story had been suggested by the final chapter of *A Window in Thrums*. The plots are similar but the treatment is different. In several earlier stories, we learn that Chairlie Grant had left Drumtochty for "Americky" and neglected his family. On his return he is introduced as speaking in a "mixed accent" but quickly slips back into Drumtochty dialect when his emotions are stirred. Leaving the railway station behind Chairlie takes the road to Drumtochty which Maclaren draws characteristically in terms of the impact of nature on the senses:

The road to Drumtochty, after it had thrown off Kildrummie, climbed a hill, and passed through an open country till it plunged into the pine-woods. The wind was fresh, blowing down from the Grampians, with a suggestion of frost, and the ground was firm underfoot. The pungent scent of ripe turnips was in the air, mingled, as one passed a stackyard, with the smell of the newly gathered grain, whose scattered remains clung to the hedges. (Maclaren 1895: 341)

The story follows a Wordsworthian pattern as the exile passes a vagabond who has been turned out of a house, gives him some money and then enters into the pastoral setting of the pines:

His pace slackened as he entered the pines, and the kindly shelter and the sweet fragrance seemed to give him peace. In the centre of the wood there was an open space, with a pool and a clump of gorse. He sat down and rested his head on his hands. (Maclaren 1895: 342)

It is in this setting that Chairlie reads over two letters by James Soutar which tell of the deaths of his grandmother and sister. The letters become an objective correlative for the emotions of loss, grief and regret – they "were almost worn away with handling". For once the sentiment does not become indiscriminate; the letters, and the letters alone, are what focus the weight of the emotion.

On another level, Chairlie's reintegration into the community is projected in higher terms as a reintegration into the community that is moving towards "oor lang hame", a colloquial expression for Heaven:

There is a certain point where the road from Kildrummie disentangles itself from the wood, and begins the descent to Tochty Bridge. Drumtochty exiles used to stand there for a space and rest their eyes on the Glen which they could now see [...] Two Drumtochty students returning in the spring with their honours might talk of learned studies and resume their debates coming through the wood, but as the trees thinned conversation languished, and then the lads would go over the stile. No man said aught unto his neighbour as they drank in the Glen, but when they turned and went down the hill a change had come over them. (Maclaren 1895: 347)

The Eucharistic image of drinking in the Glen captures the integrated vision of the real and ideal homes of Drumtochty and Heaven. The story is like a miniature *Silas Marner*, charting a movement from withdrawal and individual seclusion to integration and sociability. Anxious to avoid meeting anyone on his return, Chairlie first visits his grandmother's ruined cottage – perhaps this time an explicit echo of Wordsworth – and then the graves of his relatives. Uncomforted by private prayer, "he was minded to creep away softly and leave Drumtochty for ever – his heart full of a vain regret – when he found there was another mourner in the kirkyard" (Maclaren 1895: 355). Drawn by the feelings of communal sentiment, Chairlie speaks to his fellow mourner – Drumsheugh – and allows himself to be reintegrated into the community as he accompanies the farmer back to his house.

In George Douglas Brown's *The House with the Green Shutters* the prodigal is not welcomed back into the fold. The only community and family to which young John Gourlay can return are ones filled with spiteful gossip and murderous hate. It is precisely this celebration of community values at a time when social and cultural pressures were undermining communities – particularly religious communities – that made Maclaren's fiction unrealistic to Brown and other Kailyard critics. In Maclaren's fiction there is no cancerous growth inside the home as there is, literally and metaphorically, in *The House with the Green Shutters*; and the industrious, selfless parishioners of Drumtochty contrast sharply with the lazy, self-interested "bodies" of Barbie. Maclaren's mode, however, is pastoral and apocalyptic. F.R. Hart has written that this idyll is "subtle in its finality" and he is right to point to the overwhelming atmosphere of death and decline:

So the book ends. Chairlie will not stay, and left alone, Drumsheugh will die soon. The field is empty, the harvest safe at last. One comes home only to die; this place, living in the image of Drumsheugh's warmth and kindliness and safety, is already dead. (Hart 1978: 123).

But the ending of the story suggests otherwise. Hart is right to stress the persistent strain of death in Maclaren's stories – "Each idyll goes back to pick up some earlier strand of life and carry on the harvest, but each strand reiterates and reaffirms the all-embracing fact of death" (Hart 1978: 123) – but that all-embracing death carries a weight of association. Like the title, the final words of the idyll focus on the promise of the kindly light of Heaven: "and then Chairlie Grant went in with Drumsheugh to the warmth and the kindly light, while the darkness fell upon the empty harvest field, from which the last sheaf had been safely garnered" (Maclaren 1895: 358). Drumtochty is not dead. Rather, it is projected as the life eternal.

Chapter Five

The Marketing of Kailyard and the Debate over Popular Culture

I

In the twentieth and twenty first centuries, Kailyard has become almost synonymous with popular culture. Whether it is used in discussions of Scottish literature, cinema, television, tourism, history or politics, the term invariably stands as a synonym for kitsch. Often associated with tartanry, Kailyard has come to be seen as an expression of the worst excesses of Scottish popular culture. This association owes much to the critical concerns about Kailyard that were developed in the twentieth century. These will be discussed in full in Chapter 6. In this chapter I want to show how the roots of this association lies in the critical reception of the fiction of Barrie, Crockett and Maclaren. Analysis of the way these works were published, marketed and reviewed helps explain the seemingly peculiar situation whereby these writers have become associated with subsequent forms of popular culture and yet remained central to the Scottish literary tradition.

The association of Kailyard with popular culture has resulted in a general assumption that the works of literature most closely associated with the term must also be understood as popular culture. Beth Dickson considers that "continuing confusions about the Kailyard in Scottish criticism" are caused by a failure to "distinguish effectively between popular and literary writing" (Dickson 1997: 329). Once we understand the significance of the Kailyard as "*popular*" literature, she argues, we can "cut the Gordian knot of the Kailyard and see it at last for what it is – an outright Scottish success" (Dickson 1997: 334). Cairns Craig offers a similar argument, stating that to compare Kailyard with "high art" is to make a "simple category mistake" (Craig 1996: 107), but categories were far from being simple at the time and the issue of exactly where the work of Barrie, Crockett and

Maclaren should be placed within contemporary debates over high and low culture has never been sufficiently or effectively discussed.

Viewed retrospectively it is easy to make judgements about what constitutes serious and merely popular literature in this era. Thomas Knowles argues that as best sellers the Kailyard texts "rank low on the literary hierarchy" (Knowles 1983: 16) and Richard Cook states "it was no secret that Kailyard fiction stood outside the walls of acclaimed literature" (Cook 1999: 1054). But this is to simplify the dynamics of the literary market in the 1890s and to misrepresent the different, and often complex, ways in which the works of Barrie, Crockett and Maclaren were placed in debates over high and low culture in the 1890s. As I have argued, in his early career Crockett was highly coveted by leading publishing firms, and even Maclaren received a certain amount of serious attention in high literary circles. Commentators have also failed to grasp the fact that Barrie was seen by his contemporaries as among the most important writers of the day. As noted in Chapter 1, Margaret Oliphant and other critics were keen to separate off Barrie's work from other books by Scottish writers such as Annie S. Swan and Robina F. Hardy. Furthermore, when *The Little Minister* appeared in 1891 it was seen by reviewers as one of the two great literary events of the year, the other being *Tess of the D'Urbervilles*. To William Wallace, *The Little Minister* was "far and away the first novel of the season" (12 December 1891). W.E. Henley in the *National Observer* was even more emphatic, judging *The Little Minister* as "a book of genius" and "the novel of the year; a year, be it remarked, that has witnessed the production of work by such men as George Meredith, Thomas Hardy and Rudyard Kipling" (31 October 1891).[1] Nor was it just critics who admired Barrie's work. George Meredith wrote to him on 3 December 1891 in praise of *The Little Minister* saying "I am comforted in seeing that work like yours is warmly greeted by press and public" (Meredith 1970: II: 1051); and seven years later Joseph Conrad listed Barrie with Kipling and

---

[1] The Meredith and Kipling novels were *One of Our* Conquerors and *The Light that Failed*. Cook notes the significance of Henley's review in partial qualification of his judgement of Kailyard as popular literature (Cook 1999:1070n5).

Meredith as among "the writers who deserve attention" on the current literary scene (Conrad 1986: I: 138).

The easy identification of Kailyard with popular culture has, however, resulted in a second, more far-reaching misunderstanding. It has obscured one of the main reasons why the fiction of Crockett and Maclaren became so notorious in the 1890s. A good deal of contemporary debate about their fiction was prompted precisely because it was *not* seen as popular culture. What has never been fully appreciated is that, because of the promotional strategies of the influential editor and reviewer William Robertson Nicoll, the Kailyard (insofar as it consists of Crockett and Maclaren) was a *critical* as well as a popular success. Because of this, the term and the fiction associated with it was incorporated into discussions of high art even though its content can be argued to have paved the way for those forms of popular culture that emerged in the twentieth century in the fiction of Buchan, Compton Mackenzie and others, and in strip cartoons, music hall and film.

II

Kailyard fiction appeared at a key moment in the emergence of a marked split between high and low culture. In discussing popular fiction of the period 1860-80, R.C. Terry notes that there was a certain catholicity of taste amongst readers of fiction and a refusal to categorise novels on the part of both the reading public and reviewers (Terry 1983). By the 1890s this catholicity was splintering and the question of what constituted serious literature as opposed to mere popular success became a topic of heated debate. The reasons for the emerging stratification of levels of culture are various and complex. Broadly speaking, however, they turn on two main issues: the expansion of the market for all forms of print culture and the perceived consequence of the spread of compulsory education. Improved technological, distribution and communication networks all contributed to the massive expansion of printing production in the second half of the century. The repeal of stamp duties paved the way for the emergence of the "new journalism", typified by the periodical and newspaper ventures of George Newnes, Alfred Harmsworth and W.T. Stead. *Tit Bits* (1881), the creation of Newnes, was the first "snippet" paper, filled with trivia designed to provide readers with a fund of anecdotal – and largely useless – information. As Joseph McAleer points out, it "was both praised as a unique path towards edifying the masses and derided as the beginning of the decline of English journalism" (McAleer 1992: 23). Significantly, it also contained short stories and serial fiction, and along with its competitors, notably *Pearson's Weekly*, expanded the serial market at the same time as fracturing it along hierarchical lines.

In conjunction with these developments, the various reforms in education from the 1870s onwards led to the emergence of what was perceived as a new reading public – what became known as the "quarter-educated". In George Gissing's *New Grub Street*, *Tit Bits* is parodied in the shape of Mr Whelpdale's overwhelmingly successful *Chit-Chat* which is explicitly aimed at the "quarter-educated". Writers like Gissing responded negatively to the new developments in journalism and literature, observing a process of dumbing-down and the emergence of a market that created reputations on the strength of clever business acumen rather than artistic value. Ian Maclaren himself wrote: "reputation was never so quickly made, never so quickly dissipated in our hurried day" (Watson 1897: 81).

The important consequence of these developments was that books, periodicals and newspapers became, to a greater extent than before, important indicators of social or cultural status. Contributing to *Tit Bits* meant being associated with the "quarter-educated" which carried with it the accusation of serving the market and compromising art. But it is important to stress that in the 1890s the effects of the changes in publishing and reading practices were in the process of being formed. Joseph McAleer sees these trends contributing to a more explicit demarcation between high and low – or popular – culture in the period after 1914 (McAleer 1992: ch. 1). Whilst many novelists adopted an attitude of superiority towards the new "lowbrow" newspapers and journals, for most it remained only an attitude. As Peter Keating remarks:

viewed retrospectively, and conscious of the cultural fragmentation to come, the associations and conjunctions between novelists and periodicals at this time can appear startling. Conrad, Woolf and Joyce all submitted work to, and had it turned down by, *Tit Bits*. (Keating 1989: 38)

In the 1890s, journalism acquired a pejorative edge that it had never held in the time of Dickens. Yet an apprenticeship in journalism was not unusual for authors who had aspirations to write work of more lasting significance. Indeed, it was one of the few ways in which an author could support him or herself financially whilst writing. Barrie's journalist background has often been viewed as a fault, and as having a deleterious effect on his writing; Harry M. Geduld, for example, argues that Barrie's "shortcomings" are "directly traceable to his journalistic concessions to the tastes of the reading public" (Geduld 1971: 15). But Barrie's mastery of the practice of journalism, as espoused in his novel *When a Man's Single* (1888), was what opened the door to literature for H.G. Wells, and both Wells and Arnold Bennett became famous for their ability to exploit the opportunities of journalism at the same time as writing serious novels (Dickson 1971: 53). The idea that there was an unbridgeable chasm between journalism and literature was very much an invention of writers of the twentieth century – especially modernist writers. Richard Cook's argument that the Kailyard authors "were journalists and Kirk ministers rather than trained artists" falls into this trap and is another example of how generalisations about the Kailyard are built on characteristics pertaining to Maclaren alone.

It is within the context of these shifting attitudes to literature and journalism that we must understand the contribution to literature of William Robertson Nicoll, a man whom Donald Carswell has considered along with Harmsworth and Stead as one of the three great journalists of the closing nineteenth century (Carswell 1927: 227). Nicoll has received considerably less critical attention than these two other great luminaries, and his contribution in shaping the literary culture of the late-nineteenth and early-twentieth centuries has been underestimated, indeed barely documented. As George Blake writes:

The historian of modern journalism might decide that Sir George Newnes with his *Tit-Bits* was the true originator of the new technique. Others might say that the real start was made by a queer, immensely able Scotsman called William Robertson Nicoll. (Blake 1951: 22)

In terms of Scottish literature, the reason for the neglect of Nicoll's influence is mainly because of his association with Kailyard; it can also be attributed, however, to a general failure on the part of critics and commentators to pay due notice to the contribution of Scots to British culture.

Born in 1851, Nicoll graduated from Aberdeen University at the age of eighteen and was already an experienced and successful journalist by the time he finished his course at the Free Church Divinity Hall in 1874. During the whole of his theological course he was on the regular staff of the *Aberdeen Journal* and was also contributing to a range of other Scottish and English papers, including the *Scotsman*, *Chambers' Journal* and the *People's Friend* (Darlow 1925: 26). The latter published a critical estimate of Dickens by Nicoll in 1870 (Stoddart 1903: 35). In 1877 he was inducted as Minister of the Free Church at Kelso in the Scottish borders but his journalistic and literary interests remained strong. Two years later he became literary advisor to the Edinburgh publishing firm Macniven & Wallace where he edited a series of religious volumes, entitled *Household Library of Exposition*, and also wrote a book on Tennyson published under a pseudonym (Darlow 1925: 44). Associations with other firms followed, including Swan Sonnenschein, before in 1884 he met Thomas Stoughton of Hodder & Stoughton and agreed to become editor of the theological paper *The Expositor*. This appointment was quickly followed by an event that signalled the inception of Nicoll's lifelong devotion to literature. The effects of typhoid left him with a serious lung illness that forced him to resign his ministerial position and move south to Dawlish in Devonshire. Forbidden to preach, Nicoll devoted all his energy to literature and publishing, becoming Editor and Literary Advisor to Hodder & Stoughton in 1885, a position in which he remained until his death in 1923.

One of the first of many achievements in Nicoll's role with Hodder was to set up and edit a new penny newspaper, the *British Weekly*, which first appeared in November 1886 and soon acquired a six-figure circulation, prompting Clement Shorter to dub Nicoll as "the most successful Christian in history" (Cited in Falk 1937: 258). Subtitled "A Journal of Christian and Social Progress", the venture had a clear religious impulse but was also driven by an overt political aim. Nicoll's objective was "to reunite the Liberal Party which was split on the question of Home Rule for Ireland, and to proclaim it as the party of social progress, thereby uniting every variety of nonconformist opinion" (Attenborough 1975: 32). Apart from aiming to unite the disparate nonconformist community, the paper was an attempt to reignite the importance of religion within British national life. As Nicoll himself said:

I had always thought that religious papers did not give enough direct religious instruction, and that the leading articles should be mainly devoted to this, not to ecclesiastical matters or politics or literature chiefly, but to religion. (Cited in Darlow 1925: 81–2)

Religion and politics were the main focus of the paper but they were not the exclusive interests. From the outset, there was a broader embrace of literature and culture. Nicoll probably wrote well over half of the contents of every issue and advanced his views on contemporary literature in two review columns signed with the pseudonyms "Claudius Clear" and "A Man of Kent". Nicoll told Henry Drummond: "We mean to try and furnish a paper for Christian radicals which will be equal in literary merit to the best published" (Cited in Darlow 1925: 73). Shortly before the first number appeared he informed Macniven of his aims in setting up the paper:

I never expected to reach the masses, as the *Christian Herald* does. But I hoped to reach the vast number of nonconformists in Scotland and England who take no Christian paper and despise the Nonconformist religious papers for their want of culture. I hope especially to get the ministers.

Part of Nicoll's intention, therefore, was to bring culture to the nonconformists. As Donald Carswell notes, in this respect the project is rooted in the particular historical circumstances of the end of the century:

Chapel folk were beginning to look about and take an interest in things and even ideas. They were tenacious of their old beliefs and prejudices, yet they wanted to be

told, decently and in a way they could understand, something of the general
intellectual life of the time. (Carswell 1927: 228)

This is an important point to note because it is often wrongly assumed
that the Kailyard stories first circulated in a context where religious
writing was the principal, or only, focus. In fact, the *British Weekly* set
out to cover general intellectual life and because Nicoll had a lifelong
interest in books and literature it was not surprising that literature and
literary criticism became an essential ingredient of the paper. An
attraction of the first numbers was a series of New Literary Anecdotes,
"which included unpublished matter relating to the Brontes, George
Eliot and other authors" (Stoddart 1903: 72). Short stories and serials
began to appear and a successful column entitled "Books that Have
Interested Me" attracted such illustrious contributors as Robert Louis
Stevenson and Walter Besant.

       Although it is widely recognised that the *British Weekly* provided
an important forum for the production of Kailyard fiction – the work
of Barrie, Crockett and Maclaren is often referred to as the British
Weekly School – it is only the career of Maclaren that is absolutely
tied to the paper. As I showed in Chapter 3, Crockett's early sketches
were published in *The Christian Leader*, and it was not Nicoll but
Edward Garnett of T. Fisher Unwin who provided advice and support
for Crockett in his early career. Also, whilst several of his later novels
were published by Hodder & Stoughton, the range of publishing firms
with which Crockett became involved is an important characteristic of
his career as a professional author. Nicoll's influence on his career
was thus critical rather than editorial. So far as Barrie is concerned,
only a very small amount of his work was ever published in the
British Weekly. His novel of literary life *When a Man's Single* (which
is not remotely religious in subject matter) was first serialised in the
British Weekly (1887–88) and earlier versions of about one third of the
chapters in *A Window in Thrums* (1889) appeared between its covers.
William Donaldson, although accurately capturing the purpose of
Nicoll's venture, is wrong to lump Barrie together with its ideological
framework:

The pietistic fiction of Barrie and Maclaren was intended as a contribution to the
dilemma which called the *British Weekly* into existence, the acute crisis in English

liberal nonconformism during the last two decades of the nineteenth century. (Donaldson 1986: 147)

Nicoll was certainly an important influence on Barrie's career and was responsible for encouraging the author to turn his Auld Licht articles into a book, but Barrie operated apart from and beyond the *British Weekly* in his early career, writing on a much wider range of subjects in a variety of other newspapers and magazines.[2] Significantly, his longer novels were all published by the firm of Cassell.

Auld Licht Idylls and *A Window in Thrums* are nevertheless important volumes in the history of the publishing firm of Hodder & Stoughton. Ian Carter is wrong to label the firm as "London's foremost pulp fiction publishers" (Carter 1976: 2), though to an extent that is what they became after the First World War. At the time when Nicoll was engaged as editor and literary advisor they were predominantly publishers of religious books. Nicoll had a determination to move the firm forward and the moderate commercial success of Barrie's early books enabled him to widen the subject-base. It was not until the mid-1890s, however, with the publication of Ian Maclaren, that fiction became an essential part of the firm's strategy. Nicoll's influence on the Rev. John Watson was more absolute than it was on Barrie, as he was almost singularly responsible for encouraging, publishing and marketing his work. His publication and promotion of Maclaren's work was designed not simply to advance a particular religious position but to help shape Nicoll's vision of literary culture at the end of the nineteenth century.

III

There is some dispute over who exactly who discovered "Ian Maclaren". In his account of the publishing firm of Hodder & Stoughton, John Attenborough attests that "the author was discovered

---

[2] For an account of Barrie's early periodical writing, and the compilation of the Kailyard texts, see Nash 1998. Herbert Garland's bibliography of Barrie, though incomplete and sometimes inaccurate, reveals the sheer range of Barrie's early periodical publications (Garland 1928).

by Matthew Hodder on one of his journeys" (Attenborough 1975: 34–5) but in his biography of the author Nicoll himself claimed the credit. He was certainly responsible for encouraging Maclaren to write fiction. At the time when he was first approached by Nicoll, Watson had been ministering in Liverpool for ten years. Nicoll arranged for him to contribute a series of articles to *The Expositor* – later republished in the volume *The Mind of the Master* (1896) – but when he met Watson for the first time in London in July 1893 Nicoll did not at first take to Watson; he told Marcus Dods "he was too cynical for me" (Darlow 1925: 114). Nevertheless, in his own words he "quickly perceived that Watson could do work outside the *Expositor*" (Stoddart 1903: 95) and was entertained by Watson's tales of Scottish life drawn from the minister's experiences in Logiealmond:

> I was so much struck by the racy stories and character-sketches with which Watson regaled us, that I suggested he should make some articles out of them. The idea had never struck him, and was at first unwelcome. But I kept on persuading him. I had no success till I was accompanying him to the station, when I pressed the matter on him. Just before he said good-bye he promised to try, and in a few days the first sketch arrived. It was clever but disappointing. [...] I returned this to Watson stating objections. He sent a second sketch, also more or less unsatisfactory. Then he sent the first four chapters of what is now known as *The Bonnie Brier Bush* complete, and I knew on reading them that his popularity was assured. (Nicoll 1908: 165–6)

These circumstances of composition make clear that Maclaren did not set out to be a writer of fiction. Indeed, he was to remain a very reluctant writer throughout his career. In an interview recorded in the *Glasgow Evening Times*, Maclaren stated that he didn't enjoy writing and that he was "in cordial agreement with every unfavourable review" (28 September 1896). As Nicoll judged: "the fact is that he looked upon literature as a mere diversion from the actual work of his life, and did not consent either to stand or fall by it" (Nicoll 1908: 182).

Maclaren's first published sketch, "How we carried the News to Whinnie Knowe", appeared on 2 November 1893. It formed the second part of "Domsie", the first story in *Beside the Bonnie Brier Bush*. The first part was not published until two weeks later. Almost immediately, letters appeared in the correspondence columns of the paper from readers who believed that the author was Barrie. "'Beside the Bonnie Brier Bush' is perfection", wrote one correspondent, "but it is so manifestly Barrie's that he cannot hide himself under his change of pseudonym [...]. Not even in 'A Window in Thrums' is there pathos to surpass it" (23 November 1893). Another correspondent mooted that the signature of Ian Maclaren stood for Barrie's name: "Ian the Gaelic for John, Maclaren for which the M stands in the usual signature" (7 December 1893). No refutation of the claims was published; perhaps Nicoll was eager to milk the extra publicity arising from the confusion.

Maclaren made weekly contributions to the *British Weekly* for a period of two months; thereafter his sketches appeared once every two or three weeks until his visit to America in 1896 made his contributions more sporadic. His sketches were advertised at the top of the front page of the newspaper and as his name became more established the sketches became longer and were placed nearer to the front of the paper. From July 1895 he published articles on other subjects as well. Some of these were on social and political issues but most were on religious topics, the majority of which were collected in the volume *The Upper Room* (1896).

Unlike Barrie, Maclaren did not revise his newspaper articles for volume publication, and his first two collections were both straightforward reprints of articles published in the *British Weekly*. Both volumes were critically acclaimed, receiving positive notices in the leading reviews, such as the *Academy*, which thought *Beside the Bonnie Brier Bush* "artistically perfect", the *Athenaeum* and the *Spectator*. Like Crockett, Maclaren's work appeared in both popular magazines and highbrow periodicals. His status was not exclusively that of a popular author. One of Gissing's diary entries shows how even the most serious literary artists turned to Maclaren: "Day of mist and rain. Read Tolstoi's 'Master and Man', and Ian Maclaren's 'Beside the Bonnie Brier Bush' – Evening, some Ovid" (Coustillas 1978: 395). It is easy to forget that readers, then as now, could be catholic in their tastes, but the sandwiching of Maclaren between Tolstoi and Ovid gives an indication of the impact of his work in high literary circles.

Nor was Maclaren's work restricted to religious journals and newspapers. In 1895, the year after the publication of *Beside the*

Bonnie Brier Bush, he had work published in a range of significant magazines. *Harper's Monthly Magazine* ran the stories about Jamie Soutar that were included in *The Days of Auld Langsyne* and other sketches and essays appeared in *McClure's Magazine*, the *New York Bookman*, the *Success*, *Living Age* and *Blackwood's*. Most of these were general magazines and the spread of different publications was standard practice for authorship in this period. His presence in *Blackwood's* indicates the high literary standing he acquired as a result of the success of his early books. When asked to contribute a short story, he told William Blackwood: "to be thought worthy of being a contributor is a great thing".[3] At the time he was approached by Blackwood he was beginning to plan *Kate Carnegie*, his only novel set in Drumtochty, and his comments on that work give an impression of his sense of himself as an author. He informed Blackwood: "it may turn out that I am not able to achieve a novel and am intended to be a short story teller – but I'll minimise that vista by making the serial a series of sketches with connection." His description sums up *Kate Carnegie* precisely, and with the publication of this work Maclaren's reputation began to fall.

   Kate Carnegie and those Ministers had been commissioned by Nicoll to appear in the editor's new periodical venture, the *Woman at Home*, one of the earliest and most successful of the new wave of women's magazines. The *Woman at Home* became known as "Annie Swan's Magazine". Nicoll's shrewd sense of the selling power of an author's name encouraged Swan to put hers to the magazine; she did not edit the *Woman at Home* but was chief contributor and managed the Problem column, "Over the Teacups." The first number appeared in 1893 and the first edition of 100,000 copies sold out immediately. Nicoll conceived of the *Woman at Home* as a *Strand Magazine* for women and, however much its title and the bulk of its content was directed towards the domestic lives of women, it was far from being a special-interest magazine. Like the *British Weekly*, it had a commitment to fiction and literature and amongst the material in the first number was a short story by the New Woman novelist, Sarah Grand. Maclaren became a regular contributor; a total of six stories

---

[3] Unpublished ALS, 14 August 1895. National Library of Scotland, MS. 4640.

and essays appeared in 1896 alone. In addition, several of Sabine Baring-Gould's *Dartmoor Idylls* were first published in the magazine, as they had been in the *British Weekly*; David Christie Murray wrote a series of detective stories and H.G. Wells also published a short story, "A Perfect Gentleman on Wheels", in 1897. Barrie's only contribution was "A London Love Story", the title indicative of how he had shifted his attention away from regional stories by this time.

The nature of the magazine perhaps explains why Maclaren used the name of his heroine as the title for his serial, which is more about *"those ministers"* than Kate Carnegie. The reviewer for the *Critic* summed up the book as "a menagerie of parsons rather than a novel [...] the love-story is hardly more than an incident" (16 August 1896). The story was also serialised simultaneously in two American magazines, the New York *Bookman* and *Outlook*, and was serialised throughout Australia by a newspaper syndicate. The critical response, however, was muted. The *Critic* wrote that the man who was once "the happy owner of a name which has been one of the literary huzzas of the moment" had been overcome. The reviewer found "little to compare Dr Watson and Mr Barrie", judging "one is superior to success, and the other has been defeated by it. [...] Ian Maclaren has been conquered – that is all" (30 January 1897). As a writer of short stories, Maclaren had been seen as an artist of promise; *Kate Carnegie* revealed him unable to fulfil that promise in the full-length novel.

After *The Days of Auld Langsyne* none of Maclaren's work received the critical attention that had been given to his early volumes. Already the appearance of the second Drumtochty book led some reviewers to see Maclaren's writing as formulaic. William Wallace in the *Academy* commented on *The Days of Auld Langsyne*: "perhaps the bloom is no longer on the Kailyard" and announced that "Ian Maclaren has now exhausted Drumtochty" (18 January 1896). The response to *Kate Carnegie* was more uniformly of this nature. The anonymous *Academy* reviewer admitted to finding the Scottish parochial novel wearisome: "We know at the outset what to expect. We shall have a blend of canniness and theology, tempered by pathos, in a setting of Scotch whisky and mist" (21 November 1896). Reviews of *Afterwards*, the next full-length volume, were more sparse and predominantly negative. The reviewer for the *Critic* took issue with Maclaren's overuse of his sentimental technique:

> there can be no doubt that all this swelling of the heart, even when forcibly produced, is a good and healthful emotion. It is well to be moved by self-sacrifice, touched by generosity, stirred to "pity and terror", even though the sensations are caused by nothing more real than the words on a printed page. But eternal human nature rises up in rebellion at the high-handedness of Ian Maclaren's methods. (7 February 1899)

Once the immediate impact of his two early volumes had died away, Maclaren received fewer commissions from periodicals for stories and sketches. His non-fictional writings on religion increased, however, on the back of his successful promotion on the lecture circuit in America. In 1901 and 1903 he wrote two essays on religious topics for the *Cornhill*. In this context it is significant that *St Jude's* (1907), his final collection of fictional stories, was published not by Hodder & Stoughton but by The Religious Tract Society, a clear indication that the subject-matter, which had once been central to the trends of contemporary literature, was now fit only for a specialist audience. Maclaren's other works of fiction were barely noticed at all and are now hardly remembered. *Rabbi Saunderson* (1899), an extended story of a character introduced in *Kate Carnegie*; *His Majesty Baby and some Common Men* (1902), an eclectic collection of previously published essays and stories, ranging from an account of the Boer War to observations about farm life in Scotland; *Graham of Claverhouse* (1908), Maclaren's only genuine full-length novel, based on the Covenanters; and *Young Barbarians* (1901), a children's story, which was reprinted by Canongate in 1985.

III

Maclaren's reputation was based on the critical and commercial success of *Beside the Bonnie Brier Bush* and *The Days of Auld Langsyne*, both of which sold prodigiously. 60,000 copies of *Beside the Bonnie Brier Bush* were sold in the first year and in 1908 Nicoll reported that 256,000 copies had been sold in various UK editions and 484,000 in America, exclusive of pirated editions (Nicoll 1908: 68).

The widespread distribution of Maclaren's fiction owes much to the expansion of the book-buying public at the end of the century. The three-volume novel, which had the been bedrock of the fiction market for most of the century, all but disappeared in 1894 – the year *Beside the Bonnie Brier Bush* was published – when the two main subscription libraries, Mudie's and Smith's, revised the terms upon which they were willing to purchase volumes of fiction (Griest 1970). In the same month that Maclaren's volume was issued, Ward & Downey published William Westall's novel *As a Man Sows* in three volumes. Nicoll's expert sense of the shifting patterns of publishing ensured that Maclaren's books, by contrast, appeared in the six-shilling form from the outset and so had the opportunity of making an immediate sales impact. An additional factor in the success was the increasingly international market for books brought about by amendments in copyright law. Specifically, the harmonisation of US and UK copyright in 1891 ensured protection for British authors in America, and all three of Barrie, Crockett and Maclaren enjoyed enormous sales in America. Alice Hackett's research into best-seller lists records that *Beside the Bonnie Brier Bush* was the best-selling novel in America in 1895 (Hackett 1945: 11).

The 1890s was the era which witnessed the birth of the modern concept of the best-seller. Peter Keating records that the OED supplement attributes the earliest use of the term to a Kansas newspaper in 1889 (Keating 1989: 439). The best-seller lists were an innovation of American magazines but in Britain the *Bookman* – a literary magazine set up and edited by Robertson Nicoll – was recording data on the sales of novels from its inception in 1891. The New York *Bookman*, generally credited with popularising the term best-seller, did not commence until 1895, and in this respect the British publication laid the precedent. A recently published article in *Book History* has analysed the *Bookman* tables and produced data that enables us to analyse not only the sales of fiction in the 1890s but the geographical demand for different works (Bassett and Walter 2001). The data indicates that Crockett and Maclaren were among the best-selling novelists of the decade. The tables in the *Bookman* consisted of two types. "Sales of Books during the Month" was drawn from information submitted by bookshops across the British Isles and appeared in the first number of the journal in October 1891. From 1894 this was supplemented by a further table entitled "Monthly Report of the Wholesale Book Trade" (restricted to England until a complementary section was submitted from Scotland from 1898), which also included a summary of events in prose, compiled from information submitted by leading wholesalers.

In 1894 and 1895 *Beside the Bonnie Brier Bush* was topped in the lists only by George Du Maurier's *Trilby* – which John Sutherland considers "possibly the bestselling single novel of the century" (Sutherland 1988: 634). Maclaren's sales were certainly much greater than those of Barrie, whose early works, whilst moderately successful, cannot be considered best-sellers. Denis Mackail estimates that *A Window in Thrums* earned Barrie "eighty pounds in the first year", which, based on a royalty of one shilling per copy (the book retailed at six shillings), meant that about 1600 copies of the book were sold (Mackail 1941: 156). *The Little Minister* was much more successful; around 24,000 copies at various prices were sold in the first fourteen months but these figures hardly rank with Maclaren's (Mackail 1941: 185). What is noticeable, however, is that Barrie's works begin to sell more rapidly *after* the success of Maclaren and Crockett. *Sentimental Tommy* and *Margaret Ogilvy* generated much more immediate sales than *Auld Licht Idylls* and *A Window in Thrums* and featured prominently in the British and American best-seller charts. Nevertheless, it is wrong to conceive of Barrie as a best-selling author in the same mould as Crockett and Maclaren, just as it is wrong to look upon his critical reception as that of a popular author.

The statistical tables of best-sellers record that over the years 1891–1901 it was the works of Crockett that made the lists more often than any other author, including Marie Corelli, who is generally identified as the bestselling of all Victorian and Edwardian novelists. Maclaren takes fourth place in this survey with Kipling third and Barrie ninth. Crucially, the analysis also indicates no discernible difference between Scotland and England in the consumption of the works of Barrie, Crockett and Maclaren. Their books sold as well in Glasgow and Aberdeen as they did in London, Birmingham, Manchester and Dublin; indeed, the evidence suggests that in Scotland sales of their books were greater than those of Corelli, Hall Caine and other best-selling English novelists. For example, in April 1894, the first month of publication, *The Raiders* was recorded as the best-selling novel in Glasgow and was also listed fourth in Edinburgh and sixth in Dumfries. In England, however, it did not make the list in any town or city. In the second month it was the top-selling novel in Aberdeen and second in Edinburgh and Glasgow, bettered only by Sarah Grand's infamous *The Heavenly Twins*. It was also second in four towns in England but only sixth in London. The distinction between England and Scotland is even sharper for *The Lilac Sunbonnet*, which over September to October topped the lists in Edinburgh, Dumfries and Dundee but appeared only twice in the lists of English towns. The Dundee list for that month is especially revealing. The top four selling works of fiction were, in order, *The Lilac Sunbonnet, The Raiders, The Stickit Minister* and Annie S. Swan's *A Lost Ideal*.

Statistics for Maclaren follow a similar pattern, with Scottish readers turning to his books more quickly than English readers. In the first month of publication *Beside the Bonnie Brier Bush* topped the list in Edinburgh and was second in Glasgow. The only English lists in which it appeared were London and Newcastle (both fourth). By December 1895, two months after publication, it was the best-selling work in London as well as Glasgow and Aberdeen. The oft-repeated statement that the Kailyard novels were shunned by Scots and consumed predominantly by an English audience cannot be sustained in light of this evidence. William Donaldson's judgement that the Kailyard School "dominated the Anglo-American book-market in the closing decade of the century" and that *Beside the Bonnie Brier Bush* was "a major bestseller in England and America" makes the mistake of assuming that the English market was separate from the British market in this period (Donaldson 1986: 145–6). Crockett and Maclaren were read as widely in Scotland as they were in England and more widely than contemporary English novelists.

It is not just their considerable sales, however, that make Maclaren and Crockett typical among best-selling authors of the 1890s. Like Corelli, Du Maurier and Hall Caine, both writers acquired celebrity status, befitting the cult of personality that so characterised the age. As Peter Keating has summarised, this was an era when "what

anyone connected with books did or looked like became newsworthy"
(Keating 1989: 74). Gossip columns were an essential part of the new
magazines, such as *Tit Bits*, and the movements and habits of authors
became an integral part of the way that the profession of authorship
was presented in print culture. For example, in July 1895 readers of
the *Bookman* were informed: "After many months of hard work, Mr
George Meredith is now enjoying an entire rest. His friends think that
he looks much better and stronger than he has done for some years
past". One month later the same paper reported that "Mr J.M. Barrie
has taken up his permanent abode in London, in a house in Gloucester
Road, South Kensington". Inevitably, the obsession with authors'
movements led to the kind of misrepresentation and intrusion that we
associate with modern representations of the celebrity. A letter from
Barrie to Arthur Quiller-Couch makes clear the tenor of the times.
Writing from Kirriemuir on 25 December 1893 he remarks: "I see
from the papers that I am in Switzerland with Maarten Maartens.
Hope I'm enjoying myself" (Meynell 1942: 5).

The *British Weekly* was one of many papers to adopt this practice
of "literary gossip" – as its column was entitled – and Barrie's
movements were always hot news: "Mr Barrie is on the Suffolk coast,
working at his novel" (1 September 1892); "Mr Jerome K. Jerome and
Dr Conan Doyle have just returned from their Norwegian trip. Mr
Barrie did not accompany them" (8 September 1892); "Mr and Mrs
J.M. Barrie have returned to London and will proceed to Kirriemuir
shortly" (20 September 1894). Whereas the news of Barrie always
showed him escaping from the public eye, the reports of Ian Maclaren
indicate how he was brought irresistibly before it. Whether it be his
opening a bazaar in Barrie's home town of Kirriemuir; his lecturing
on 'Certain Traits in the Scottish Character' at Grindelwald; his
speaking at Badenoch and Laggan, the YMCA in Stirling, or in any
number of places and situations, the public were told about it. The
same was true of Crockett. As David Christie Murray, a contemporary
observer, noted:

The curiosity with which a section of the newspaper press has been inspired as to Mr.
Crockett's personal whereabouts, as to his comings and goings, his engagements for
the future, and his prices 'per thousand words', would have seemed to indicate that in

him we had discovered a person of considerably more than the average height. (Murray 1897: 99–100)

The extent of Crockett's celebrity status can be witnessed in an anonymous poem printed in the *British Weekly* on 30 August 1894. Three happy "maidens" glimpse Crockett getting off a train and react with the sort of nervous excitement now afforded to footballers or pop stars:

Then one of them suddenly started,
And exclaimed in a whisper low,
"It's Crockett himself! S.R. Crockett!
We heard he was coming you know."

And gazing forgetful of manners,
They watched till he drove away,
And one wrote in her diary that evening,
"We saw S.R. Crockett to-day."

Some novelists, such as James and Conrad, looked with scorn upon this intrusive obsession with authors' lives and personalities. James referred to the "mania for publicity" and provided the perfect rebuttal of the trend in *The Aspern Papers* (1888). In this context it is significant that J.M. Barrie positioned himself firmly in the James camp. Throughout his career Barrie remained suspicious of media representations of his life and work. Like Conrad, he refused to have his photograph published in magazines, declined invitations to talk at public events and turned down requests for interviews. In a letter of 3 January 1894, he told Quiller-Couch:

McClure's magazine dogs me as if it wanted my hand in marriage. There must be a mistake about Gilbert Parker. I only met him once (and liked him enormously) but remember no talk on any such matter. He wrote about interviewing me for this magazine, and I declined. Never shall man or maid interview me. (Meynell 1947: 5)

Whereas Barrie resisted every attempt to pin down his personality, Maclaren and Crockett revelled in this aspect of contemporary literary life and eagerly lapped up the public interest in their lives. Both authors responded to the American innovation of the personal interview, which was a regular feature of British magazines in the

1890s. Raymond Blathwayt, "the most famous exponent of the genre" (McDonald 1997: 8), interviewed Maclaren for *Great Thoughts*, and further interviews with both Crockett and Maclaren were published in a variety of magazines.[4] In such articles there was little discussion of the writers' books, but plenty of background information about their lives, ways and habits. Pictures of their homes, desks, libraries and gardens mingled with photographs of Galloway or Drumtochty. The contemporary cultural interest was thus vested as much in the authors' personalities as it was in their books. Even if only for a short time, Ian Maclaren the man became as significant a presence in the literary world as Ian Maclaren's work. Even a writer like Rudyard Kipling, so temperamentally and artistically different from his contemporary, declared in a letter of 21 July 1897 that "I should much like to have met Ian Maclaren" (Kipling 1990: II: 306).

Nowhere was the impact of the personality of Maclaren felt more than in his visits to America. Thomas Knowles has explored the success of the Kailyard in America, arguing that "a public taste habituated to Scottish themes and history, with a propensity for the religious in fiction and receptive to local colour undoubtedly favoured the success of the Kailyard novels in America" (Knowles 1983: 78). Maclaren's appeal in America was as much religious as national. His form of Christianity appealed to many Americans. Nicoll records that immediately before leaving America he was presented with an address from the Brotherhood of Christian Unity where he was thanked for his work in "awakening and uniting the deepest sympathies of our common human nature" and "formulating a Creed of Christian life which embodies the spirit and essence of Christ's teachings" (Nicoll 1908: 198). The emphasis here on unity, common human nature, and Christ's teachings reflect Maclaren's religious principles and goes a long way to explaining his success in America.

Maclaren first toured America in the winter of 1896, shortly before *Kate Carnegie* was published. J.B. Pond arranged as many as 96 engagements over October–December. His lecturing was attended

---

[4] For similar articles on Maclaren see Noble (1895), Paton (1896) and the unsigned articles in the *Glasgow Evening Times* (28 September 1896), *McClure's Magazine* (1896), *Sunday Strand* (1900) and *Young Man* (1901).

and admired by such luminaries as Andrew Carnegie and Theodore Roosevelt. Gerald Stanley Lee, who reported on one of the lectures for the New York *Critic*, noted how Maclaren's appeal was emotional rather than intellectual:

> It is apparent that it is an essentially pastoral genius which has taken its artistic form in Ian Maclaren. The more intellectual emphasis which would have characterised the same work in another man would probably have failed to get such a complete cross-section of the public as has fallen to the lot of the Drumtochty parson. (Lee 1896)

A large part of the appeal of these lectures, especially to the Scottish emigrants, was the nostalgic strain of the Drumtochty stories. In an interview printed in the *British Weekly*, Maclaren recounted his "impressions of America", and recorded that he was often introduced as "an old friend, whom we all know well" (31 December 1896). A contemporary article also suggests the nostalgic appeal:

> the people, especially the settlers from Bonnie Scotland, thought it a very little thing to travel two or three hundred miles, to hear the man who could write so exquisitely of the land of Wallace and Burns. (Pearson 1901: 660)

The trips to America brought many American visitors to Liverpool and to the church at Sefton Park. Pond offered Maclaren $24,000 for a further lecture tour of twelve weeks but it was not until 1899 that Maclaren embarked on a second visit.

Maclaren's tours to America limited the time he had to spend writing, and Nicoll is surely right in his assessment that the numerous requests to give speeches and lectures that followed on from his successful tour of America were "injurious to his literary work" (Nicoll 1908: 213). Giving lectures was a standard practice for the best-selling author, however, and it is quite possible that Maclaren, emulating Dickens, made as much money from his lectures and public readings as he did from the considerable sales of his books. Nicoll reported in the *British Weekly* that the receipts of the three lectures he gave in Chicago were 'not below 8,000 dols." (26 November 1896). Major Pond, the organiser of the tours, was reported in the same paper as saying that Maclaren was "in greater demand than any foreigner who has ever come to America" (13 August 1896). Given this, it is perhaps not surprising that Maclaren was invited to lunch with the President.

None of this is true of Barrie and the association of his work with that of Maclaren has led to continued misrepresentations of his activities in America. Thomas Knowles claims that Barrie and Maclaren both made "overwhelmingly successful promotional visits" to America (Knowles 1983: 66) and John Caughie links Barrie with Harry Lauder as someone who openly promoted the "stifling 'kailyard' mythology" through being "almost as popular on the American lecture circuit as was Lauder on the stage" (Caughie 1990: 16). But Barrie never gave lectures in Britain or America. The *British Weekly* reported that Pond invited Barrie to "deliver from eighty to a hundred lectures in America, but the proposal [had] been respectfully declined" (16 July 1896). G.W. Cable gave a report of Barrie's time in America in *Symposium* remarking "I doubt if anyone [...] had any revealing converse with Mr Barrie as to his views on the literary art or his methods of writing".[5] Such was Barrie's attitude to the media of the age.

V

The reason why Kailyard became so notorious within contemporary literary debates and within the historical understanding of Scottish culture cannot, however, simply be explained by the commercial success of Crockett and Maclaren. Commenting on Ian Campbell's book, *Kailyard*, David S. Robb posed a question that remains as pertinent now as it did in 1983:

> The question seems to me to be, not, why is kailyard writing so poor and why is so much Scottish literature tainted by its tendencies, but why was it ever mistaken for really serious and important Scottish literature? (Robb 1983: 31).

The answer lies in the promotion of Crockett and Maclaren as high art and the subsequent reaction against this by contemporary critics.

---

[5] Quoted in *British Weekly*, 24 December 1896.

Without Nicoll's marketing strategies the term Kailyard would probably never have acquired the lasting notoriety it has, and the books associated with it would have been forgotten – in the same way as many other Victorian best-sellers have been forgotten – as fleeting novelties.

Nicoll's role as literary editor to Hodder & Stoughton was a considerable one but it wasn't just his effect on the internal affairs of a publishing house that made him such a giant in the literary world at the turn of the century. His extraordinarily penetrative reviewing strategies enabled him to exert a remarkable control over the decisions of a section of the reading public and, consequently, over the reputations of countless authors. In the words of Dixon Scott:

Every Thursday, in the *British Weekly*, Sir W. Robertson Nicoll addresses an audience far more numerous, far more responsive, far more eagerly in earnest, than that controlled by any other living critic. He praises a book – and instantly it is popular. He dismisses one, gently – and it dies. He controls the contents of the bookshelves of a thousand homes – they change beneath his fingers like bright keyboards – and every alteration means the modification of a mind. What Claudius Clear reads on Wednesday, half of Scotland and much of England is reading before the end of the week. (Scott 1927: 99)

Nicoll's considerable industry made him a master of the art of multiple-reviewing, a famous case being the tremendous debunking of Arthur Conan Doyle's comic work of fiction, *A Duet*. When this book appeared in 1899 no less than six reviewers charged it as immoral. The six were anonymous writers in the Daily Chronicle, the American *Bookman* and the London *Bookman*; "Claudius Clear" and "A Man of Kent" in the *British Weekly* and "O.O." in *The Sketch*. All six were Robertson Nicoll, and when Conan Doyle found out he wrote in protest to the *Daily Chronicle*, precipitating an exchange of letters with Nicoll on "The Ethics of Criticism".[6]

In such ways Nicoll developed a much-respected if rather dubious reputation as a man who could single-handedly make or destroy a book. For some writers this made the prospect of an association with Hodder & Stoughton a lucrative one. Arnold Bennett

---

[6] The correspondence is reprinted in Gibson and Green 1986: 54–7.

found himself so tempted when seeking to find a new publisher for *The Old Wives' Tale* in 1909. He wrote to his agent J.B. Pinker:

it would not be bad thing to have some slight connection with H & S because such a connection would undoubtedly influence Claudius Clear's criticisms. I have the greatest contempt for them as an artist [...] but the effect of his criticisms is undeniable. (Hepburn 1966: 140)

Nicoll gave the book a good review and then, when Hodder duly issued an edition in 1910, had what Bennett called "his sickly praise" emblazoned across the front binding of the book (Hepburn 1966: 152). Bennett was appalled.

Nicoll's most remarkable and controversial log-rolling success, however, was his promotion of Barrie and, more critically, Crockett and Maclaren in the 1890s. There is no great mystery as to why Nicoll took such an interest in these writers. The shared national and religious background undoubtedly fuelled the association, although Nicoll had more in common with Maclaren than with Crockett on religious questions. As noted, he did not think much of the comic representation of religion in *The Lilac Subonnet* and Crockett's ambivalence towards the ministry makes his case different from Maclaren, who used his fiction to advance a particular religious ideology, one inkeeping with Nicoll's own views. Nicoll would have approved of Maclaren's attitude towards Biblical scholarship, for example. Donald Carswell reports that at college, "unlike most of his fellow-students he was perfectly immune from the effects of the new theological wine that [William] Robertson Smith had brought from Germany" (Carswell 1927: 221–2). Nicoll would also have welcomed Maclaren's stories for more literary reasons. He had a firm belief that literature should have a moral basis and, as Knowles has noted, feared and distrusted the influence of naturalist developments in fiction (Knowles 1983: 35–8). For this reason, the sentimental technique of Maclaren and its allied vision of a universal religious community based on feeling, rather than doctrine, appealed to both his moral and cultural values.

If Nicoll did not greatly influence the production of Barrie's work, he certainly played an important role in promoting it. Christopher Harvie argues that Barrie was a "pioneer product of the literary industry of agents, bestseller strategies, and advertising campaigns" (Harvie 1985: 321–2). Whilst this judgement applies more fully to Crockett and Maclaren – Barrie's early books were not bestsellers and he never used an agent for his fiction – he did benefit from a promotion campaign in the pages of the *British Weekly*. In July 1891 the paper issued, as a free supplement, a sixteen page "literary and biographical portrait". With a full-size photograph on the front page, the portrait outlined Barrie's background in literary journalism and offered a laudatory account of his books. As A. Whigham-Price notes: "this was perhaps one of the earliest deliberate attempts to sell an author's personality" (Whigham-Price 1994: 78) but as I have already discussed, the *Bookman* was not alone among reviews in its ecstatic enthusiasm for Barrie's work and Barrie always distanced himself from such strategies of authorial presentation.

Nicoll's personal role in the discovery of Ian Maclaren gave him an even stronger reason for booming *Beside the Bonnie Brier Bush*. Two weeks before the book was published, it was announced in the *Bookman* that it was "confidently anticipated by many competent judges that the book will place the author in the first rank" (August 1894). Then, when the book was published in October 1894, Nicoll devoted an entire front page of the *British Weekly* to reviewing it, claiming that "from the artistic point of view it is an unquestionable and marked success", and declaring that Maclaren was "unsurpassed by any living writer in the gift of pathos" (11 October 1894). His review of Crockett's *The Stickit Minister* the previous year had been similarly outlandish, claiming that the book gave the author "a very high place among his fellow artists", and concluding: "one is tempted to say that Mr Crockett is a man of genius" (6 April 1893). When he reviewed another Crockett novel two years later he was still making extravagant comparisons, suggesting that "if anyone wishes to understand why Mr Crockett is so popular, and why it is well he should be popular, let him do as I did – read 'The Men of the Moss Hags' and follow it immediately with the last instalment of Mr Hardy's 'Hearts Insurgent'" (26 September 1895). Nor was this simply a case of Nicoll being characteristically prudish about the serial that was to become *Jude the Obscure*; Frank Swinnerton recalled that Nicoll greatly admired Hardy and considered him "the most winning literary man" he had ever met (Swinnerton 1956: 53).

Nicoll must have been aware that not everyone was likely to agree with his assessment of Crockett and Maclaren, and he attempted to validate their achievement further by repeatedly claiming that their work was difficult to produce. On 11 April 1895 he published a letter in the *British Weekly* entitled "To a Writer of Scottish Idylls", which purported to be a reply to an author who had sent Nicoll some of his work. It is impossible to say whether the letter is genuine or merely a clever publicity gimmick, but whatever the case, Nicoll was clearly setting out to refute the claims that were now being made that it was all too easy to write "Scottish idylls":

> When you read in the newspapers of the immense circulation and fame which some Scottish Idylls have achieved, you are apt to imagine that the writers have found the easiest way to the top which was ever revealed to man. When the experiment is made, it will be seen that no kind of work is more difficult than theirs.

The first critic to launch an attack on Nicoll's reviewing methods was the writer who first applied the term Kailyard – J.H. Millar, writing in the *New Review* in 1895. Among other things, Millar attacked the way Crockett was "almost wholly the result of the modern method of reviewing":

> Not only has he enjoyed the benefit of the ingenious system of log-rolling consistently practised by a portion of the so-called religious press, but many other newspapers and reviews have conspired to overwhelm him with fulsome and exaggerated flattery. (Millar 1895: 393)

These sentiments were echoed by the young John Buchan in an article entitled "Nonconformity in Literature" published in the *Glasgow Herald* in the same year. The title referred not to religious issues but to the taste for novelty which Buchan considered characterised current trends in fiction. Buchan drew attention to what he saw as the inappropriate categorisation of certain works as serious literature:

> Idylls of humble country life have lately grown upon us thick and fast; charming pieces of literature many of them; nigh perfect in their narrow sphere. [...] But some gentlemen of the press, whose interest is to puff such books, do not let the matter rest

here. These unpretentious and delightful volumes are gravely set above work with which they are scarcely even comparable. (Buchan 1895)

The criticism was not lost on Nicoll who responded in the *British Weekly* by combining notice of the article with a short review of Buchan's *Sir Quixote*, which he took to be little more than imitation Crockett. "I hope Mr Buchan will some day do some good work", he wrote, "and meanwhile he need not trouble his head about the Scottish school. The little finger of the least of them is as yet much thicker than his loins" (7 November 1895).

Buchan's article had concluded with a view of artistic production that was characteristic of its age. Calling Crockett at his worst "only a boisterous talker", he wrote: "no man, however high his spirits and rich the life within him, can hope to be a great writer save by the restraint, the pains, the hard and bitter drudgery of his art." The ease with which certain writers like Crockett and Maclaren seemed to be able to achieve popular success contributed to this alternative image of the "true" artist compelled, like Reardon in Gissing's *New Grub Street* (1891), to labour on in financial ruin in the service of his art. Buchan had his revenge on Nicoll when he portrayed him satirically in one of his novels, *Castle Gay* (1930).

It is important to realise, then, that much of the contemporary attack on Kailyard fiction was to do with debates over high and low culture and with the etiquette of reviewing. Buchan's criticisms were repeated by the English novelist David Christie Murray, who in his critical book, *My Contemporaries in Fiction*, complained of "the 'boom' which has lately filled heaven and earth with respect to the achievements of the new Scotch school" (Murray 1897: 115). Like Millar and Buchan before him, Murray singled out Crockett, remarking:

the unblushing effrontery of those gentlemen of the press who have set him on a level with Sir Walter is the most mournful and most contemptible thing in association with the poorer sort of criticism which has been encountered of late years" (Murray 1897: 100)

Murray added a further assault with regard to Maclaren, saying that "here is another case where the hysteric overpraise of the critics has done a capable workman a serious injustice" (Murray 1897: 111).

As Thomas Knowles notes, H.G. Wells levelled similar charges against the puffing of Crockett and Maclaren (Knowles 1983: 52) but the most interesting of all these critics was a writer in the *Glasgow Evening Times* signing himself "Rix", who wrote an article published on 6 January 1897 entitled "The Slump in Kail Runts". "Rix" declared the Kailyard to be in decline and proceeded to attack it on a number of counts. He was concerned about the future understanding of Scottish literary history and feared that a lot of second-rate material might become indelibly marked upon tradition. Posterity has proved him right. As I noted in my introduction, he began with a prophetic statement:

Most readers must be weary of the outworn word itself, as they are of the class of writing for which it stands. But the word has become part of the language, and will probably survive the books which it connotes.

Significantly, "Rix" was quick to exclude Barrie from what he understood as the Kailyard, considering him to have been "brought, somewhat unfairly, into the same gallery". But it wasn't so much the word that distressed him as the whole question of reputation. Of Crockett and Maclaren, he wrote: "their absurdly inflated reputations has been made by an ingenious system of log-rolling, whose perfect construction and success in working are without parallel in modern literary records." Nicoll was clearly the target of this attack and he replied in his column "A Man of Kent" in the *British Weekly* a week later, quoting "accurate and verified figures of sales for 1896" that amounted, when the "three best known of these writers" were taken into account, to "over half a million". Given this, Nicoll argued that "articles about the slump might perhaps in the circumstances be held over" and proceeded to offer a general defence of the Kailyard books:

Nobody says that these Scotch books have made anyone think less of Scotland; nobody can say that they have done anything to corrupt the minds of their readers. They have made everywhere for tenderness, for purity, for a higher standard of life. (14 January 1897)

The response given by Rix in the *Glasgow Evening Times* reveals the clear difference in opinion between the two critics over what constituted literary success:

"A Man of Kent" asks if I "can tell him of anything in the least degree comparable in contemporary literature." I frankly admit I cannot tell him of anything in the least degree comparable in contemporary bookselling. Why this perpetual dragging in of America? And why this continual harping upon sales, as if they formed the first and last tribunals before which all authors must come? (21 January 1897)

In discussing whether good sales should be taken as an indicator of literary value, the debate between Nicoll and "Rix" is characteristic of its age. What is perhaps surprising is that it is a writer in an evening newspaper who is adopting the cultural high ground. For Nicoll, good sales indicated success. As he wrote in the *British Weekly*:

When you see a man put out one difficult book after another with a circulation steadily sagging, with a spirit inflamed and rebellious, you see a tragedy. One such, whose name I will not mention, died among us lately. He had, I think, a far more genuine literary gift than many who were popularly successful, but he stiffened and hardened and went to the wall. Of course, if a man cannot condescend to a certain style of writing and cannot bring over the public to like his style of writing, it is best for him to give up authorship. (Nicoll 1926: 81)

Nicoll might easily have been talking about Edwin Reardon in Gissing's *New Grub Street* (1891), whose refusal – or inability – to condescend to a certain style of writing forces him to give up authorship and leads ultimately to his death. It would be wrong to suggest that Nicoll held sales as the only criterion for the judgement of value but in the debate which took place in the 1890s over the commercialisation of literature there is absolutely no doubt on which side he stood. In his column in the *British Weekly* for July 16, 1896, he set out his idea of literary value. "What makes a Novel successful?" he asked himself:

By successful I mean circulation. I do not mean favourable reviews, or the good opinion of a select but limited class [...] I sometimes see in reviews of Scottish books that high praise is accompanied by the high certificate "This is not in the Kail-yard style of Ian Maclaren and Crockett." This may or may not be altogether pleasant to the author criticised. What it means is that he gets a certain number of friendly reviews in superior papers, and that his book struggles on to seven hundred copies or so, while the remaining three hundred appear much knocked about and linger for a long time as remainders on the bookstalls.

To many writers and critics of the time, good sales necessarily indicated artistic compromise, and this inverse relation between popularity and literary value became a fundamental part of Modernism.[7] It is in this wider context that we must place Nicoll's multifarious editing and reviewing strategies and the critical reception of the Kailyard. Nicoll differed from the modernists in that he wanted to work with the new reading public, and was thus keen to find works of literature that were appealing to the masses but also serious-minded as well as ethically sound. The "Scottish Idyllists" were, for him, the best example.

The most scathing attack on Nicoll came in T.W.H. Crosland's attack on all things Scottish, *The Unspeakable Scot*. It seems certain that animosity towards Nicoll alone drove Crosland to his unflinching diatribe, but it is easy to miss the importance and specificity of what he is saying beneath the unabashedly racist rhetoric. His satirical attack on Nicoll's editorial characteristics is worth quoting in full as an accurate portrait of what really took place in the pages of the *British Weekly*:

Any author who is doing well – that is to say, any author whose record of sales entitles him to be considered a success – may always reckon on a large hospitality in Dr. Nicoll's journals, and will always find Dr. Nicoll and his merry men beaming round the corner and hat in hand. It is a matter of what would you like, sir? all the time. Are you spending your holiday cruising on the blue Mediterranean in the Duchess of Puttleham's yacht? Very good. Paragraph in the column signed "Man of Kent", with a delicate reference to your last great novel. Have you projects? Equally good. Mr So-and-So is, I understand, hard at work on his next great novel. Will your new book, 30,000 copies of which have been sold before the day of publication, make its appearance on April 1? Capital. Send us portraits of yourself at all ages from three months to the present day, pictures of the modest tenement in which you were born, and of your present town-house and little place in the country, and, bless your heart, we will do the rest. Do people say that the great novel, of which you have sold fifty million copies in England and America, is a pot-boiler and a failure? Dear, dear me! You have our heartiest sympathies sir, and if you would like to vindicate your

---

[7] See Carey 1992; Rainey 1998.

character as an artist in a couple of pages in the British Weekly, why, my dear sir, they are at your service. (Crosland 1902: 65–6)

Crosland went on to map out a clear reason for his resentment of Nicoll's methods by writing: "I do not say that there is any terrific harm in this species of enterprise. That it pleases the mass of mankind and therefore sells papers goes without saying. On the other hand it is quite subversive of the best interests of letters" (Crosland 1902: 66). It was as a result of the success of publications like those created by Robertson Nicoll that the question of what was "the best interest of letters" became such a heated topic of debate in the final decades of the century.

There is, however, something more positive to say about Nicoll within this very context. It is easy to be too one-sided about his interests and tastes. However much he invested value in popularity, and however much he mistrusted naturalism and took the sentimental piety of Maclaren as his touchstone for literary excellence, he nevertheless admired, advised and wrote warmly of such diverse figures as Gissing, Hardy and Yeats. Nor did he acquire his exalted position on the contemporary literary scene by a fluke. He was enormously well-read and took an eager interest in the dissemination of literature and literary knowledge. Nicoll has received considerable attention for his political, religious and moral outlook. What has been less documented is the serious ambition he held in the literary sphere. Of course his morals, politics and religious beliefs affected his opinions on literature, but he was greatly interested in the history and development of literature in itself. Even within the pages of the *British Weekly* – a newspaper with a strong political and religious accent – it is clear that literature and writing were Nicoll's most favoured subjects. At Hodder & Stoughton he oversaw a number of ambitious publishing projects that sought to provide a grand history of nineteenth-century literature, and at the time of his death he was planning to write a single-authored history of that period himself.

In all of his publishing and editorial ventures Nicoll tried to be responsive to the new demands of the increased readership and mass markets brought about by the reforms in education. His most important and successful venture in this respect was the launching of the *Bookman* in 1891. This magazine remains a neglected landmark in Victorian literary publishing and represents a major attempt to shape the course of British literary culture. Set up and run by Nicoll, it soon took over from the *Athenaeum* as the main site of book advertising and reviewing and was not only "the most widely read literary periodical in Britain" (Keating 1989: 338) but was also a serious-minded literary magazine. It was the first successful magazine of its kind devoted entirely to literature, and Nicoll's aims were specifically to fill a gap in the market. As he wrote to Marcus Dods:

> My experience is that there is a great class of literary aspirants whose wants are met in no way. Then a great many like to know about books and to be guided, but they don't wish it more than once a month, and they can't wade through reviews like the Athenaeum and Academy. Who can read a complete number of either? (Cited in Darlow 1925: 98)

In the words of Frank Swinnerton, the *Bookman* "united moderately serious literary criticism with gossip to an extent previously unknown in London journalism" (Swinnerton 1956: 52). Swinnerton was perhaps a little too cautious. Whilst *The Bookman* was never aimed at a scholarly or academic readership it acquired considerable literary respectability. Writers were not embarrassed to be associated with it as they were *Tit Bits* and other examples of the new journalism, and it boasted among its contributors some of the most important writers and critics of the day: Hardy, Swinburne, Pater, Chesterton, Barrie, Quiller-Couch, Lang, Lionel Johnson, George Saintsbury, and, most strikingly, W.B. Yeats, who contributed reviews and essays to all but the first of the opening ten numbers.

As easily the most widely-read literary magazine of the day, the *Bookman* was crucial in disseminating opinion, and the pages were liberally filled with articles and features on Scottish authors and topics. Maclaren and Crockett were afforded as privileged a place within its covers as any other contemporary novelist, carrying their work still further into a paradigm of high art. Both were given full-length, six page articles and featured in the supplements that were issued with each volume on leading nineteenth-century authors. In this context they were grouped not only with near-contemporaries like Meredith, Ruskin and Hardy, but with Austen, Scott and Dickens as well, and were thus identified as an integral part of the British literary tradition.

Nicoll's success in placing Scotland at the centre of British literary culture at the turn of the century cannot be overlooked, however much subsequent critics have disapproved of his political and national outlook. In his prospectus to the *Bookman*, Nicoll recorded his hope that the magazine would make "some real contribution to that final history of the Victorian literature which cannot yet be written" (Stoddart 1903: 92). It was the elevation of Maclaren and Crockett into that final history that explains, in part, why, along with Barrie, these writers' books became part of what was seen as the Scottish literary tradition, and the term Kailyard was fixed as the co-ordinate around which twentieth-century writers would understand their cultural heritage.

Chapter Six

The Critical Kailyard

I

The cultural impact of Barrie, Crockett and Maclaren, and the nature of the critical reception of their work, made it inevitable that the Kailyard debate would inflect subsequent creative writing. In her novel *A Young Dragon* (1900), Sarah Tytler included a reference to Kailyard and Ian Maclaren in her description of a bleak moorland farm:

everybody in the neighbourhood knew that if roses were still to be found at Garden-rose they were of the commonest and prickliest description, the very "brier-bushes" of ancient "kail-yards"; yet what so unapproachably fresh and fragrant as these brier bushes – only one stop removed, and that in the direction of Nature's exquisite scents, from the wild rose of the heath and hedgerow? (Tytler 1900: 1)

Seven years earlier, Tytler had contributed an article on Barrie to *Atalanta*, praising his "broad humour" and "exquisite pathos" and holding his fiction up as a model of realism (Tytler 1893: 60). The impact of Maclaren's fiction in the intervening years meant that Tytler was now confronted with a different model and in alluding to the dominant trends of recent Scottish fiction on the very first page of her novel she distances her story from the "fresh and fragrant" conventions of Maclaren and the Kailyard. One year later, George Douglas Brown offered a more sustained reaction in *The House with the Green Shutters* (1901), a novel that has come to be seen as a landmark event in Scottish literature; the beginnings of a counterblast against the Kailyard and of the foundations of modern Scottish literature.

Brown commented in the early 1890s when at Oxford: "No one pictures the real Scottish village life [...] I will write a novel and tell you all what Scottish village life is like" (Veitch 1952: 57). As Ian Campbell has argued, his method is to set up a typical Kailyard village populated by recognisable Kailyard characters only to explode this conventional world of fiction from within (Campbell 1974: 65). Barbie may look like Drumtochty on the surface but it emerges as a town filled with spiteful gossip and petty hatreds. The familiar characters of the minister, the dominie and the local "bodies" are the antithesis of their Kailyard counterparts. All community spirit is broken and Maclaren's idealistic vision of Christian redemption is nowhere to be found; indeed, as Alistair McCleery notes, "the Church itself as a physical landmark in the village is missing" (McCleery 1989: 47) and Brown deleted references to the Church in his revision to the first draft of the novel.

Brown's novel contains a more subtle and far-reaching reaction against the conventions of Kailyard fiction in its treatment of social change. As we have seen, the presentation of a static world resistant to outside interference and to modern improvements is one of the characteristics of Maclaren's fiction. In *The House with the Green Shutters* the effects of social change on the individual and the community drive the narrative. The novel charts the fall of John Gourlay from his position of eminence in the town as he is usurped by the outsider, Wilson, whose superiority rests in his greater knowledge of agricultural improvements. The similarities to Hardy's *The Mayor of Casterbridge* and the story of Michael Henchard and Donald Farfrae have often been noted and Gourlay's weakness of character is what drives the plot to its inevitable tragic denouement. The novel is less a response to the Kailyard's neglect of social realities as a reaction against its vision of human nature. What makes Barbie "rotten to the core" (Campbell 1974: 70) is not its exposure to social and economic pressures but the attitudes and personalities of its inhabitants, above all the vindictiveness of the "bodies", delighting in the downfall of Gourlay and not lifting a finger to help his son or his family, the victims of the man's destructive pride.

It is wrong to see Brown's novel as nothing more than an inversion of the Kailyard, but the author himself acknowledged that in his determination to present an alternative view he affected the balance. As he wrote to Ernest Barker:

There is too much black for the white in it. Even so it is more complimentary to Scotland, I think, than the sentimental slop of Barrie, and Crockett, and Maclaren. It was antagonism to their method that made me embitter the blackness; like old Gourlay I was going to "show the dogs what I thought of them". (Veitch 1952: 153)

Some critics have judged Brown harshly on this issue, notably Hugh MacDiarmid, who found the novel "mere reversal, the same thing disguised as its opposite" (MacDiarmid 1995: 342). But in addition to the formal patterning and the treatment of social change, Brown's novel is valuable for its portrayal, through the character of young John Gourlay, of the theme of imagination. Brutalised by his father, John's vivid imagination can find no outlet in an environment which is presented as both hostile and sterile. He briefly glimpses the pleasures of a different world at university but his indulgence in alcohol and his inability to discipline his imagination with philosophy defeats him. In this context, Brown's novel can be compared to Barrie's *Tommy* novels, which also explore the collision of reality and the imagination and the relationship between social environment and the creative mind. In a convincing essay, Beth Dickson has suggested that this preoccupation with the workings of the artistic imagination in novels by Barrie, Brown and Neil Munro constitutes the "Foundations of the Modern Scottish Novel" (Dickson 1987). Viewed from this perspective, Barrie's fiction can be seen – as it was before it was associated with Kailyard – as the inception of a new, modern tradition rather than the summation of a debilitating past tradition.

Brown's novel represents the most sustained creative response to Kailyard fiction, but the centrality of Kailyard to Scottish literature lies in the way that the critical criteria embedded in the term came to structure debate over the subject in the twentieth century. As I argued in Chapter 1, the Kailyard term was applied at a key moment in the shaping of the discipline of Scottish literature within academia and the publishing world. The various surveys and histories published in the last quarter of the nineteenth century formed part of a critical climate that aimed to investigate the possibility of a distinctively Scottish literature. As a term of literary criticism Kailyard soon formed part of this investigation.

The critical parameters of the Kailyard structure aspects of G. Gregory Smith's *Scottish Literature: Character and Influence* (1919), a study which proved crucial in determining the theoretical approach taken to Scottish literature in the twentieth century (Crawford 1998: 232–8). In his chapter "Lets and Hindrances", Smith grapples with the anxiety over provincialism raised by the Kailyard debate. Tracing the influence of Burns on the themes and idioms of nineteenth-century Scottish writing, Smith judges that whereas Burns "laid hold of the universal" his successors descended into the "provincial":

> There, and especially in the later period, in the ingle-pathos and tavern-fun, even amid the most artificial sentimentalism, the free appeal is certainly hampered by "parochial" claims. There is no denying the fact that the Scot seldom strays from the village-pump and the familiar gable-ends. Nor is this surprising, when we find the habit of intimacy so engrained in the literary character; nor strange that it should be exaggerated in the special conditions of modern Scotland. A small country, made guardian of its own destinies, runs the risk, but the sheer energy and success of its self-reliance, of finding an ever-growing satisfaction in the things that lie at hand and are familiar. The Scot may be a great wanderer […] but the Scot at home, accepting circumstances with like readiness, busies himself, happily enough, with the tasks of neighbourhood and gossipry imposed by a rigorous tradition. (Smith 1919: 45–6)

The tradition of Burns imposes a ready-made set of conventions which makes it inevitable that any renaissance will "protest that these things poorly answer her longing and smack too much of outworn convention" (Smith 1919: 51). Viewed in this way, it is easy to see why Burns became an anxiety of influence for MacDiarmid.

The historical importance of Gregory Smith's study arises from its engagement with the issue of whether Scottish literature could be seen as distinct from English or British literature as a subject in its own right. T.S. Eliot gave his own answer to this question in the title of his review of Smith's book in the *Athenaeum* – "Was there a Scottish Literature?" (1 August 1919). Smith's investigation into "the character or habit" of his subject carried with it "the author's confession that he knows how difficult it is to set forth a corporate literary character or to indicate the direction of a literary influence" (Smith 1919: v). In the final chapter he reviewed the main thrust of his discussion:

> The reader may ask whether all that has been said about persisting traits in Scottish literature and about its influence upon others is of more than historical interest. Modern conditions seem to put the thesis of a well-defined and sustained Scotticism

to a very severe test [...]. The literary historian finds, as he passes from Hume to Sir Walter, that it is increasingly difficult to segregate his "Scottish" writers, and that he has often no better excuse for a label than the accident of birth or residence, or the choice of subject or dialect. The public of to-day does not trouble itself about the matter, except when, roused by the accent of Drumtochty, it convinces itself that it hears the "true Scottish note". (Smith 1919: 276)

The only visible tradition was the "accent of Drumtochty" – the Kailyard – and on that issue Smith was unequivocal. If an independent Scottish literary tradition was to be detected then "we rule out the whole company of 'stickit ministers' and all the things done and said within reach of bonnie brier bushes" (Smith 1919: 277). Like Margaret Oliphant in the 1890s, Smith is preoccupied with the construction of the Scottish literary tradition; and like Millar and the other contemporary Kailyard critics he is wary that the accent of Drumtochty will be seen as the true accent of Scotland and Scottish literature. And it should be noted that, like Oliphant and Millar, Smith excludes Barrie from his summary of Kailyard, grouping him instead with Stevenson and Lang as writers to whom "serious criticism dares to look for the deeper and abiding differences in literary character" between Scotland and England (Smith 1919: 278).

As Robert Crawford argues, in Smith's study "the germ of a theory of Scottish literature emerges" (Crawford 1998: 232), one that was to prove crucial to Hugh MacDiarmid who seized on Smith's concept of the "Caledonian antisyzygy" – the idea that the distinctive characteristic of Scottish literature was its "antithesis of the real and the fantastic" (Smith 1919: 4, 20). MacDiarmid also picked up on Smith's rejection of the Kailyard. More than any other writer, MacDiarmid was responsible for placing Kailyard at the centre of discussions over Scottish literature in the twentieth century. In the editorial to the first edition of *The Scottish Chapbook* (1922), he outlined "A New Movement in Scottish Literature".[1] This foundational statement of the Scottish renaissance begins with an attack on the standards of literary criticism in Scotland with the comment that Scottish literature has been written about "almost

---

[1] *The Scottish Chapbook* was edited by C.M. Grieve. I have referred to Grieve's penname of MacDiarmid throughout.

exclusively by ministers", an obvious reference to William Robertson Nicoll, who is mentioned in the same paragraph (MacDiarmid 1992: 3). The main thrust of the essay, however, builds on the criticisms levelled at Kailyard by J.H. Millar and the contemporary critics discussed in Chapter 1. MacDiarmid argues:

> for several generations Scottish literature has neither seen nor heard nor understood what was taking place around it. For that reason it remains a dwarf among giants. Scottish writers have been terrified even to appear inconstant to established conventions. (Good wine would have needed no "Bonnie Brier Bush"). (MacDiarmid 1992: 4)

As with Gregory Smith, who saw the "accent of Drumtochty" as the only visible tradition, MacDiarmid here takes issue with the assumption that Maclaren's fiction stands for Scottish literature. The "established conventions" set in place by the Kailyard are inadequate to deal with what is taking place around Scotland.

At the end of the same essay, MacDiarmid makes a reference to another Kailyard text. He recounts a meeting with an Edinburgh artist who asked him to "visualise a typical Scotsman":

> When I assured him that I had this mythical personage clearly established in my mind's eye, he turned to a blackboard and rapidly sketched a Glasgow "keelie", a Polish pitman from Lanarkshire, a Dundee Irishman, an anarchist orator of a kind frequently seen at the Mound in Edinburgh on Sunday nights, a Perthshire farmer, a Hebridean islander, and a Berwickshire bondager.

These, the artist declared, helped "to show that the Window in Thrums gives an obsolete outlook on Scottish life" (MacDiarmid 1992: 7–8). For MacDiarmid and the Edinburgh artist, Barrie's text stood for an outmoded expression of Scotland, both socially and aesthetically.

Throughout his criticism, MacDiarmid developed this idea that Kailyard representations of Scotland were obsolete and constituted a false representation of Scottish literature. Unlike Smith, however, who positioned Barrie outside the Kailyard, MacDiarmid made the author of *Peter Pan* the representative writer of his argument. The only work by Barrie that MacDiarmid admired was *Tommy and Grizel* – which contained "certain rare elements of psychologising subtlety" (MacDiarmid 1995: 14) – but Barrie's commercial success and popular reputation made him responsible in MacDiarmid's eyes for propagating a false image of Scotland. In the final essay of *Scottish Scene* (1934), entitled "The Future", MacDiarmid laments how "Kailyairdism" is "all of Scottish literature that is known to or appreciated by the great majority of Scottish people" (Gibbon and MacDiarmid, 1934: 278); the book then closes with a poem, "Envoi", which wishes "Away, away" to "Auld Lichts, wee Frees, Burnsians, London Scots!" and concludes by again seeing Barrie as the embodiment of a false tradition of Scottish literature:

Peter Pan nae langer oor deity'll be
And oor boast an endless infantilism.
Awa, wi' the auld superstitions. Let the sun up at last
And hurl a' sic spoons into their proper abysm. (Gibbon and MacDiarmid, 1934: 288)

MacDiarmid's use of the Kailyard term turned in part on the issue of language. In an early passage in *Lucky Poet* (1943), he discusses the use of Scots in his poetry and refers to "the influence of Sir J.M. Barrie [...] and the other writers of the Kailyard School" (MacDiarmid 1994: 17). It is the only positive reference to Kailyard in MacDiarmid's writing. Some twenty years earlier, when "Introducing 'Hugh M'Diarmid'", he had directly opposed the Kailyard against his campaign for the revival of the Doric:

The value of the Doric lies in the extent to which it contains lapsed or unrealised qualities which correspond to "unconscious elements of distinctively Scottish psychology. The recovery and application of these may make effectively communicable those unexpressed aspects of Scottish character the absence of which makes, say, "Kailyaird" characters shallow, sentimental, humiliating travesties. (MacDiarmid 1992: 11)

MacDiarmid was the first writer to use the term consistently to refer to a poetic tradition. In an article of 1923 in the *Scottish Nation* – one of MacDiarmid's own periodicals – he railed at the appearance of a collection of Gilbert Rae's verse, arguing: "it is verse in the Kailyaird tradition, sentimental, moralitarian, and unreal [...] It is to this pass that the Kailyaird tradition has driven us" (MacDiarmid 1996: 128, 130).[2]

MacDiarmid's association of the Kailyard term with a poetic tradition was built around his antagonism towards the Vernacular Circle of the London Burns Club, which in the early 1920s embarked on a programme to revive and preserve the Scots vernacular. MacDiarmid saw the programme as regressive and in an entry in his "Leaves from a London Scottish Diary", contributed to the *Scots Pictorial* on 12 May 1923, he accused the London "Vernacular Revivalists" of failing to respond to the social conditions of the modern world:

These men make a fetish of reactionary provincialism in the heart of London. They forget the consequences of rural population. The great majority of the Scottish people today have entirely changed in temperament and tendencies from the stock conceptions of the Kailyard School. There is little relationship between Thrums and Clydebank. We cannot restore the conditions that obtained prior to the commencement of the industrial era. The problem is to transplant the Doric in so far as it still possesses any evolutionary momentum into the soil of contemporary civilisation. (MacDiarmid 1996: 48)

In one respect this criticism anticipates that of George Blake in emphasising the need for Scottish writers to attend to the realities of urban Scotland. But the criticism is conceived not solely in terms of social representation; it is bound up with MacDiarmid's theory of nationalism and internationalism. He argues that the London Vernacular enthusiasts are guilty of neglecting continental affairs:

I have often had cause to stress the fact that where there is a national literary renaissance nowhere else is interest in contemporary foreign literature more keenly manifest. Nationalism and Internationalism presuppose and confirm each other [...] renaissances do not grow in kailyairds. (MacDiarmid 1996: 46)

Kailyard stands here for a force in culture that turns inwards and neglects international developments. In this way, Kailyard came to encapsulate MacDiarmid's politically motivated critique of provincialism. MacDiarmid's argument was that within British

---

[2] MacDiarmid later adopted the more conventional spelling of Kailyard.

literature Scotland could only ever be provincial; English cultural influences had to be purged and continental ones embraced. As he wrote in an essay on William Jeffrey:

One of the main preliminary aims of the Scottish Renaissance [...] must be to bring every other Scottish writer of any consequence to a like conscious confrontation of the fact that he is Scottish and that his work cannot be proceeding along the lines calculated to enable him to express himself and realise his artistic potentialities most fully unless it offers an unmistakable practical equivalent – in contrast if not also in form and language – of the difference in psychology and cultural background between any Scot and any Englishman. (MacDiarmid 1995: 97)

Writers who had absorbed English cultural influences were considered de-nationalised or Kailyard.

MacDiarmid's construction of Kailyard emerges most fully in *Contemporary Scottish Studies* (1926), where he took the term to the centre of his critical and creative agenda. *Contemporary Scottish Studies* has been considered a "landmark in modern Scottish literature" (Riach 1995: vi) and is MacDiarmid's fullest articulation of his early manifesto for a Scottish renaissance. First published in the *Scottish Educational Journal* between 1925 and 1927, most of the essays were issued as a book in 1926. MacDiarmid used the term Kailyard throughout these studies but it was not until the thirty-eighth essay on "Newer Scottish Fiction" that he referred specifically to the "Kailyaird School of Novelists". In most of the other essays the term is used in relation to poetry where it forms part of MacDiarmid's attack on the influence of Burns on Scottish verse. "Kailyairdism" becomes interchangeable with "Burnsianism" (MacDiarmid 1995: 61) and is used to sum up a whole tradition of Scottish poetry in the nineteenth century. For MacDiarmid, "the Kailyaird canon" is "what generally passes – and is still largely in use – as 'Braid Scots'" (MacDiarmid 1995: 372). In the essay on Lewis Spence and Marion Angus entitled "The New Movement in Vernacular Poetry", he accuses the "great majority of vernacular enthusiasts" of perpetuating the "traditional and deepening rut of post-Burnsian Kailyairdism" (MacDiarmid 1995: 196–7). Spence and Angus, in contrast, exhibit the "true creative approach to the vernacular" which represents "a radical departure from the methods of Kailyairdism" (MacDiarmid 1995: 200).

Kailyard was thus a phrase for MacDiarmid to use to make swift and easy judgements on the kind of Scottish writing he rejected. Alexander Gray is judged to be operating on "a pedestrian Kailyaird level" and Peter Taylor has not "succeeded in liberating himself from the Kailyaird pressure to any vital extent" (MacDiarmid 1995: 334, 329). By contrast, Muriel Stuart's "directness of statement" is what emphasises "the gulf between her and the soul-destroying sentimentalities of the Kailyaird School" and Violet Jacob, though she "may seem through her choice of subject and angle of treatment to be merely a belated and somewhat etherealised Kailyairder", is really pursuing a "direction [that] is subtly but none the less completely different." (MacDiarmid 1995: 156, 28).

Part of MacDiarmid's intention in *Contemporary Scottish Studies* is to raise the profile of neglected writers whom he believed had been subordinated by Kailyardism and the Burns cult. In the article on James Pittendrigh Macgillivray he condemns

the vast majority of self-styled lovers of Scottish poetry who are bogged in an overwhelming admiration for Burns and a few others such as Motherwell and Ferguson, who belong to the same school and indifferent to, and indeed for the most part entirely ignorant of, the Old Makars on the one hand and on the other of Scottish poets wholly outwith the kailyaird traditions such as Robert Buchanan and John Davidson, not to mention some of our great Gaelic bards. (MacDiarmid 1995: 50)

Kailyard traditions have become poetic traditions but in this essay the term forms part of MacDiarmid's larger argument about the need to reject British influences on Scottish culture:

Macgillivray's work is for the most part – despite certain resemblances which would only further baffle naïve readers going to it with popular predilections – at the furthest remove from what is commonly understood – especially by Scots themselves – as "Scotch poetry." Despite certain superficial similarities he has nothing whatever in common with any of the amazing array of mediocrities represented in the endless series of volumes of Mr D.H. Edwards' *Modern Scottish Poets* – all of whom were dreadful examples of the excesses of self-parody into which imitative post-Burnsianism has been forced under conditions of progressive Anglicisation. Macgillivray's work, constitutionally incapable of being affected by Anglicising influences, remains free from any such distortion and degradation. The consequence is that it does not appear Scottish at all to those accustomed to wallow in the obviousnesses of Kailyardism: while, on the other hand, it is so far removed from stock-conceptions of what is Scottish, as to be for the most part inappreciable by any non-Scot. For foreign, and especially English, readers it can only be seen in its true aspect once the independent literary traditions of Scotland are re-established in general estimation as a distinctive department of *welt-literatur*, and effectively purged of the denationalised elements which have been progressively obscuring and corrupting them for the past hundred years or more. In other words, Macgillivray cannot be properly approached except *via* a thorough knowledge and genuine appreciation of the Old Makars, from whom he stands in the direct line of descent – and, in some important respects, stands entirely alone. (MacDiarmid 1995: 48)

The "obviousness of Kailyairdism" are part of the misunderstanding of Scotland's "independent literary traditions" which have been obscured by the force of progressive Anglicisation. In another essay he states that the differences between English and Scottish poets:

derive in unbroken descent from the Old Makars and constitute and perpetuate the independent literary traditions of Scotland which, on close analysis, have always been discernible even when Scottish letters have seemed most submerged in English – better preserved there, indeed, than in the Kailyairdism which ostensibly exemplifies them. (MacDiarmid 1995: 76)

Kailyardism "ostensibly exemplifies" the Scottish tradition but is in fact a distortion and not the real tradition at all. This is why, to MacDiarmid, Kailyard is a "disease" with "evil effects" working "subterranean mischief" (MacDiarmid 1995: 342). It claims to represent what he believes it doesn't – a Scottish tradition independent of English literature. For MacDiarmid, Kailyard is not just a negation of Scottish identity but a parading of a false national identity.

In a letter to the *Scottish Educational Journal* reprinted in *Contemporary Scottish Studies* MacDiarmid clarified his position, arguing that by adopting "the idioms, vocabulary, etc., of Dunbar and Henryson and the other old Makars" Scottish writers will avoid "the degeneracies inherent in all later Scots" and so "obtain a language adapted to every form of literary expression and not suitable for kailyaird purposes only" (MacDiarmid 1995: 122). Kailyard here is about a limitation of possibilities for the Scottish writer, one intimately associated with language and Scotland's historical status within the United Kingdom. The term becomes for MacDiarmid a word to conceptualise this central problem:

the fact that Scotland has not yet been realised as Scotland – Anglicisation has thrust its problems out of the sphere of practical politics, and as a consequence created a public opinion which, aided by the Anglo-Scottish Press, finds them unreal and negligible, while irrelevant issues assume the guise of reality and monopolise the mind. (MacDiarmid 1995: 71)

Irrelevant, "Kailyard" issues, under the thumb of Anglicisation, assume the guise of reality and monopolise the mind whilst the real Scotland remains unrealised. As a result of MacDiarmid arguing that 'Scotland has not yet been realised as Scotland' the idea of replacing Kailyard representations with alternative discourses became a leitmotiv of much subsequent criticism.

The construction of Kailyard as a false tradition in Scottish literature is at the heart of MacDiarmid's criticism and also inflected his poetry. In the long poem *A Drunk Man looks at the Thistle* (1926), MacDiarmid's Drunk Man laments the way Dunbar has been "owre the Kailyaird wa' flung" (MacDiarmid [1978] 1985: 106). The real independent literary traditions of Scotland that derive from Dunbar have become obscured by a Kailyard wall. He revisited the theme in his next major poem, *To Circumjack Cencrastus* (1930). The central section of this poem is entitled "Frae Anither Window in Thrums", an allusion to the painting by William McCance, which itself takes issue with the implicit (if never intended) claim of Barrie's text to speak for Scotland. Alan Bold explains that this particular section of the poem was "once figured as the title poem of a proposed collection", to be entitled *Another Window in Thrums* (Bold 1988: 256, 520-1n). The use of Barrie's title by both artist and poet indicates the extent to which Barrie and the Kailyard texts had become iconic of a particular way of representing Scotland in art. Barrie is not mentioned in *To Circumjack Cencrastus* but is a ghostly presence throughout, indicating how, through Thrums, his writing had come to stand for Scotland. In a letter to George Ogilvie, MacDiarmid explained that "where the *Drunk Man* is in one sense a reaction from the 'Kailyaird', *Cencrastus* transcends that altogether – the Scotsman gets rid of the thistle, 'the bur of the world' – and his spirit at last inherits its proper sphere" (MacDiarmid 1984: 91).

The construction of Kailyard as the improper sphere of Scottish literature meant that the term became a context from which both the criticism and the creation of a national literature could take place. Other writers of the renaissance movement followed MacDiarmid in using the term as a marker against which to position their own work. In 1927 Neil Gunn wrote: "The Renascent Scot is – must be – intolerant of the Kailyairder, that is of the parochial, sentimental, local-associative way of treating Scotland and the Scots" (Gunn 1987: 90). The Kailyard debate continued to influence literary representations of Scotland. In *Sunset Song* (1932), the first part of his trilogy *A Scots Quair*, Lewis Grassic Gibbon located his fictional Kinraddie within a literary context:

So that was Kinraddie that bleak winter of nineteen eleven and the new minister, him they chose early next year, he was to say it was the Scots countryside itself, fathered between a kailyard and a bonnie brier bush in the lee of a house with green shutters. And what he meant by that you could guess at yourself if you'd a mind for puzzles and dirt, there wasn't a house with green shutters in the whole of Kinraddie. (Gibbon [1932] 1988: 24)

What he meant – or rather what Grassic Gibbon meant – was that any fictional representation of a Scottish village had the fiction of Maclaren and Brown – and the structures of Kailyard and Anti-Kailyard – as its anxiety of influence. Twentieth-century novelists who wrote of rural or small town life inevitably courted association with the Kailyard. Lorna Moon's collection of stories, *Doorways in Drumorty* (1925, 1926) appears to invite such contextualisation, with the seeming allusion to Maclaren's Drumtochty. Glenda Norquay suggests that "while she may have wished to profit by the generic associations, she certainly didn't want to be seen as producing exactly the same kind of fiction as Kailyard authors" (Norquay 2002: 13). Moon's fiction inclines more to the anti-Kailyard model of *Sunset Song* as well as containing a perspective that is reflective of her status as a woman writer of the 1920s.

The extent to which the Scottish renaissance defined itself against the Kailyard is witnessed in George Campbell Hay's poem

"Kailyard and Renaissance", included in the volume *Winds on Loch Fyne* (1948). Hay sets out a flyting between a "Kailyairder" and a "Renaissance Chiel" which begins with the Kailyarder's objection to the attack on his type:

oor kailyaird wa's dung doon an' scattert,
oor kailyaird sangbuiks raxt an' spattert
wi ink o infamy an' slander
it ryses e'en a Yairder's gander. (Hay 1948: 26)

Admitting of Kailyard verse that "twasna Homer, Virgil, Dante or Spenser", the Kailyairder maintains "it had hert, was warm and tender". The Renaissance chiel's reply describes a Kailyaird poet as "Cronnan the Sangs his Mither Sang [...] he slorps his cauld kail het again" (Hay 1948: 27). Complaining of the "snivellan greetan'" of "This thowless, sornan, thirled North Briton", the poem concludes with an image of the Kailyard poet

swaiveran, slaiveran, stumblan, mumblan,
while ootbye life's white spate gangs tumblan,
an' deif, he disna hear it rumblan. (Hay 1948: 28)

Hay's poem captures not only the stylistic objections and the criticism of realism that the Renaissance poets levelled at Kailyard writers but also the wider cultural argument developed by MacDiarmid – that Kailyard verses were expressions of North Britain not Scottish national literature.

MacDiarmid's construction of Kailyard as a false tradition in Scottish literature affected the subsequent structuring of the subject in at least four ways. Firstly, in associating Kailyard with forms of popular culture MacDiarmid created an indelible link between the term and popular representations of Scotland. Secondly, by labelling much of Victorian Scottish literature as Kailyard, MacDiarmid set out the agenda by which that period would come to be understood by literary and cultural critics. Thirdly, by identifying Kailyard as a fake tradition of Scottish literature, MacDiarmid promoted that emphasis on authenticity that characterised much of the rhetoric of the Scottish literary renaissance and much of the criticism about Scotland and

Scottish literature in the twentieth century. Finally, in identifying Kailyard as a provincial expression of North Britain, MacDiarmid set in place the political emphasis that has characterised debates over the provincialism of Scottish culture.

II

In Chapter 5, I showed how the debate carried out in the *Glasgow Herald* by "Rix" turned on the issue of popular culture and the question of what constituted the Scottish literary tradition. Like Rix, and a number of other contemporary critics, the Kailyard phenomenon signalled for MacDiarmid the onset of a new popular culture and indicated the emerging conflict between popularity and literary value. In his discussion of the New Movement in Vernacular Poetry, MacDiarmid asked:

Is literary English coincident with spoken English – and do the majority of the most significant and important writers of England or any other country write for the mass of the people? Is popular taste and the mass of contemporary understanding not invariably intent on the products of mediocrity and averse to the best product of its period? (MacDiarmid 1995: 197)

MacDiarmid's writing is everywhere infected by the cultural snobbery that makes his criticism characteristically modernist. Writing in the *Dunfermline Press* in 1922, he attacked the Scottish reading public:

No doubt thousands of Scottish people would be prepared to swear on oath that Annie S. Swan is an immortal genius: but that wouldn't make her one [...] The truth of the matter is that it doesn't matter one way or another what the general public think, on any literary matter. They are not in a position to have or to express opinions. (MacDiarmid 1996: 34–5)

The irony implicit in the fact that MacDiarmid is making these comments in a provincial newspaper should not go unnoticed. It was characteristic of "highbrow" or modernist writers to use the organs of mass culture to attack its forms. As Glen Murray notes, MacDiarmid was effective in "cultivating, manipulating or creating media for his writing" (Murray 1996: x); he could alternate between contributions to *avant-garde* periodicals and work on provincial newspapers in Scotland and elsewhere. Like George Orwell, he used the modern media to spread his social and cultural agenda.

MacDiarmid's attitude towards popular culture lies behind his attack on J.M. Barrie and other commercially successful writers. In *Contemporary Scottish Studies* he wrote: "Barrie's immense popularity is no evidence of his literary quality" and in the same series stated that Neil Munro's popularity is "simply a commercial phenomenon, an element (of a comparatively restricted nature) in contemporary entertainment, of no particularly literary consequence at all" (MacDiarmid 1995: 17, 19). This form of cultural elitism has had a debilitating effect on the understanding of Scottish culture. As Gavin Wallace argues, MacDiarmid's "defensiveness, and his corresponding wariness of the popular" has been "counter-productive in that much has been expelled from what has been deemed to constitute the nation's valid literary inheritance" (Wallace 1987: 244).

In the twentieth century, Kailyard came to be used pejoratively in relation to a variety of forms of popular culture, some of which are only tangentially related to the fiction of Barrie, Crockett and Maclaren. MacDiarmid's transformation of the term ensured that Kailyard was seen throughout the century as a continuing force of malevolence in Scottish life and letters. In 1927 Neil Gunn could still refer to the "Kailyard" as the "recent written expression" of the spirit of Scottish literature (Gunn 1987: 88) and in 1933 Angus Macdonald wrote: "the 'Kailyard' school is always with us; and year after year fresh samples are given us of Thrums or Drumtochty renewing its youth, or disguised with a new set of side-whiskers". Macdonald pointed to the work of Joseph Laing Waugh, R.W. McKenna and O. Douglas, suggesting that whilst "the 'Kailyard' type can offer a refuge from the overgrown commercialism of our lives, we feel that it is at once too 'precious' and too narrow in scope ever to make a national novel" (Macdonald 1933: 163). The examples point to a force in popular fiction that was quickly identified as the legacy of the fiction of Barrie, Crockett and Maclaren. In the 1920s MacDiarmid saw Waugh (1868-1928) as the bottom-line of the "Kailyaird School of novelists" (MacDiarmid 1995: 342) and in 1951 George Blake detected the maintenance of the "Kailyard strain" in J.J. Bell's sketches of "Wee Macgreegor" and "Joseph Laing Waugh's popular figure 'Rabbie [*sic*] Doo' (Blake 1951: 83).

Joseph Laing Waugh came from Thornhill in Dumfriesshire and set much of his fiction in the district. By far his most successful character was Robbie Doo, a humorous raconteur, reminiscent of those found in Barrie's and Maclaren's early stories. *Robbie Doo: His Reminiscences*, first published in Dumfries in 1912, is written in discursive Scots prose and is set back in the mid-nineteenth century. The volume begins: "I daursay there are very few fouk in Thornhill at the present time wha mind o' the auld laigh smiddy at the fit o' the toon" (Waugh 1912: 1). In a preface, Waugh claims that "these delightful glimpses of the auld lang syne of his eventful life" were related to him personally by Robbie "in the beautiful native Doric" (Waugh 1912: ix). Robbie is presented as a real life person and in the preface to the second edition Waugh recorded that "in exploiting Robbie Doo" he wrote out of a love for his "native village and for all the dear old worthies whose honoured names grace the pages of its history" (Waugh 1914: v). Waugh was certainly interested in local history. In 1903 he published *Thornhill and its Worthies*, a volume of his own reminiscences similar in style to those discussed in Chapter 1, which was reprinted several times following the success of Robbie Doo.

In 1914 Hodder & Stoughton published *Cracks wi' Robbie Doo* and in the same year reissued the *Reminiscences* in a shilling paperback. A review in the *Scotsman* quoted on the back cover of this edition declared that Waugh "has made Thornhill comparable with Thrums and Drumtochty". In its backward glance, its use of spoken Scots, its small-town setting and its focus on a local eccentric, Waugh's books certainly exploit aspects of the fiction of Barrie and Maclaren. What makes his fiction characteristic of its own time is the pursuit of humour. In this respect it can be compared to J.J. Bell's *Wee Macgreegor* (1902). The genesis of Bell's famous creation has similarities to that of Barrie's *Auld Licht Idylls*. The sketches first appeared in the *Glasgow Evening Times* but publishers thought their appeal was "too local" to justify the risk of volume publication (Bell 1933: xii). The book was published at the author's expense by the Scots Pictorial Publishing Co. which hoped for a modest sale in

Glasgow and the West of Scotland. Unexpectedly, 20,000 copies were sold within the first six weeks and Wee Macgreegor soon became a phenomenon of print culture. As Bell recalls, there was Wee Macgreegor "lemonade, matches, china, 'taiblet', picture postcards, sardines" (Bell 1933: xiv). A second book appeared in 1904 after which the character grew up, finding love in *Courtin' Christina* (1913) and entering the war in *Wee Macgreegor Enlists* (1915). Bell found the book's appeal to the English reader "inexplicable" and he did not think of taking out copyright in America where it was soon pirated. To the American publishers, however, Wee Macgreegor was insufficiently Scottish. They dispensed with the now famous illustration on the front cover and instead portrayed "effigies of little boys [...] in full Highland costume" (Bell 1933: xv).

Consisting substantially of dialogue written in a West of Scotland, Glaswegian Scots, the early Macgreegor sketches focus on the everyday life of the young son of a working-class family in Glasgow – visiting the zoo; attending the Sunday school soiree; receiving aunts and grandparents to tea. George Blake considered Bell's success "perhaps the last, wild wave of enthusiasm for a product of the Kailyard" (Blake 1951: 83). The use of mundane objects or events, such as a teapot or a new hat, as the focus for the narrative is consistent with the almost suspension of narrative in some of Barrie's and Maclaren's stories. Furthermore, the substantial use of dialect suggests that the novelty taste for Scots in literature continued beyond the 1890s. Although Bell wrote that he never made any effort to "learn the speech of the people of the period" (Bell 1933: ix), his handling of Scots is confident and alert to the nuances of region and character. Bell also commented that the stories had never struck him as "particularly funny" (Bell 1933: xi–xii) but it is clear that, like Maclaren's sketches, humour revealed through dialogue is an important part of the appeal of *Wee Macgreegor*.

Opinion still divides over Bell's creation. Moira Burgess asks if *Wee Macgreegor* is "a classic of Scottish humour", "a social document" or "a true flower of the kailyard" (Burgess 1998: 80–1). As with Barrie, Crockett and Maclaren, however, it is not so much the stories themselves as the context of their appeal and consumption that has led to them being seen as a product of the Kailyard. Like Waugh's

Robbie Doo books they were published cheaply and Bell commented that the paper-covered volume was in more demand than the cloth and leather editions. This gave the stories a mass appeal which to MacDiarmid denied them any artistic relevance. The fact that they had first appeared in a Scottish publication might also have indicated that what was once seen as an émigré vision had now become embedded within Scotland itself.

This point could also be made in relation to Neil Munro who, under the alias "Hugh Foulis", created a host of successful Scottish comic figures in the *Glasgow Evening News*. The most famous of these was Para Handy and the crew of the Clyde puffer "The Vital Spark". The original Para Handy sketches were closely linked to contemporary events. The sketches began in 1905 and were first published in volume form by Blackwood in 1906. Para Handy was turned into a successful television series in 1960 and was revived in 1994-5. Once again the association with Kailyard turns on the popular appeal and the use of humour which, as in Bell's sketches, emerges in the dialogue. George Blake put Munro in the "Kailyard group" but considered that he "elevated the trick to a minor art" (Blake 1951: 81).

Kailyard has also been seen to encompass the later comic tradition typified by the Highland comedies of Compton Mackenzie. *Whisky Galore* (1947) which became more widely known as a film (1949) picks up on a characteristic of Maclaren's stories in the comic presentation of a community threatened by, but ultimately triumphing over, hostile outside forces. The irony implicit in Mackenzie's humour pre-empts criticism of mockery, however, both here and in the satirical presentation of Ben Nevis of "Glenbogle" in *The Monarch of the Glen* (1941) and other Highland comedies. A stubborn anglicised laird, resistant to change and blissfully ignorant of the realities of modern life taking place outside his castle, Ben Nevis cuts a ludicrous figure; only a very perverse reading could see Mackenzie as identifying essential Scottishness in his fictional characters. It is noticeable that, like Munro who wrote historical novels as well as comic sketches, Mackenzie alternated between different fictional modes. Well before he discovered the strain for comedy he achieved critical success with *Sinister Street* (1913), a novel that was admired by Henry James and banned by the circulating libraries. Later on,

almost contemporary with the Highland comedies, he produced the
vast saga *The Four Winds of Love* (1937–1945). The ability to exploit
– or manipulate – a popular taste whilst exploring alternative artistic
modes perhaps suggests that Kailyard could be an enabling as well
disabling legacy for subsequent authors. Significantly, MacDiarmid
contrasted the comedy of Mackenzie and others to "the antics of Sir
Harry Lauder and the other Scotch 'coamics'" (MacDiarmid [1943]
1994: 52).

MacDiarmid's conception of Kailyard also helped forge the link
with non-literary forms of popular culture. As Colin McArthur writes:
"the immense popular success of the Kailyard novels in the UK and
the USA ensured that they would rapidly become cinema fodder"
(McArthur 1982: 42). Film adaptations of Maclaren's *Beside the
Bonnie Brier Bush* (1921) – actually based mainly on *Kate Carnegie* –
Crockett's *The Lilac Sunbonnet* (1922) and four versions of Barrie's
The Little Minister consolidated the impact of their work on cultural
representations of Scotland. The international taste for Scottish subject
matter also contributed to the development of Scottish music hall.
Although the tradition of the "Scotch comic" had developed in the
1880s it was not until after the Kailyard boom that Scottish performers
achieved success outside their native towns (Bruce 2000). The central
figure here is Sir Harry Lauder, whom MacDiarmid explicitly linked
to Kailyard on several occasions. In the *Scottish Nation* he referred to
"our rhymsters of the Kailyaird-cum-Harry-Lauder school"
(MacDiarmid 1996: 97) and when "Introducing Hugh M'Diarmid" in
The Scottish Chapbook he positioned himself against "the grotesque
clothes of the Canny-Sandy cum Kirriemuir Elder cum Harry Lauder
cult" (MacDiarmid 1992: 12). The link was more than casual.
Lauder's use of Scots, the subject matter of his songs, his mixing of
humour and piety, his nostalgic appeal to a transatlantic audience and
his close identification with the British political establishment were all
things that MacDiarmid had identified with Barrie, Crockett and
Maclaren.

Lauder served his apprenticeship in music halls throughout
Scotland but moved to London at the turn of the century and made
successful yearly tours of the United States from 1907. He was
enthusiastically received in America, recording that "the expatriated

Caledonians sure rallied to my support during my early trips to the Dollar land" (Lauder 1922: 158). That Lauder paraded a fabricated Scottishness to his expatriated audiences – and believed in that Scottishness – is evident by his remark that "the folks in New Zealand are more Scottish than the Scots themselves" (Lauder 1922: 175). His tours led to him becoming an "unofficial ambassador of Britain" and during the war he was used as political propaganda, lecturing to Americans on his war experiences as well as entertaining the troops at home and on the western front (Lauder 1922: 157, 195). His book *A Minstrel in France* (1918) documents his involvement in the war effort which concluded with the financing of a fund for maimed Scottish soldiers and sailors.

Such identification with the British political establishment would have appalled MacDiarmid but his main quarrel was with Lauder's use of Scots. Although Lauder saw Burns, Hogg and Tannahill as his "heroes", his songs drew mainly on established music hall traditions. He was the first "Scotch comic" to achieve lasting fame outside Scotland and he put his success down to his resolution to "sing my songs in English ... *but with a Scottish accent*" (Lauder 1922: 96). As a result it was easy for MacDiarmid to link his songs with the Kailyard tradition of poetry, and in a review of John Buchan's anthology *The Northern Muse* he complained that "the Kailyard and Harry Lauder schools" had set a "false trail" for the use of Scots in poetry (MacDiarmid 1996: 187).

Lauder's songs mixed humour with sentiment; he considered "Scottish sentiment" a "tremendously real and eternally vibrant thing" and he liked to end each performance with a serious – usually religious – song or speech (Lauder 1922: 256). In this, however, he was breaking with the tradition of Scottish music hall to which he had himself contributed before he turned to London. His songs were sanitised for southern audiences, cleansed of those bawdy elements that "went down well in the 'rough-houses' in the Glasgow halls" (Bruce 2000: 36). Ivor Brown criticises Lauder on this point:

The Scots comedians when they stay at home work with homely jest; they do not exploit in Pantomime or Summer Show the kilted absurdity so dear to the English. They draw on the stuff of Scottish town-life [...]. They broaden the authentic, of course, but they do not debase. (Brown 1952: 145)

In the same book Brown defends Barrie and Maclaren but he considers "the music-hall Kailyard" to be "the most tiresome of all the 'quaint Scot' forms of nonsense" (Brown 1952: 146).

Throughout his career Lauder was accused of extravagant self-publicity. He denied this in his memoirs but admitted that he had "never been under any misapprehension as to the publicity value of my own kith and kin throughout the world (Lauder 1922: 174). His apparent keenness to exploit shallow notions of national character led to the criticism that, like Kailyard fiction, his performance validated a false image of Scotland. As one commentator has written: "The image of Scotland which Harry Lauder so assiduously propagated during the Edwardian period was irritatingly trite and trivial where it was not downright spurious" (Hill 1976: 59). All of these attributes are what led MacDiarmid to write that "Harry Lauderisation is the only policy the majority of Anglo-Scots and Englishmen can conceive as appropriate to Scotland (MacDiarmid 1996: 59). The fact that Lauder fitted exactly into MacDiarmid's transformed conception of Kailyard goes a long way to explaining why the term became indelibly associated with popular culture in the twentieth century.

As a form of popular entertainment, music hall can be grouped together with popular magazines and comic strips. The association between Kailyard and popular culture has been developed more than anything else by the impact of popular newspapers and magazines, especially those produced by the firm of D.C. Thomson, "the newspaper Mussolini of Dundee" (McAleer 1992: 162). George Blake wrote in 1951:

It is even more to the point that one of the most highly-successful and efficient periodical publishing firms in Scotland, the Thomson-Leng firm of Dundee, flourishes largely by the careful cultivation of the Kailyard strain. (Blake 1951: 85)

The Thomson firm dates from 1886. Publishers of the *Dundee Courier*, the *Weekly News* and other papers, Thomson acquired a controlling interest in the rival Dundee firm of John Leng & Co in 1906. Leng was publisher of the mass-market newspaper the *People's Journal* and the popular weekly the *People's Friend*. Whereas in the nineteenth century these papers were vital organs of the Scottish democracy (Donaldson 1986), in their twentieth century incarnation they have been viewed as the worst excesses of a politically reactionary popular culture. This is especially true of the *Friend*, which cashed in on the growing demand for romance fiction and published scores of serial stories by Annie S. Swan. The *People's Friend* had a loyal Scottish readership and the *Sunday Post* – another of Thomson's publications – got an even greater backing. Described by Christopher Harvie as a "Kailyard gold-mine"(Harvie 1998b: 152) and by Michael Gardiner as "classic latter-day kailyard" (Gardiner 2005: 182), the *Sunday Post* retains a large circulation within Scotland. The reason for its association with Kailyard lies partly in its lowbrow popular appeal and right-wing politics but mainly as a result of its successful comic strips, "Oor Wullie" and "The Broons". These icons of Scottish culture first appeared in a comic supplement in 1936. Both strips use a form of dialect. "Oor Wullie" charts the pranks and adventures of a harmless young tearaway – a loose connection might be made with Crockett's *Cleg Kelly* – whilst "The Broons" follows the domestic adventures of a large, loyal, working-class family, who live in a flat in a tenement block in an unnamed city. As Michael Gardiner judges, the Broons "started out as D.C. Thomson's idea of the typical Scottish family, but they have remained unchanged as the world changes around them" (Gardiner 2005: 182). It is this representation of an unchanging world and the idealised portrayal of community life that, together with their mass consumption, has led to the identification of these comic strips as Kailyard. Whilst earlier generations might have recognised in "The Broons" much that was typical of a certain type of Scottish family, the passage of time made their habits and values seem outmoded and sentimental. Yet whilst the strips have been seen by some modern commentators as having a pernicious impact on Scottish life, they demand to be investigated more carefully. As with Kailyard fiction there has been a tendency to prioritise representation over issues of genre. "Oor Wullie" and "The Broons" may be caricatures, but it is in the nature of cartoons to be so; and, like *Wee Macgreegor* and Harry Lauder, some consideration must be given to the rhetoric of humour, which historically has always been an important part of Scottish culture.

In 1961 Maurice Lindsay judged the readers of *The Sunday Post* and *The People's Friend* as "the modern Kailyarders, for whom current international standards mean nothing at all and who only want to escape into a fanciful past" (Lindsay 1961: 121). Such an attitude indicates the maintenance of MacDiarmid's revulsion at popular taste and anticipates the lines upon which criticism of Scottish nationalism would take place in the seventies and eighties.

III

MacDiarmid's construction of the term made it inevitable that Kailyard came to refer to the whole Victorian period in Scottish literature. The most important writer in this context is George Blake, whose book *Barrie and the Kailyard School* (1951) has had a major influence on the understanding both of Kailyard and of Barrie. As I noted in my introduction, despite the title, Blake's book is not really about Barrie but is a lament for Scotland's failure to respond imaginatively to industrial life in the nineteenth century:

> The bulk of the Scottish people were thus condemned to a purely urban, sophisticated, and mainly ugly sort of life during the nineteenth century. A really dramatic, often beastly revolution was taking place. And what had the Scottish novelists to say about it? The answer is – nothing, or as nearly nothing as makes no matter. They might as well have been living in Illyria, as in the agonised country of their birth. (Blake 1951: 9)

To Blake – the pioneer of the twentieth-century Industrial novel – this was a "massive evasion" and a "betrayal of the realities of Scottish life". Blake drew contrasts with the course of English literature, noting that "industry and its effects were the themes of gifted writers from Gaskell to D.H. Lawrence" (Blake 1951: 10). In Scotland, by contrast, "the industrial fret was completely ignored":

> The Scots storyteller either followed Scott and Stevenson through the heather with a claymore at his belt, or he lingered round the bonnie brier bush, telling sweet, amusing little stories of bucolic intrigue as seen through the windows of the Presbyterian manse. (Blake 1951: 13)

Blake's assessment of the period after the death of Scott is not unusual. Earlier writers had made similar judgements. J.M. Reid argued in 1945 that the generation of Scottish writers after Scott "closed their eyes to the life of the cities where most of them wrote, and even in dealing with the life of the countryside they preferred to ignore most of what had happened since Scott's death" (Reid 1945: 13). Edwin Muir also regarded the Kailyard as an escape from industrialism:

> The flight to the Kailyard was a flight to Scotland's past, to a country which had existed before industrialism [...] To anyone living in Glasgow or Dundee even the Kailyard must have seemed heaven [...] It was the increasing bestiality of industrial Scotland that turned the countryside of fiction into a *Schlaraffenland*, and made Scottish literature for a time mainly a literature written by sentimental ministers. (Muir [1935] 1979: 68)

In his study Blake develops this argument into outright criticism. Whilst his assessments of Barrie, Crockett and Maclaren are not without merit or substance, they are conditioned by his assumptions of the novelist's responsibilities:

> We expect him, in his task of creating "the willing suspension of disbelief", to be something of a social historian as well. His work must be to some extent what is nowadays called "documentary" in character. (Blake 1951: 7)

In an argument where it is stated that "novelists are the reporters and colourists of history" it is inevitable that the author of *Peter Pan* gets short shrift. It is arguable that the misrepresentation of Barrie within the context of Kailyard and Scottish literature can be attributed to an accident in literary publishing. Blake's book is not really about Barrie but it was included in a series called "The English Novelists". Putting aside the troublesome adjective, this presumably required the author to include the name of a novelist in his title. Indeed, Blake spares Barrie from the deeper cuts of his hatchet job, repeatedly reminding his reader of the quality of Barrie's writing and his achievement in the theatre. He also suggests that George Douglas Brown and Barrie "were not so terribly far apart in their attitude to the peasant Scot as some may think" (Blake 1951: 97). Circumstances demanded, however, that Barrie's name be put on the title page and as a consequence he became the representative figure for the failure of the

whole of Victorian Scotland to produce a novel based on industrial
life.

Blake's book has had a massive influence on the way Barrie's
work has been understood within the context of Scottish literature.
More than any other study it has been responsible for tying Barrie up
with the critical context Kailyard. That context has had a peculiar
effect on the way Barrie's work is positioned within literary history.
Canons are inevitably and necessarily selective but it is unusual to
find one that consciously excludes an author's best work and includes
his weakest. In *The Mainstream Companion to Scottish Literature*,
Trevor Royle offers separate entries for two of Barrie's works: *Auld
Licht Idylls* and *The Admirable Crichton*. Barrie's more ambitious
novels, and his most famous work – *Peter Pan* – do not form a major
part of "Scotland's own very distinctive voice as reflected in its
national literature" (Royle 1993: 8). Virtually all histories or surveys
of Scottish literature have followed the same path. Although the
Tommy novels are briefly discussed in Roderick Watson's one-volume
history, the chronological table at the back of that book represents
Barrie's fiction only by *Auld Licht Idylls* and *A Window in Thrums*
(*Peter Pan* is the only other work listed). Similarly, the most recent
full-scale survey by Marshall Walker lists these three texts in addition
to *The Little Minister* and *Margaret Ogilvy*. So far as Scottish literary
history is concerned, the *Tommy* novels and *The Little White Bird*
have no place. Contextualised in a negative paradigm, Barrie's fate is
sealed before his best work is even considered.

The misrepresentation of Barrie is not the only consequence of
the mapping of the Victorian period as Kailyard. The critical criteria
embedded in the term influenced the narrative of Scottish literary
history that was constructed in the twentieth century. It led to the
diagnosis of Scottish literature in the period after the death of Sir
Walter Scott as one of decline or failure. In the words of David Craig:

In the mid-19th century the Scottish literary tradition – the writing by Scotsmen of
fiction and poetry of more than parochial interest – paused; from 1825 to 1880 there is
next to nothing worth attention. (Craig 1961: 273)

Kurt Wittig also concluded that, apart from the isolated achievements
of Hugh Miller and William Alexander, "the less said about the two

generations after Scott the better" (Wittig 1955: 254); and William Power was in agreement, arguing that "With the deaths of Scott, Hogg, Galt and Wilson, Scots literature fell at once from a national to a provincial level" (Power 1935: 117). This diagnosis has for long shaped understanding of Victorian Scottish culture. In the fourth volume of the *Edinburgh History of Scotland* (1968), William Ferguson argues that "Loss of confidence led to a virtual collapse of Scottish culture" in the nineteenth century as "literature degenerated into mawkish 'kailyard' parochialism and painting into 'ben and glen' romanticism" (Fergusson 1968: 317). The same argument underpins the structure of the Aberdeen University Press *History of Scottish Literature* (1987-9). The nineteenth-century volume in that series begins with a chapter by Paul H. Scott, whose first words rehearse the standard reading of the period after the death of Scott:

The late 1830s mark one of the most obvious and drastic turning points in the literary history of Scotland. Before lay a long period of high achievement: Ramsay, Fergusson and Burns, the Gaelic poets of the eighteenth century, the philosophers and historians of the Enlightenment, Scott, Galt and Hogg. Afterwards there was a loss of cohesion and self-confidence, a decline which lasted about 50 years. (Scott 1988: 13)

The fact that both Scott and Craig date the revival to 1880 – i.e. *before* the fiction of Barrie, Crockett and Maclaren – is an indication of the way that the work of these three writers is being used to open up a larger debate about the trajectory of Scottish literary history.

This reading of Victorian Scottish literature's evasion or failure proceeds directly from the critical preoccupations that had been built into Kailyard by MacDiarmid and Blake. The issues of false tradition and national misrepresentation underpin David Craig's "social history of literature" *Scottish Literature and the Scottish People 1680–1830* from which I have already quoted. Craig adopts a Marxist approach, arguing that "no literature can exist without embodying the human nature and habits of life actually there in the country it comes from" (Craig 1961: 72). He sets himself the task of bringing to light "the basic issues – questions of real of fake idiom, ample or cramped culture – which make up the 'social history of literature'" (Craig 1961: 12). Inevitably, nineteenth-century Scottish literature emerges as fake because it fails to reflect prevailing social conditions. Like

Blake, Craig sees Kailyard fiction as the culmination of a century-long
tradition of literature that "recoiled, immersing itself in the country
ways" at the very moment when Scotland "grew into a modern town-
centred nation" (Craig 1961: 145). Discussing the line of poetry
leading to and from Robert Burns, he argues:

Appreciation of this line, which is mainly comic, was for long debased into a relish
for the "Kailyaird" – sly farce or nostalgic escapism in which social life is brought
exclusively inside the range of country ways and values, and these values (as in S.R.
Crockett, J.M. Barrie, or Iain [*sic*] Maclaren) become more and more unreal as the
main initiative of the nation sets in from the towns. (Craig 1961: 72)

As ever, Barrie, Crockett and Maclaren are brought in to illustrate a
discussion of the whole of nineteenth-century Scottish writing. The
consequence of this pattern is that their work is assessed in so far as it
represents a whole period and a whole culture. Ignoring for the
moment the fact that Crockett and Maclaren wrote some stories based
in the city, the country values of their work are only unreal in so far as
they represent Scotland as a whole. In this kind of criticism, the
individual writer becomes a part standing for the whole. Kailyard
values are "unreal", "fake", not truly Scottish, because they do not
reflect the values of the whole of Scotland; they do not embody a
whole culture. David Craig's conclusion is that this can only mean
that Scottish literature in its native tradition ceases to exist: "the end of
the 19th century was reached and still an aware Scotsman could not
feel that his country had found its literature" (Craig 1961: 148).

In *The Scots Literary Tradition* (1940, 1962), John Speirs
reaches the same conclusion. Although his book is an account of
literature written in the Scots language, Speirs includes a discussion of
The House with the Green Shutters. A preface to the 1962 edition of
his book explains why:

I wanted to include a book to represent nineteenth-century Scotland – or, more
specifically, to indicate some of the things that may have gone wrong with nineteenth-
century Scotland and that might explain why it did not achieve a literature. (Speirs
1962: 19)

What follows is an account of "the clarity of the social criticism"
offered by Brown's novel, and Speirs' implies that it is only when a

literary tradition offers "social criticism" that it could be said to exist – to have been "achieved."

Cairns Craig has argued that, in its emphasis on tradition, David Craig's study typifies the approach taken to Scottish literature in the twentieth century. As he notes, in constructing his story "as the story of Scotland's loss of tradition" (Craig 1996: 17), David Craig was responding to the cultural parameters developed both by MacDiarmid and by Edwin Muir. Although they disagreed about the remedy, MacDiarmid and Muir both diagnosed the problem with Scottish literature in terms of tradition, concluding that in the nineteenth century the Scottish tradition had run down. Whereas MacDiarmid believed that "the proper business of any Scottish imaginative writer is to found or to further a Scottish – not an English – tradition" (MacDiarmid 1995: 33), Muir argued that "a Scottish writer who wishes to achieve some approximation to completeness has no choice except to absorb the English tradition" (Muir 1936: 15). As Cairns Craig points out, however, the understanding of Victorian Scottish literature as fake, unreal or unachieved depends upon a comparison with the English tradition, and such a comparison negates the possible significance of Scottish cultural traditions by assessing writers according to an external – or alien – model of culture or tradition, viz. Blake's comparisons with Gaskell and Lawrence. Furthermore, as Robert Crawford has argued, the construction of the tradition of English literature since the eighteenth century owes much to cultural impulses from outside England including, not least, Scotland (Crawford 1992). Such revisions to the critical parameters of Scottish literature have led in recent years to a loosening of the association between Kailyard and the Victorian period. In the four decades that followed on from Blake's landmark study of 1951, however, that association remained strong.

On one level, the criticism of Blake, David Craig and Speirs is simply a matter of uneasiness with certain literary forms. Craig's assessment of both Scott and Stevenson reveals his distrust of romance:

If Scott had been more aware of the society around him, he might have been less prone to the irresponsibility of romance-writing and plot-making; and a proper awareness need not have precluded a deep feeling for the past. (Craig 1961: 155-6)

Such a view is comparable to Blake's judgement that the novelist must be "documentary" in character. But the suspicion over romance forms part of a larger argument about Scotland's constructed self-image. In an essay on Robert Louis Stevenson, Andrew Noble argues that "Scottish identity has largely been since the eighteenth century a thing of synthetic symbols", a "policy" of which the Kailyard "with its soporific pastoralism was a central feature" (Noble 1983: 150). This argument involves consideration of a wide range of material, not least the poems of James Macpherson's Ossian and the novels of Sir Walter Scott but once again Kailyard is seen as the summation of a long tradition in Scottish writing that allegedly deals in the synthetic and the fake. MacDiarmid's construction of Kailyard as a term indicating a false tradition allowed for the development of this critical model; it enabled the construction of a binary opposition between real and fake within which to assess literary and cultural representations of Scotland. At the end of his book on eighteenth-century Scottish literature, Kenneth Simpson argues that because of the cultural effects of the Union Scotland failed to develop the central tenets of Romanticism:

when the first stirrings of Romanticism began to be felt Scotland was no longer a nation, and as a people she was already preoccupied with an image of herself that was rooted in a distant and largely unreal past. Ironically, Romanticism did much to encourage just such sentimental nationalism. Only in Scotland did Romanticism help to guide people along the way to, not self-realisation and self-advancement, but a predominantly self-willed stereotyping. (Simpson 1988: 9)

The important phrase in that sentence is "self-willed." Scottish writers conspire in the promotion of an image of themselves that is divorced from reality and are predisposed to favour the fake idiom over the real because there is no real tradition or culture to support them, only a set of synthetic symbols.

IV

The writings of MacDiarmid and Blake have also had a major influence on those critics who have employed Kailyard in wider discussions of Scottish culture. In one of the most influential books published in the last quarter of the twentieth century, Tom Nairn used the term to help structure his analysis of Scottish nationalism, figured in what he projected as *The Break-Up of Britain* (1977, 1981). Attempting to account for the failure of nationalism in the nineteenth century, Nairn diagnosed the problem of what he called "cultural sub-nationalism" – a neurosis at the heart of Scottish identity. The two most prominent strands in this neurosis were the connected phenomena of "cultural emigration and the Kailyard School"; underlying them both was the "significant popular cultural-reality" of "vulgar tartanry" (Nairn [1977] 1981: 156). It is from Nairn that the association between Kailyard and tartanry – which became almost indelible in the last two decades of the twentieth century – takes root.

Nairn's use of the term opens up two important issues that dominated critical discussion about Scotland in the last quarter of the century – the function of myth and the issue of indigenous cultural traditions. Taking his lead from David Craig, as well as historians such as William Ferguson, Nairn draws attention to the "intellectual emigration" in the nineteenth century that emptied the country of its literary talent and left only a "rootless vacuum" and a "great 'absence'" (Nairn [1977] 1981: 156–7). Into this absence "increasingly from the 1820s onwards, until it became a vast tide washing into the present day, was the Scots 'Kailyard' tradition" (Nairn [1977] 1981: 157). This Kailyard tradition was a false tradition because it evaded reality and dealt in myths and because it was the product of an émigré vision. Nairn notes that "Thrums", "Drumtochty" and "Tannochbrae" – the location of A.J. Cronin's Dr Finlay stories – "were all creations of émigrés" and were produced "very largely for a foreign reading public" (Nairn [1977] 1981: 160). Although it is not quite accurate to see Thrums as the creation of an émigré – Barrie wrote most of his Thrums stories in Kirriemuir and returned to his native home during the writing of *The Little Minister* – an essential part of the criticism of Kailyard fiction is that the image of Scotland presented in these works is compromised for the sake of an outside audience. Edwin Muir considered that "the one thing that clearly distinguishes" the fiction of Barrie, Crockett and Maclaren and that of Gunn, Gibbon or MacColla was that the older writers intended their Scottish characters "primarily, like Harry Lauder's humour, for foreign consumption. They were designed for the popular English taste; they were exports" (Muir 1934: 147). By strengthening the understanding of Kailyard as a false émigré vision, and by making it central to political arguments about the trajectory of Scottish history, Nairn helped establish a focus on the question of indigenous cultural traditions that was developed in the 1980s and 1990s.

Related to this point is Nairn's construction of Kailyard as a synonym for myth. Like Blake, Nairn laments the failure of nineteenth-century Scottish writers to attend to contemporary life: "They did not ponder mightily and movingly upon the reality of 19th century Scotland – on the great Glasgow bourgeoisie of mid-century and onwards, the new class conflicts, the continuing tragedy of the Highlands" (Nairn [1977] 1981: 157). At the time when Scotland should have been orchestrating for itself a place on "the great and varied stage of European nationalism" (Nairn [1977] 1981: 144), all that it had to offer was Kailyard – a "surrogate nationalism", a "sub-culture" which Scotland has produced for itself:

It was a kind of self-imposed, very successful *Kulturkampf*, one which naturally appears as "neurosis" in relation to standard models of development. Because of its success the elements of "pathology" inherent in it have become embedded as modern "national traits". (Nairn [1977] 1981: 153)

This is a replication of MacDiarmid's idea of a false, apolitical tradition which modern Scots misrecognise as the real tradition. Although Nairn considered the Kailyard's "major triumphs" to have occurred at the end of the century, and judged that Barrie remained "the master of the *genre*", he nevertheless argued that Kailyardism "arose before 1880" and continued to prosper in the present day in television series such as *Dr Finlay's Casebook* and the "cabbage-patch publishing mafia, the D.C. Thomson gang" (Nairn [1977] 1981: 157-8). In an earlier essay on Scottish nationalism, Nairn had concluded with the words: "As far as I'm concerned, Scotland will be reborn the day the last minister is strangled with the last copy of the *Sunday Post*" (Nairn 1970: 54). Here two great emblems of Kailyard were seen as impediments to national self-definition.

Nairn's employment of the Kailyard term forms part of a Marxist interpretation of national and cultural development that has been challenged by several writers, notably Craig Beveridge and Ronald Turnbull in *The Eclipse of Scottish Culture* (1989). Yet as Cairns Craig wrote in 1996, the argument of *The Break-Up of Britain* "still forms the essential substratum of much of the analysis of Scotland's cultural situation and the nature of its identity" (Craig 1996: 88). Chiefly as a result of Nairn's book, Kailyard came to signify a particular diagnosis of Scottish culture that spread across academic disciplines in the last quarter of the century. Political and cultural commentators set out to expose the way Scotland had conspired to represent itself through distorting myths. Kailyard became a convenient label to sum up this distorting impulse and was often used in arguments about the cultural effects of the Union. In the conclusion to his book *The Strange Death of Scottish History*, Marinell Ash referred to the state of historiography in Victorian Scotland as "a succession of historical kailyards" (Ash 1980: 152). What he meant was that the narrative of Scottish history in the nineteenth century had been constructed as one of failure – Scottish culture, as a discrete entity independent of British culture, did not exist. Coming one year after the devolution referendum, Ash's book had an important influence on the movement to recover the narratives of Scottish history from beneath – or beyond – British historiography. In 1992 Michael Fry endorsed Ash's view when he criticised the Whig interpretations of Scottish history that were promulgated by late nineteenth century historians. Such writers, Fry argued, had condemned Scottish historical culture to be "locked for safekeeping in the 'kailyard'" (Fry 1992: 83).

The use of the term to signify a general tendency towards distortion or evasion allowed commentators with different agendas to use Kailyard to structure their own particular discussion. In *The Rousing of the Scottish Working Classes*, the Marxist historian James Young linked the Kailyard to the failure of the Scottish labour movement in the late nineteenth century. To Young, the bourgeois nationalist movement of the turn of the century "isolated themselves from the mainstream of Scottish life" by failing to recognise that "the

Kailyard school of novelists and comedians" was the logical outcome of the class-based Scottish Enlightenment:

> The "kailyarders" inspired the continuity of propagandist images of a Scottish society as a rural idyll remote from strife or class conflict [...] the dominance of these images in Kailyard novels, together with the systematic indoctrination of working people in church and school, made it exceptionally difficult for the labour movement to popularise their quite moderate critique of the capitalist system. (Young 1979: 168)

Such a view of the Kailyard texts depends heavily on Maclaren's story of Burnbrae discussed in Chapter 4 – if it depends directly on anything. It is hard to believe that one short story would do so much damage. Young offers no definition of Kailyard, nor does he link the term to a body of texts or authors. His use of the term depends on the set of assumptions that, by the late 1970s, had been built into it.

In an essay published one year previously, Young had deplored "the whole Kailyard myth" of the past from which "modern Scots [are] struggling to rescue the country" (Young 1978: 3). The synonymity of Kailyard and myth meant that the term formed part of the Scotch Myths debate that dominated Scottish culture in the 1980s. Within this debate, Kailyard came to be used interchangeably with tartanry to indicate a false historical and cultural consciousness that blighted the nation and impeded meaning self-definition. The failure of the 1979 referendum bred various analyses of Scottish culture which set out to expose the myths that informed Scottish identity. The most significant of these was *Scotch Myths*, an exhibition of 1981 devised by Barbara and Murray Grigor, Subtitled "An Exploration of Scotchness", the programme described the exhibition as

> an exploration and enquiry into the residue of fatigued romanticism and home-grown caricature, which blossomed in the period before the first world war, but is still very much alive today [...]. Our principal aim is to question a culture that continues to portray itself in distorted national stereotypes.[3]

---

[3] Quotations are taken from a copy of the exhibition programme held in St Andrews University Library (shelfmark StAN1470.C8).

These national stereotypes were shown to have descended from the cultural impact of the poems of Ossian and the novels of Sir Walter Scott, but the exhibition broke new ground by focusing on the representation of Scotland in forms of popular culture and advertising. The emphasis on picture postcards and food-product labels showed up the extent to which the stereotyped images had been deployed in mass markets and, very likely, soaked up by an international audience. The growth of picture postcards dates from the 1890s – exactly contemporary with the application of the Kailyard term – and indicates how developments in media at the turn of the century contributed to the construction of an image of Scotland that was exported to an international audience. The exhibition showed that the vital moment for the development of this stereotyped international image was the early years of the twentieth century; the years when Harry Lauder – whose presence was a leitmotiv in the exhibition – was parading an image of Scotland on the transatlantic stage. One exhibit depicted a music hall scene on Broadway from 1907:

In the music hall, the tartan of Walter Scottland and Balmorality is still in evidence but transferred from red haired giants to knock-kneed dwarfs and transvestites who exhibit the national traits of mean, drinking, fighting Scots. The bastard offspring of Kailyard and romance. It is caricature, of course. A picture of the Scots which owed little to the often grim reality of life in the urban wastelands of bonny Scotia.

The exhibition prompted considerable debate including a whole forum in the *Bulletin of Scottish Politics*, which included contributions from Lindsay Paterson and Paul H. Scott. Paterson saw in the exhibition a "grotesque amalgam of the romantic and the kailyard [...] a whole array of mythic symbols, of dubious national character traits, of false social experience" which, like all myths, "operated as an ideology to help people to adjust to their environment" (Paterson 1981: 69–70). Like many other commentators, Paterson concluded that what was needed to build "a genuinely decentralised democracy" in Scotland was:

a national self-image that might inspire social change rather than offer escape from its urgent necessity: It requires a national ideology – a view of Scotland – that engages with social reality, rather than with a fabulous Highland fairy tale [...]. And it requires a national movement that has its roots not in the cheap distortions of the tartan Myths

(part of which is the xenophobia of the kailyard), but rather in a positive aspiration to
a self-confident, realistic national awareness. (Paterson 1981: 71)

Like the Kailyard wall in *A Drunk Man*, the Kailyard, with its
xenophobic fear of anything outside its own patch, is here cast as a
restrictive force, imprisoning Scotland in the Union.

The association of Kailyard with tartanry, and the construction of
both terms as the embodiment of Scotland's distorting myths, was
taken up in the discussion of Scottish cinema that developed in the
early 1980s. The pioneering collection of essays *Scotch Reels* (1982),
which was accompanied by an affiliated three-day discussion of
Scottish film culture at the Edinburgh International Film Festival, has
been identified as "the most influential critical and cultural analysis"
of Scottish cinema (Petrie 2000: 2). Taking its impulse from the
writings of Tom Nairn and the Scotch Myths debate, *Scotch Reels*
used the terms "Tartanry and Kailyard" as the defining contexts within
which to initiate debates over Scottish film culture which hitherto had
lacked   any   "self-definition"   (McArthur   1982a: 1).   As   in
MacDiarmid's criticism, Kailyard is here being used as a critical term
to help define an aspect of Scottish culture.

Employing Nairn's construction of Tartanry and Kailyard as
signifying "deformed" and "pathological" discourses of Scotland, the
Scotch Reels critics set out to expose "the seriously stunting effects
Tartanry and Kailyard have had on the emergence of alternative
discourses more adequate to the task of dealing with the reality of
Scottish life" (McArthur 1982a: 3). The lack of "alternative traditions
of   representation   with   comparable   power"   meant   that   any
representation of Scotland on film was drawn "towards the armature
of images, characters and stories making up tartanry and Kailyard"
(McArthur 1982b: 45). The criticism turns on matters of form,
ideology and popular consciousness. In several essays in *Scotch Reels*
and elsewhere, Colin McArthur developed a Marxist critique of
Scottish cinema that used the term Kailyard as a synonym for myth.
From this Marxist perspective, Kailyard is presented as a discourse
that serves to mask the real conditions of class oppression and social
and economic life. In a response to the Scotch Myths exhibition,
McArthur had concluded, in a phrase borrowed from Althusser, that

Scottish people were "[i]nterpellated within an armature of discourses of which Tartanry and Kailyard are the most important at the level of popular consciousness" (McArthur 1981: 21). In *Scotch Reels* his conception of Kailyard film is similar to Ian Campbell's understanding of Kailyard literature; he labels as "Kailyard" those films which fail to subvert, or render problematic, existing conceptions about Scotland (McArthur 1982b: 63). In contrast to the "modernist sensibility which stresses play, paradox and contradiction", Kailyard films are seen to have "eschewed the problematic and the contradictory in favour of the celebratory" (McArthur 1982b: 64, 58).

In McArthur's conception of the term, Kailyard discourses seek to maintain the *status quo* through offering viewers the illusion of a real identity. As he writes in a separate study of *The Maggie* (1953):

it is the essence of ideology that what has been historically constructed appears natural and timeless. ...the tradition of Kailyard – the dominant discourse of *The Maggie* – is not a system of representation traceable in history but "the way things are" in Scotland. (McArthur 1983a: 11)

As in MacDiarmid's use of the term, Kailyard signifies a misunderstanding and a misrecognition of the real identity of Scotland and Scottish culture. McArthur interprets *The Maggie* as a text that disables political awareness: "In true Kailyard style, what is not achievable at the level of political struggle is attainable in the delirious Scots imagination" (McArthur 1982b: 47–8).

The conception of Kailyard developed by the *Scotch Reels* critics and the assessment of individual films was driven by a political agenda that was both nationalist and Marxist. In a chapter on Scottish television, John Caughie demanded the mobilisation of "positive images of Scotland [...] as the basis for political action" (Caughie 1982: 116). The *Scotch Reels* critics argued that the myths of Tartanry and Kailyard needed to be deconstructed and dismantled and alternative discourses investigated and mobilised. Colin McArthur drew attention to "ostensibly progressive and 'realistic' feature films" such as *Floodtide* (1949), a film based on a novel by the Kailyard's harshest critic, George Blake, which engages with modern, industrial Scotland. To McArthur, the film's attempt "to define the meaning of

Scotland in relation to the Clyde" was "extremely progressive" (McArthur 1982b: 52). Similarly, in a chapter on Scottish television, John Caughie suggested that:

> To break with the Tartanry/Kailyard tradition would involve an active engagement with other traditions and other versions of history: the traditions, for example, of the literature and theatre based in working-class experience which, since the twenties, have seemed to offer the only real consistent basis for a Scottish national culture. (Caughie 1982: 121)

Scotch Reels prompted considerable debate and counter-debate and sparked concerns that a new Kailyard myth might come to replace the old. As Cairns Craig wrote, in the forum "'Scotch Reels' and After":

> What is worrying in the contemporary situation is the way that the death-throes of industrial West-Central Scotland have become the touchstone of authenticity for our culture. [...] That decaying industrial world – Peter McDougall's plays inhabit them, as does William McIlvanney's *Laidlaw* and the Jimmy Boyle myth – remakes the emblems of tartanry and kailyard in a new form. (Craig 1983: 9)

For Craig this was an indication that "the cultural dilemma that produced Tartanry and Kailyard continues unabated" and in his book *Out of History* (1996) he examines this dilemma in the context of theoretical debates over myth, authenticity and history. To be fair, the *Scotch Reels* critics had recognised this danger themselves. Colin McArthur had found fault with the representation of Scottishness in *Floodtide* even when acknowledging its "progressive" intentions and later acknowledged that in Clydesidism there was another discourse to be put alongside "the other pernicious discourses [...] within which representations of the Scots have been constructed" (McArthur 1983b: 2).

Like Tom Nairn, the *Scotch Reels* critics linked the issue of myth to that of cultural emigration and the failure of Scottish cultural institutions. The discourses of Kailyard and Tartanry were seen as having had "a cruelly stunting effect on Scots actors which, in terms of the growth of individual talents, could only be remedied by working outside Scotland and within different, non-Scottish discourses" (McArthur 1982b: 66). The failure of Scotland to grow anything more than cauld kail pushed Scots outside the confines of their own yard and in so doing negated their national identity. On the other side of the same coin was the important argument that "the dominant filmic representations" of Scotland "have been articulated elsewhere". Colin McArthur complained that:

the indigenous Scottish institutions which exist to foster film culture have never articulated as a priority the helping of Scottish film-makers towards the discourses which would effectively counter the dominant ones (McArthur 1982b: 58).

This argument compares with MacDiarmid's criticism that Scottish literature lacked support from an indigenous periodical and publishing culture. The *Scotch Reels* critics saw the failure of Scottish film culture in the same way as MacDiarmid saw the failure of Scottish poetry – as a failure of cultural institutions. This issue of indigenous cultural production would re-emerge in the discussions over devolution at the end of the 1990s.

Analysis of Scottish film has moved on since *Scotch Reels*, and in the next major study of the subject, *A Scottish Film Book*, John Caughie acknowledged the flaws inherent in the original project, particularly the application of kailyard as a homogenous discourse (Caughie 1990). More recently, Duncan Petrie has produced a survey of *Scotland on Screen* that employs the familiar tropes of Kailyard, Tartanry and Clydesidism but which attempts to move away from the "profound negative connotations associated with them" (Petrie 2000: 8). The influence of the *Scotch Reels* analysis, however, was such that it strengthened the now almost ubiquitous use of the term Kailyard in Scottish culture to refer to a fake, regressive, parochial representation of Scotland that was inimical to authentic national expression. It also had the effect of making Kailyard the opposite of irony. By constructing Kailyard as a discourse that was unproblematic, unsubversive and celebratory, the *Scotch Reels* paved the way for subsequent critics to assess representations of Scots on film and television according to whether they celebrated or deconstructed Scottish myths. So, for example, one commentator can put one television series, *Dr Finlay's Casebook*, in the "kailyard frame", and excuse another, *Hamish Macbeth*, on account of its ironic, "postmodern" deployment of "high-tartanry and strategic kitsch" (Gardiner 2005: 179–80).

In the years after Scotch Myths and *Scotch Reels*, tartanry and Kailyard became almost interchangeable in cultural discourse. Christopher Harvie argued in 1988 that "Tartnary" attained its fullest extent in the shrewd marketing of the Kailyard authors of the 1890s" (Harvie 1988: 27–8). As David McCrone writes: "Two disparate cultural formations have combined into a hegemonic system which locks Scots into a sense of their own inferiority in the face of a powerful Anglo-British culture" (McCrone 1992: 186). Kailyard became even more ubiquitous a term and even more central to the critical idiom than it had under MacDiarmid's influence in the 1920s and 1930s.

V

In the 1990s, the Kailyard diagnosis of Scottish culture was questioned from a variety of disciplinary perspectives. The first major challenge to the interpretation of the Victorian period as Kailyard came a few years previously in William Donaldson's *Popular Literature in Victorian Scotland* (1986). Donaldson investigated the publication of imaginative literature – stories, sketches and serials – in local Scottish newspapers, specifically those in Aberdeen and Dundee. Although his study deals mainly with the period 1850–1880, he positions his argument against the fiction of Barrie, Crockett and Maclaren who stand as representatives for the period after 1832:

According to the prevailing view of Scottish culture, the nineteenth century after the death of Scott was a period of decline and failure, in which Scottish writers, recoiling from the spectre of industrialisation, immersed themselves in rural fantasy following Sir James Barrie, "Ian Maclaren" (Dr John Watson) and other writers of the "Kailyard School". The present study seeks to modify this view, suggesting that Scottish culture was (and is) a popular culture, and that its major vehicle during the period was not the London-dominated book trade, but the Scottish newspaper press, owned, written, and circulating within the country. (Donaldson 1986: xii)

The word "following" indicates the extent to which writers at the end of the century had come to stand for the period after 1850.

Donaldson's research challenges the Kailyard understanding of Victorian Scottish literature in several ways. He draws attention to thousands of novels serialised in the popular press, most of which were never republished in volume form. Most were set in the present and a considerable proportion dealt with urban life and the impact of industrialisation. Written in a vigorous Scots – "the language of the people" – the fiction contributed to a period of "resurgence, renewal and growth" in vernacular culture (Donaldson, 1986: 35, 71). All of these characteristics enable Donaldson to argue for a wholesale shift in perspective:

> On the whole popular fiction in Victorian Scotland is not overwhelmingly backward-looking; it is not obsessed by rural themes; it does not shrink from urbanisation or its problems; it is not idyllic in its approach; it does not treat the common people as comic or quaint. (Donaldson 1986: 149)

Most importantly of all, Donaldson argues that this newspaper market represents an indigenous Scottish culture and so challenges the view that Scottish culture was constructed by émigrés and was dependent upon the demands – and constraints – of an audience outside Scotland:

> At the same time as the Scottish bookmarket declined as a proportion of the total Anglo-American market, and the Scottish bourgeoisie became an all-UK London-centred middlebrow culture, there arose in Scotland a new publishing medium, controlled in Scotland, written in Scotland and selling in Scotland, and with it a whole new wave of popular novelists writing for a specifically Scottish audience. (Donaldson 1986: 99)

In this context Barrie, Crockett and Maclaren are seen as part of an Anglo-American book culture which was not popular in Scotland and was "substantially different from the basically realist thrust of contemporary Scottish fiction" (Donaldson 1986: 147).

As I have argued in relation to Crockett, the distinction Donaldson makes between the newspaper market in Scotland and the London-centred book market was beginning to break down by the end of the century when the different forms of publication – newspaper and book – were also coming together. Furthermore, as I showed in the previous chapter, Barrie, Crockett and Maclaren were not unpopular with Scottish readers and were in fact more popular in Scotland than contemporary English novelists. There is a wider issue here, which turns on Donaldson's rather wilful anticipation that in time the fiction of Barrie and Maclaren will "take its place where it belongs: in the intellectual annals of England and the United States" (Donaldson 1986: 147). If this argument were followed through into the twentieth century almost all of Scottish literature would be condemned to Anglo-American culture. As cultural representations of Scotland written by Scottish writers, the works of Barrie and Maclaren form part of the history of Scottish literature, even if they cannot be seen as a wholly indigenous culture. Representations of Scotland that are not exclusively produced and consumed within Scotland are still part of Scottish culture. Furthermore, even if Scottish Victorian culture did not wholly consist of Kailyard fiction, and was not wholly dependent upon its themes and values, the greater cultural authority of books ensured that it was this fiction that became representative and, as a result, impacted upon subsequent cultural patterns.

If some literary historians have been slow to respond to Donaldson's challenge to the canon – William Alexander is nowhere mentioned in Marshall Walker's survey *Scottish Literature since 1707* (1996) – cultural historians have incorporated his work into their own critique of the Kailyard diagnosis of Victorian Scotland. In *The Autonomy of Modern Scotland*, Lindsay Paterson argues that "the belief that Scottish popular culture in the nineteenth century was parochial and reactionary cannot be sustained: the literature of which that is true – the kailyard – was produced largely for a market of expatriates" (Paterson 1994: 60). Tom Devine makes a similar point in his book *The Scottish Nation*, noting that "Scottish culture in the later nineteenth century was much more than the Kailyard school" and that the record of achievement hardly suggests that "Scottish culture was in crisis" (Devine 1999: 297–8). This reaction against the Kailyard diagnosis forms part of a widening sense of the Victorian period as one of cultural achievement rather than decline. Devine is one of several historians who have rejected Tom Nairn's reading of Scottish history by arguing that the absence of a strong political nationalism did not indicate the absence of a strong national identity. Scotland's civil autonomy within a largely decentralised United Kingdom meant that the middle classes had "no reason to seek parliamentary independence or to adopt a nationalism which was hostile to the British state". Furthermore, the British Empire, rather than diluting the sense of Scottish identity, "strengthened it by powerfully reinforcing the sense of national esteem and demonstrating that the Scots were equal partners with the English in the great imperial mission" (Devine 1999: 289). Historians have also been keen to stress that institutional and political developments in the second half of the century signified not the final collapse of the country into the Kailyard but "the re-creation of Scotland as a nation"; the 1890s "were the high summer of a renewed national consciousness" (Lynch 1993: 34–5). Wider investigation into Scottish philosophical traditions in the nineteenth century has led to a renewed awareness of the importance of Scotland to the development of modern culture. Devine is one of many commentators to point to the achievements of anthropologists such as James Frazer and social reformers such as Patrick Geddes in contributing to what has come to be seen as the first Scottish Renaissance. A biologist, sociologist, educational reformer, city planner, and much else besides, Geddes's ambition was "to recreate in Edinburgh an active centre [and] arrest the tremendous centralising power of the metropolis of London" (Sharp 1912: II, 49).

The challenge to the Kailyard diagnosis of Scottish culture has created its own problems, however, principally because in their critique of Kailyard as a homogenising discourse critics have taken a homogenous view of Kailyard itself. This point emerges in David McCrone's study *Understanding Scotland* (1992). This sociological analysis of "a stateless nation" has been cited as "one of the most celebrated books written on Scotland" (Gardiner 2005: 24) McCrone argues for a post-modern perspective on Scottish identity commenting, thirteen years after the publication of *The Break-Up of Britain*, that in spite of the "cultural renaissance" in Scotland in the seventies and eighties "the dominant analysis of Scottish culture remains a pessimistic and negative one, based on the thesis that Scotland's culture is 'deformed' and debased by sub-cultural formations such as tartanry and Kailyardism" (McCrone 1992: 12-13). Like Devine, McCrone argues that the discourses of tartanry and

Chapter Six

Kailyard "are far less dominant than is made out, nor is their influence quite so unproblematic and pernicious" (McCrone 1992: 175). He cites the revisionary accounts of William Donaldson and Thomas Knowles which "help to undermine the view that Scottish culture was overly dependent on Kailyard themes and values" (McCrone 1992: 175, 180).

The argument is repeated in McCrone's later study on Scottish Heritage, *Scotland – the Brand*, co-authored with Angela Morris and Richard Kiely (1995). In both books, however, the determination to undermine the power of the Kailyard discourse leads McCrone to fall into the same trap as those who have employed the term by reading it monolithically. As I noted in Chapter 3, McCrone builds his understanding of Kailyard on the "lad o' pairts" motif. By using this image as his definition of Kailyard culture McCrone concludes that because there is no female equivalent of the "lad o' pairts" Kailyard is "entirely masculinist" (McCrone et al. 1995: 69). Yet if one looks at the aesthetic rather than the sociological effect of much Kailyard fiction, one can argue that with its emphasis on the sentimental Kailyard offers a feminised vision. Much of the criticism of Kailyard fiction in the twentieth century came from male writers, such as George Blake, who reacted against the presentation of Scottish life within an aesthetic of feeling or sympathy. It is for this reason that popular women novelists such as Annie S. Swan and O. Douglas have been considered "Legacies of the Kailyard" (Dickson 1997).

There are plenty of other arguments that could be mobilised in this discussion. One might note, for example, that in *The Raiders* Crockett's heroine saves her injured lover by killing the bloodthirsty dogs of the gypsies, and that in Barrie's *The Little Minister* it is Babbie who is presented as the dominant force over Gavin Dishart. The proto-feminism of Barrie's plays also complicates the argument (Jack 1995). The problem is that McCrone's understanding of Kailyard is drawn from other critics – mainly George Blake and Gillian Shepherd – not from a consideration of literary texts. In both books he defines Kailyard as "a popular literary style from about 1880 until 1914" and argues that "the Kailyard School probably failed to survive the Great War"; he even suggests that it was Blake himself who coined the term (McCrone 1992: 177-8; McCrone et al. 1995:

61–2). Such errors and generalised assumptions about literary history illustrate how understanding of Kailyard has been built on a set of critical attitudes rather than an investigation of the literature itself.

Nevertheless, the fact that McCrone, in his exposition of Kailyard, simplifies and misunderstands the literature involved, proves the point that Scottish culture "cannot in any serious way be reduced to the discourses of tartanry and Kailyard" (McCrone 1992: 193). The Kailyard term has been constructed by literary critics into a discourse that is at odds with much of the literature that was actually produced in the period concerned. It is important to stress, however, that the rejection of Kailyard as a diagnosis of Scottish culture entails reinvestigation – not rejection – of the texts which have commonly been associated with the term.

In spite of the fact that the Kailyard diagnosis of Scottish culture has been exposed as unrepresentative and inadequate, the term has remained useful for critics discussing different periods of Scottish literature and culture. In an essay entitled "Designer Kailyard", Deidre Chapman uses the tools of the critical Kailyard to analyse "modern writers of romantic and light fiction", such as Rosamunde Pilcher, Jan Webster and Christine Marion Fraser. Readers of such fiction are judged to enjoy the "strong comfort factor in recognition" of a "parochial Scottish setting: neutered by diminutives, walled in by teacups" (Chapman 1995: 537). For their part, writers are shown to appeal to "the kailyard in the Scottish reader" – to draw from an "emotional parish", to "lean heavily on unexamined kailyard conventions" and exploit the "kailyard reflex" of reader recognition (Chapman 1995: 538, 539, 541). The term is transformed in a similar way by Moira Burgess in her critical study of the Glasgow novel. Burgess uses the term "urban kailyard" to refer to "fiction with an urban setting which otherwise shares the attributes of the kailyard proper" (Burgess 1998: 69). Burgess sees Kailyard as "a body of work characterised by sentimentality, narrowness of vision, and the acceptance of a code of unshakeable assumptions regarding conventional conduct and belief" (Burgess 1998: 68). She assesses the work of various Glasgow writers of the first two decades of the twentieth century – "the height of the urban kailyard vogue" – judging, for example, that Neil Munro is "not wholly free of kailyard

sentimentality", and at times "captures the very tone of the urban
kailyard, couthy and contented, with an eye for the customs and
curiosities of its own small world" (Burgess 1998: 88–9). Such
evaluations indicate the flexibility of a critical tool that serves
criticism through having an inbuilt set of critical criteria.

The Kailyard term has not gone away. Instead, the noun that
became an adjective has acquired adjectives of its own. In 1998
Andrew Collier attacked the Scottish media group for "preferring to
ditch relatively expensive serious programmes and instead feed its
viewers a relentless diet of trash from the electronic kailyard" (Collier
1998). In the same year Christopher Harvie, in the *Glasgow Herald*,
charged Irvine Welsh with writing "books for people who don't read
books" and thus "exploiting a chemical generation kailyard" (Harvie
1998a). The point is repeated in the third edition of Harvie's *Scotland
and Nationalism*:

There may originally have been a political purpose in these tales of the semi-qualified
insecure of McWorld and their instant gratification, but the mark of the MBA was
there. Welsh shrewdly commodified the result into "books for people who don't read
books, exploiting the satanic Kailyard of the chemical generation as professionally as
No Mean City had milked working class Glasgow in the 1930s, or as "Ian MacLaren
[*sic*]" had played the Mid-West in the 1890s. (Harvie 1998b: 222)

Harvie sees Welsh's books as evidence not of "a new and positive
international society" but as a typical product of a commodity culture
which breeds only mediocrity.

Both Collier and Harvie were responding in their criticism to the
change in Scotland's political status following the devolution
referendum of 1997. The debate both before and after the referendum
gave Kailyard something of a renewed lease of life. An article in the
Sunday Times wondered whether proposed changes in the school
curriculum would involve "more tales of the kailyard" rather than "a
lesson in modern Scotland" (Martin 1997). The fear that "Scotland
might become a cultural ghetto if it becomes introspective" was part
of the discussions about the likely cultural consequences of
devolution. In the *Scotsman* Allan Massie wrote:

The fear is that the spirit of devolution will be primarily defensive; that it will lead us
to withdraw into ourselves and become introspective, self-absorbed, content to

cultivate only our own Kailyard, indifferent to the rest of the United Kingdom, parochial and myopic. (Massie 1999)

Kailyard, as a critical tool, is here being used to focus discussion on the larger topic of whether a devolved cultural base breeds an insular or an international outlook. As a synonym for parochialism, Kailyard thus retains its usefulness. In a symposium held in 1998 to discuss the future of the BBC under a Scottish parliament, the question of parochialism was central and resulted in the Secretary of State resorting to what Magnus Linklater dubbed "The K-word":

> I am not saying, not for a moment, that devolved broadcasting would necessarily mean Kailyard programming, if I can put it like that. But I am saying that it is not self-evident that separating out a Scottish BBC would be for the best. (Linklater 1998)

The debate continued in Westminster a few days later when the Labour MP John Macallion responded to the use of the term by arguing that the Scottish Parliament was being treated like a Kailyard institution.[4]

In the article in the *Glasgow Herald* quoted at the very beginning of this study, "Rix" argued that the term Kailyard deserved "to be completely pensioned off". But the word which was probably first intended as a joke became the context from which much of the study of Scottish culture was shaped in the twentieth century. From literature and light entertainment, through political history, film, sociology and the Scottish Parliament, Kailyard remains an essential term of reference. All the more reason why a proper awareness of its use in critical and cultural debates is essential for a proper understanding of Scotland and Scottish culture.

---

[4] *Hansard*, 4 March 1998, Column 1113. Electronic version. (http://www.Publicationsparliament.uk/pa/cm199798/cmhansrd/vo980304/debindx/80 304-x.htm).

Bibliography

References to manuscript material are made in the footnotes. References to contemporary reviews of literary works are embedded within the text.

Anderson, Eric. 1979. "The Kailyard Revisited" in Campbell, Ian (ed.) *Nineteenth–Century Scottish Fiction: Critical Essays*. Manchester: Carcanet. 130–47.

Anderson, Linda. 1998. *Bennett, Wells and Conrad: Narrative in Transition*. Basingstoke: Macmillan.

Anderson, R.D. 1985. "In Search of the 'Lad of Parts': the Mythical History of Scottish Education" in *History Workshop* 19: 82–104.

Ash, Marinell. 1980. *The Strange Death of Scottish History*. Edinburgh: Ramsay Head Press.

Attenborough, John. 1975. *A Living Memory: Hodder and Stoughton, Publishers, 1868–1975*. London: Hodder & Stoughton.

Barrie, J.M. 1888. *Auld Licht Idylls*. London: Hodder & Stoughton.

—. 1889a. *A Window in Thrums*. London: Hodder & Stoughton.

—. 1889b. "Thomas Hardy: The Historian of Wessex" in *Contemporary Review*. July. 57–66.

—. 1891a. *The Little Minister*. London: Cassell.

—. 1891b. "Mr. Kipling's Stories", *Contemporary Review*. March. 364–72.

—. 1896a. *Sentimental Tommy*. London: Cassell.

—. 1896b. *Margaret Ogilvy*. London: Hodder & Stoughton.

—. 1896c. "Introduction" in *The Novels, Tales and Sketches of J.M. Barrie, Volume 1: Auld Licht Idylls and Better Dead*. New York: Charles Scribner.

—. 1900. *Tommy and Grizel*. London: Cassell.

Bassett, Troy J. and Christina M. Walter. 2001. "Booksellers and Bestsellers: British Book Sales as documented by *The Bookman*, 1891–1906" in *Book History* IV: 205–36.

Bell, J.J. 1933. *Wee Macgreegor, with an introduction by the author, telling the story of the Book*. Edinburgh: The Moray Press.

Beveridge, Craig and Ronald Turnbull. 1989. *The Eclipse of Scottish Culture: Inferiorism and the Intellectuals*. Edinburgh: Polygon.

Blake, George. 1951. *Barrie and the Kailyard School*. London: Arthur Barker.

—. 1955. *Annals of Scotland 1895–1955*. London: British Broadcasting Corporation.

Blathwayt, Raymond. 1899. "A Talk with 'Ian Maclaren'" in *Great Thoughts* XXX: 288–90.

Bold, Alan. 1983. *Modern Scottish Literature*. New York and London: Longman.

Bremner, Robert A. 1894. "An Afternoon in Thrums" in *Scots Magazine*. December. 16–21.

Brown, Ivor. 1952. *Summer in Scotland*. London: Collins.

Brown, Stewart J. 1982. *Thomas Chalmers and the Godly Commonwealth in Scotland*. Oxford: Oxford University Press.

Brown, Callum G. 2000. "Rotavating the kailyard: re-imagining the Scottish 'meenister' in discourse and the parish state since 1707" in Aston, Nigel and Matthew Cragoe (eds) *Anticlericalism in Britain, c.1500–1914*. Stroud: Sutton. 138–58.

Bruce, Frank. 2000. *Scottish Showbusiness: Music Hall, Variety and Pantomime*. Edinburgh: NMS Publishing.

Buchan, John. "Nonconformity in Literature" in *Glasgow Herald* (2 November 1895).

Burns, John. 2001. "Introduction" in Crockett, S.R. *The Raiders* [1894] Edinburgh: Canongate.

Burgess, Moira. 1998. *Imagine a City: Glasgow in Fiction*. Arundell: Argyll Publishing.

Butcher, Rev. J. Williams. 1897. "The Fiction of Scottish Life and Character: a comparative study of Barrie, Crockett and 'Ian Maclaren'" in *Great Thoughts*. August–September. 307–8, 331–2, 346.

Byrde, Margaretta, 1898. "Thrums" in *Great Thoughts*, XXIX: 325–6.

Caird, J.B. 1977. "A Scotsman on the Make: a note on Barrie's novels" in *Brunton's Miscellany* 1(1): 25–7.

Campbell, Ian. 1974. "George Douglas Brown's Kailyard Novel" in *Studies in Scottish Literature* 12(1): 62-73.

—. 1981. *Kailyard*. Edinburgh: Ramsay Head Press.

—. 1988a. "Nineteenth-Century non-Fictional Prose" in Gifford, Douglas (ed.) *The History of Scottish Literature, Volume 3: Nineteenth Century*. Aberdeen: Aberdeen University Press. 169–88.

—. 1988b. "The Scottish Short Story: Three Practitioners" in *Journal of the Short Story in English* 10: 17–44.

Carey, John. 1992. *The Intellectuals and the Masses: Pride and Prejudice among the Literary Intelligentsia, 1880–1939*. London: Faber and Faber.

Carswell, Donald. 1927. *Brother Scots*. London: Constable.

Carter, Ian. 1976. "Kailyard: The Literature of Decline in Nineteenth Century Scotland" in *The Scottish Journal of Sociology* 1(1): 1–13.

Caughie, John. 1982. "Scottish Television: What Would it Look Like?" in McArthur, Colin (ed.) *Scotch Reels: Scotland in Cinema and Television*. London: British Film Institute Publishing. 112–22.

—. 1990. "Representing Scotland: New Questions for Scottish Cinema" in Dick, Eddie (ed.) *From Limelight to Satellite: A Scottish Film Book*. London: British Film Institute Publishing. 13–30.

Chalmers, Patrick. 1938. *The Barrie Inspiration*. London: Peter Davies.

Chapman, Deirdrie. 1997. "Designer Kailyard" in Gifford, Douglas and Dorothy Macmillan (eds.) *A History of Scottish Women's Writing*. Edinburgh: Edinburgh University Press. 536–48.

Colby, Robert and Vineta. 1979. "Mrs Oliphant's Scotland: The Romance of Reality" in Campbell Ian (ed.) *Nineteenth-Century Scottish Fiction*. Manchester: Carcanet. 91–104.

Collier, Andrew. 1998. "Milking of Cowcaddens" in *Scotsman* (24 July 1998).

Collin, Dorothy W. 1991. "Edward Garnett, Publisher's Reader, and Samuel Rutherford Crockett, Writer of Books" in *Publishing History* XXX: 89–121.

Conolly, M.F. 1869. *Fifiana: or, Memorials of the East of Fife*. Glasgow: John Tweed.

Conrad, Joseph 1986. *The Collected Letters of Joseph Conrad* (ed. Frederick R. Karl and Lawrence Davis). 5 vols. Cambridge: Cambridge University Press.

Cook, Richard, 1999. "The Home-ly Kailyard Nation: Nineteenth-Century Narratives of the Highland and the Myth of Merrie Auld Scotland" in *English Literary History* 66(4): 1053–73.

Coustillas, Pierre (ed).. 1978. *London and the Life of Literature in late Victorian England: the Diary of George Gissing, Novelist*. Hassocks: Harvester.

Craig, Cairns. 1979. "The Body in the Kit Bag: History and the Scottish Novel" in *Cencrastus* I: 18–22.

—. 1983. "Visitors from the Stars: Scottish Film Culture" in *Cencrastus* XI: 6–12.

—. 1996. *Out of History: Narrative Paradigms in Scottish and British Culture*. Edinburgh: Polygon.

—. 1998. "Regionalism and the Scottish Novel" in Snell, K.D.M. (ed.), *The Regional Novel in Britain and Ireland*. Cambridge: Cambridge University Press. 221–56.

—. 1999. *The Modern Scottish Novel: Narrative and the National Imagination*. Edinburgh: Edinburgh University Press.

Craig, David. 1961. *Scottish Literature and the Scottish People: 1680–1830*. London: Chatto & Windus.

Crawford, Robert. 1992. *Devolving English Literature*. Oxford: Clarendon.

—. 1998. "Scottish Literature and English Studies" in Crawford (ed.) *The Scottish Invention of English Literature*. Cambridge: Cambridge University Press. 225–46.

Croal, D. 1873. *Sketches of East Lothian*. Haddington: Haddington Courier.

Crockett, S.R. 1893. *The Stickit Minister and Some Common Men*. London. T. Fisher Unwin.

—. 1894. *The Lilac Sunbonnet*. London: T. Fisher Unwin.

—. 1895. *Bog-Myrtle and Peat. Tales Chiefly of Galloway gathered from the Years 1889 to 1895*. London: Bliss, Sands and Foster.

—. 1896. *Cleg Kelly*. London: Smith, Elder.

—. 1899. *Kit Kennedy*. London: James Clarke.

—. 1900. "A Romancer's Local Colour" in *Windsor Magazine* XII: 3–14.

—. 1904. *Raiderland: All About Grey Galloway, its Stories, Traditions, Characters, Humours*. London: Hodder & Stoughton.

—. [1894] 2001. *The Raiders*. Edinburgh. Canongate.

Crosland, T.W.H. 1902. *The Unspeakable Scot*. London: Grant Richards.

Cunningham, Ellen Painter. 1896. "Margaret Ogilvy: A Visit to Mr J.M. Barrie's Mother" in *Outlook*. September. 552–4.

Cunninghame Graham, R.B. [1896] 1899. "A Survival" in *The Ipane*. London: T. Fisher Unwin.

Cuthbertson, Gill. 1997. "Barrie and Striptease" in *Scotlands* 4(2): 53–65.

Darlington, W. A. 1938. *J. M. Barrie*. London and Glasgow: Blackie.

Darlow, T.H. 1925. *William Robertson Nicoll: Life and Letters*. London: Hodder & Stoughton.

Davie, George. 1961. *The Democratic Intellect: Scotland and her Universities in the Nineteenth Century*. Edinburgh: Edinburgh University Press.

Davies, Laurence. 1974. "R.B. Cunninghame Graham: The Kailyard and After" in *Studies in Scottish Literature* XI: 156–77.

Devine, T.M. 1999. *The Scottish Nation: 1700–2000*. Harmondsworth: Penguin.

Dickson, Beth. 1987. "Foundations of the Modern Scottish Novel" in Craig, Cairns (ed.) *The History of Scottish Literature, Volume 4: Twentieth Century*. Aberdeen: Aberdeen University Press.

—. 1997. "Annie S. Swan and O. Douglas: Legacies of the Kailyard" in Gifford, Douglas and Dorothy Macmillan (eds.) *A History of Scottish Women's Writing*. Edinburgh: Edinburgh University Press. 329–46.

Dickson, Lovat. 1971. *H.G. Wells*. London: The Readers Union.

Donaldson, Islay Murray. 1985. "S.R. Crockett and the Fabric of *The Lilac Sunbonnet*" in Drescher, Horst W. and Joachim Schewnd (eds) *Studies in Scottish Fiction: Nineteenth Century*. Frankfurt: Peter Lang. 291–305.

—. 1989. *The Life and Work of Samuel Rutherford Crockett* Aberdeen: Aberdeen University Press. 1989.

Donaldson, William. 1986. *Popular Literature in Victorian Scotland*. Aberdeen: Aberdeen University Press.

Douglas, George. 1893. "The Stickit Minister and Some Common Men" in *Bookman* IV: 146.

Dryerre, Jno. Meldrum. 1894. "'Ian Maclaren' (The Rev. John Watson, M.A.)" in *Great Thoughts* XXII: 136–8.

Duncan, T. 1895. "An Interview with a Kailyard Novelist" in *Glasgow Herald* (21 December 1895).

Edwards, D.H. 1897. *Modern Scottish Poets*, sixteenth series, Brechin: D.H. Edwards.

Eliot, George. [1859] 1980. *Adam Bede* (ed. Stephen Gill). Harmondsworth: Penguin.

—. [1856] 1992. "The Natural History of German Life" in *George Eliot: Selected Critical Writings* (ed. Rosemary Ashton). Oxford and New York: Oxford University Press.

—. 1954. *The George Eliot Letters* (ed. Gordon S. Haight). London and New Haven: Yale University Press.

Ellmann, Richard. 1987. *Oscar Wilde*. London: Hamish Hamilton.

Falk, Bernard. 1937. *Five Year's Dead*. London: Hutchinson.

[Ferguson, J.M.]. *Auld Ayr: Sketches and Reminiscences, chiefly descriptive of Ayr since the beginning of the 19th century*. Ayr: Observer Office.

Ferguson, William. 1968. *The Edinburgh History of Scotland, Volume 4: Scotland 1689 to the Present*. Edinburgh: Edinburgh University Press.

Findlater, J.H. [1899] 1904. "The Scot of Fiction" in *Stones from a Glass House*. London: James Nisbet & Co. 89–110.

Forrester, David A.R. 1992. "The 'Lad o' Pairts': a Study of the Literary Myth" in Carter, Jennifer J. and Donald J. Witherington (eds) *Scottish Universities: Distinctiveness and Diversity*. Edinburgh: John Donald. 156–62.

Frierson, William. 1928. "The English Controversy over Realism in Fiction" in *PMLA* 43: 533–50

Fry, Michael. 1992. "The Whig Interpretation of Scottish History" in Donnachie, Ian and Christopher Whately (eds) *The Manufacture of Scottish History*. Edinburgh: Polygon. 72–89.

Gardiner, Michael. 2005. *Modern Scottish Culture*. Edinburgh: Edinburgh University Press.

Garland, Herbert 1928. *A Bibliography of the Writings of Sir James Matthew Barrie* London: Bookman's Journal.

Gatrell, Simon. 2003. *Thomas Hardy's Vision of Wessex*. Basingstoke and New York: Macmillan.

Geddie, John. 1897. "The Land of Barrie" in *Ludgate* IV: 544–8.

—. 1898. "Thrums" in *Ludgate* VI: 120–5.

Geduld, Harry M. 1971. *Sir James Barrie*. New York: Twayne.

Geikie, Archibald. 1904. *Scottish Reminiscences*. Glasgow: Maclehose.

Gibbon, Lewis Grassic. 1934. "Literary Lights" in Gibbon and Hugh MacDiarmid, *Scottish Scene, or, the Intelligent Man's Guide to Albyn*. London: Jarrolds. 163–75.

Gibbon, Lewis Grassic and Hugh MacDiarmid, 1934. *Scottish Scene, or, the Intelligent Man's Guide to Albyn*. London: Jarrolds.

Gibbon, Lewis Grassic. [1932] 1988. *Sunset Song*. Edinburgh: Canongate.

Gibson, John Michael and Richard Lancelyn Green. 1986. *The Unknown Conan Doyle: Letters to the Press*. London: Secker & Warburg.

Gilmour, Robin. 1989. "Regional and Provincial in Victorian Literature" in *The Literature of Region and Nation*, ed. R.P. Draper. Basingstoke: Macmillan. 51–60.

Graham, Kenneth. 1965. *English Criticism of the Novel*. Oxford: Oxford University Press.

Gray, Robin. 1894. "S.R. Crockett. A Chat about the Author of 'The Raiders'", *Great Thoughts*, XXI: 328–30.

Griest, Guinevere L. 1970. *Mudie's Circulating Library and the Victorian Novel*. Bloomington: Indiana University Press.

Gunn, Neil M. 1987. *Landscape and Light: Essays by Neil M. Gunn* (ed. Alastair McCleary). Aberdeen: Aberdeen University Press.

Hackett, A.P. 1945. *Fifty years of Best Sellers*. New York: Bowker.

Hammerton, J.H. 1929a. *Barrie: the Story of a Genius*. London: Sampson Low & Marston.

—. 1929b. *Barrieland: a Thrums Pilgrimage*. London: Sampson Low & Marston.

Hardy, Thomas. [1887] 1998. *The Woodlanders* (ed. Patricia Ingham). Harmondsworth: Penguin.

Harper, Malcolm McL. [1907]. *Crockett and Grey Galloway: the Novelist and his Works*. London: Hodder & Stoughton.

Hart, Francis Russell. 1978. *The Scottish Novel: A Critical Survey*. London: John Murray.

Harvie, Christopher. 1982. "Drumtochty Revisited: The Kailyard" in *Scottish Review* 27: 4–11.

—. 1985. "The Barrie who Never Grew Up: An Apologia for *The Little Minister*" in Drescher, Horst W. and Joachim Schwend (eds) *Studies in Scottish Fiction: Nineteenth Century*. Frankfurt and Bern: Peter Lang. 321–35.

—. 1988. "Industry, Religion and the State of Scotland" in Gifford, Douglas (ed.) *The History of Scottish Literature, Volume 3: Nineteenth Century*. Aberdeen: Aberdeen University Press. 23–42.

—. 1998a. "Celts with Attitude". *Glasgow Herald*, 21 February 1998.

—. [1977, 1994] 1998b. *Scotland and Nationalism: Scottish Society and Politics 1707–1994*, 3rd edition. London: Routledge.

Hay, George Campbell. 1948. *Winds on Loch Fyne*. Edinburgh and London: Oliver & Boyd.

Hepburn James, (ed). 1966. *The Letters of Arnold Bennett, Volume 1: Letters to J.B. Pinker*. Oxford: Oxford University Press.

Herbert, W.N. 1991. "The Significance of Gregory Smith" in *Gairfish: Discovery*. Bridge of Weir: Gairfish.

Hill, C.W. 1976. *Edwardian Scotland*. Edinburgh and London: Scottish Academic Press.

Hunter, Shelagh. 1984. *Victorian Idyllic Fiction: Pastoral Strategies*. London and Basingstoke: Macmillan.

Jack, R.D.S. 1989. *The Road to the Never Land: A Reassessment of J.M. Barrie's Dramatic Art*. Aberdeen: Aberdeen University Press.

—. 1992. "Art, Nature and Thrums" in Schwend, Joachim et al. (eds) *Literature in Context*. Frankfurt am Main: Peter Lang. 155–64.

—. 1995. "Barrie and the Extreme Heroine" in Whyte, Christopher (ed.) *Gendering the Nation*. Edinburgh: Edinburgh University Press. 137–67.

Jackson, Rev. George. 1894. "A Visit to Thrums" in *Young Man*. February; May. 52–5; 164–7.

James, Henry. [1884] 1985. "The Art of Fiction" in Eigner, Edwin M. and George J. Worth (eds) *Victorian Criticism of the Novel*. Cambridge: Cambridge University Press. 193–212.

Kaplan, Fred. 1987. *Sacred Tears: Sentimentality in Victorian Literature*. Princeton: Princeton University Press.

Keating, Peter. 1989. *The Haunted Study: A Social History of the English Novel 1875–1914*. London: Secker & Warburg.

Kennedy, John. 1930. *Thrums and the Barrie Country*. London: Heath Cranton.

Kipling, Rudyard. 1990. *The Letters of Rudyard Kipling* (ed. Thomas Pinney). 4 Vols. Baskingstoke: Macmillan.

Knowles, Thomas D. 1983. *Ideology, Art and Commerce: Aspects of Literary Sociology in the late Victorian Scottish Kailyard*. Goteburg: Acta Universitatis Gothoburgensis.

Lauder, Sir Harry. 1922. *Roamin' in the Gloamin'*. London: Hutchinson.

Law, Graham. 2000. *Serialising Fiction in the Victorian Press*. Basingstoke and New York: Palgrave.

Lawson, Alexander. 1891. *Tales, Legends and Traditions of Forfarshire*. Forfar, Edinburgh and Glasgow: [n/p].

Lee, Gerald Stanley. 1896. "Ian Maclaren as a Lecturer" in *Critic* (10 October 1896).

Leclaire, Lucien. 1954. *A General Analytical Bibliography of the Regional Novelists of the British Isles 1800–1950*. Claremont: G. de Bussac.

Leicester Addis, M.E. 1900. "A Harvest Home in Thrums" in *Lippincott's Monthly* LXVI: 553–8.

Letley, Emma. 1988. *From Galt to Douglas Brown: Nineteenth–Century Fiction and Scots Language*. Edinburgh: Scottish Academic Press.

Levine, George. 1981. *The Realistic Imagination; English Fiction from Frankenstein to Lady Chatterley*. Chicago and London: University of Chicago Press.

Lewins, George. 1896. "Ian Maclaren" in *Primitive Methodist Quarterly Review* 18: 465–74.

Lindsay, Maurice. 1961. *By Yon Bonnie Banks: A Gallimaufray*. London: Hutchinson.

—. 1977. *History of Scottish Literature*. London: Robert Hale.

Linklater, Magnus "Towards a separate future for Scotland's broadcasters", *Scotland on Sunday* (1 March 1998).

Low, Donald. 1974. *Robert Burns: the Critical Heritage*. London: Routledge.

Lownie, Andrew. 1995. *John Buchan: The Presbyterian Cavalier*. Edinburgh: Canongate.

Lynch, Michael. 1993. "Scottish Culture in its Historical Perspective" in Scott, Paul H. (ed.) *Scotland: A Concise Cultural History*. Edinburgh and London: Mainstream. 15–45.

—. 2001. *The Oxford Companion to Scottish History*. Oxford: Oxford University Press.

M'Bain, J.M. 1887. *Arbroath: Past & Present: Being Reminiscences Chiefly relating to the Last Half Century*. Arbroath: Arbroath Herald.

Macara, D. 1881. *Crieff; Its Traditions and characters with Anecdotes of Strathearn*. Edinburgh: D. Macara.

MacDiarmid, Hugh. 1984. *The Letters of Hugh MacDiarmid* (ed. Alan Bold) Athens: University of Georgia Press.

—. [1978] 1985. *The Complete Poems of Hugh MacDiarmid* (ed. Michael Grieve and W.R. Aitken) Harmondsworth: Penguin.

—. 1992. *Selected Prose* (ed. Alan Riach). Manchester: Carcanet.

—. [1943] 1994. *Lucky Poet* (ed. Alan Riach). Manchester: Carcanet.

—. 1995. *Contemporary Scottish Studies* (ed. Alan Riach). Manchester: Carcanet.

—. 1996. *The Raucle Tongue: Hitherto uncollected prose*, Volume 1 (ed. Angus Calder, Glen Murray and Alan Riach). Manchester: Carcanet.

MacDonald, Angus. 1933. "Modern Scots Novelists" in Grierson H.J.C. (ed.) *Edinburgh Essays on Scots Literature*. Edinburgh: Oliver & Boyd. 149–73.

Mackail, Denis. 1948. *The Story of J.M.B.* London: Peter Davies.

Maclaren, Ian. 1894. *Beside the Bonnie Brier Bush*. London: Hodder & Stoughton.

—. 1895. *The Days of Auld Langsyne*. London: Hodder & Stoughton.

—. 1896. *Kate Carnegie and Those Ministers*. London: Hodder & Stoughton.

—. 1897. "Among My Books: Ugliness in Fiction" in *Literature* II: 80–1.

—. 1898. *Afterwards and other Stories*. London: Hodder & Stoughton.

—. 1902. *His Majesty Baby, and Some Common People*. London: Hodder & Stoughton.

—. 1907. *St Jude's*. London: The Religious Tract Society.

—. [1901] 1985. *Young Barbarians*, 1907. Edinburgh: Canongate.

Maclean, Neil N. 1874. *Life at a Northern University*. Glasgow and London: John S. Marr and Simpkin, Marshall.

Macmillan, Duncan. 1994. "The Canon in Scottish Art: Scottish Art in the Canon" in *Scotlands* 1: 87–103.

Martin, Iain. 1997. "Yet More Tales of the Kailyard?" in *Ecosse, Sunday Times* (18 May 1997).

Massie, Alan. 1999. "Cool Heads, not Brave Hearts" in *The Scotsman* (5 May 1999).

McAleer, Joseph. 1992. *Popular Reading and Publishing in Britain: 1914–1950.* Oxford: Oxford University Press.

McArthur, Colin. 1981. "Breaking the Signs: 'Scotch Myths' as Cultural Struggle" in *Cencrastus*. VII: 21–5.

—. 1982a. (ed.) *Scotch Reels: Scotland in Cinema and Television*. London: British Film Institute Publishing.

—. 1982b. "Scotland and Cinema: The Iniquity of the Fathers" in McArthur (ed.) *Scotch Reels: Scotland in Cinema and Television*. London: British Film Institute Publishing. 40–69.

—. 1983a. "The Maggie" in *Cencrastus*. XII: 10–14.

—. 1983b. "'Scotch Reels' and After" in *Cencrastus*. XI: 2–3.

McCleery, Alistair. 1989. "'The Devil Damn Thee Black' – a note on *The House with the Green Shutters*" in *Scottish Literary Journal* 16(1): 43–50.

McClure, J. Derrick. 1995. *Scots and its Literature*. Amsterdam and Philadelphia: John Benjamins Publishing Company.

McCrone, David. 1992. *Understanding Scotland: the sociology of a stateless nation.* London and New York: Routledge.

McCrone, David, Angela Morris and Richard Kiely. 1995. *Scotland – the Brand: the making of Scottish heritage*. Edinburgh: Edinburgh University Press.

McDonald, Peter D., 1997. *British Literary Culture and Publishing Practice: 1880–1914* Cambridge: Cambridge University Press.

McIlvanney, Liam. 2002. *Burns the Radical*. East Linton: Tuckwell.

McK, F.A. 1891. "Mr J.M. Barrie and 'The Little Minister'" in *Literary Opinion* VII: 141.

Meredith, George. 1970. *The Letters of George Meredith* (ed. C.L. Clive). 3 vols. Oxford: Oxford University Press.

Meynell, Viola (ed.) 1942. *The Letters of J.M. Barrie*. London: Peter Davies.

Millar, J.H. 1895. "The Literature of the Kailyard" in *New Review* XII: 384–94.

—. 1903. *A Literary History of Scotland*. London: T. Fisher Unwin.

Mills, John F. 1896. *Through Thrums: A Handbook for Visitors to Kirriemuir and District*. Kirriemuir: W.B. Mills.

Moffat, Dr James. 1910. "J.M. Barrie and his Books" in *Bookman* 39: 21–6.

Morgan, Edwin. 1974. "The Beatnik in the Kailyard" in *Essays*. Cheadle: Carcanet: 166–76.

—. 1988. "Scottish Poetry in the Nineteenth Century" in Gifford, Douglas (ed.) *The History of Scottish Literature: Volume 3 Nineteenth Century*. Aberdeen: Aberdeen University Press. 337–50.

Muir, Edwin. 1934. "Literature in Scotland" in *The Spectator* (25 May 1934).

—. 1936. *Scott and Scotland: The Predicament of the Scottish Writer.* London: Routledge.

—. [1935] 1979. *Scottish Journey.* Edinburgh: Mainstream.

Muir, Hugh. 1890. *Reminiscences and Sketches. Being a Topographical History of Rutherglen and suburbs.* Glasgow: Bell & Bain.

Mullett, Mary B. 1900. "Real Thrums" in *Ladies Home Journal* 17: 11–12.

Murray, David Christie. 1897. *My Contemporaries in Fiction.* London: Chatto & Windus.

Murray, Glen 1996. "MacDiarmid's Media 1911-1936" in MacDiarmid, Hugh. *The Raucle Tongue: Hitherto uncollected prose,* Volume 1 (ed. Angus Calder, Glen Murray and Alan Riach). Manchester: Carcanet. x-xix.

Murray, Isobel and Bob Tait. 1984. *Ten Modern Scottish Novels.* Aberdeen: Aberdeen University Press.

Nairn, Tom. 1970. "The Three Dreams of Scottish Nationalism" in Miller, Karl (ed.) *Memoirs of Modern Scotland.* London: Faber.

—. [1977] 1981. *The Break-Up of Britain: Crisis and Neo-Nationalism.* Second edition. London: Verso.

Nash, Andrew. 1996. "Re-reading the 'Lad o' Pairts': the myth of the Kailyard myth" in *Scotlands* 3(2): 86–102.

—. 1997. "The Cotter's Kailyard" in Crawford, Robert (ed.) *Robert Burns and Cultural Authority.* Edinburgh: Edinburgh University Press. 180–97.

—. 1998. "The Compilation of J.M. Barrie's *Auld Licht Idylls*" in *The Bibliotheck* 23: 85–96.

—. 1999a. "From Realism to Romance: Gender and Narrative Technique in J.M. Barrie's *The Little Minister*" in *Scottish Literary Journal* 26(1): 77–92.

—. 1999b. "'Trying to be a Man': J.M. Barrie and Sentimental Masculinity" in *Forum for Modern Language Studies* 35(2): 113–25.

—. 1999c. "'A Phenomenally Slow Producer': J.M. Barrie, Scribner's and the publication of *Sentimental Tommy*" in *Yale University Library Gazette* 74(1–2): 41–53.

—. 2000. "Understanding the Land in Scot(t)land" in Hagemann, Susanne (ed.) *Terranglian Territories.* Frankfurt am Main: Peter Lang. 631–40.

Neish, J.S. 1881. *In the By-ways of Life: A Series of Sketches of Forfarshire Characters.* Dundee: The Weekly Press Office.

Nicoll, William Robertson. 1889. "The Correspondence of Claudius Clear – A Visit to Thrums" in *British Weekly* (2 August 1889).

[—]. 1892a. "The Auld Lichts; their ministers and their Kirk. A historical Resume" in *British Weekly* (31 March 1892).

—. 1892b. "An Auld Licht Causerie" in *The National Review.* September. 132–5.

—. 1908. *"Ian Maclaren": Life of the Rev. John Watson.* London: Hodder & Stoughton.

—. 1926. *People and Books: From the Writings of W. Robertson Nicoll.* London: Hodder & Stoughton.

Noble, Andrew. 1982. "Versions of Scottish Pastoral: the Literati and the Tradition 1780–1830" in Markus, Thomas A. (ed.) *Order in Space and Society: Architectural Form and its Context in the Scottish Enlightenment*. Edinburgh: Mainstream. 263–310.

—. (ed.) 1983. *Robert Louis Stevenson*. London: Barnes & Noble.

—. 1985. "Urbane Silence: Scottish Writing and the Nineteenth-Century City" in *Perspectives of the Scottish City*, ed. George Gordon. Aberdeen: Aberdeen University Press, 64–90.

—. 1988. "John Wilson (Christopher North) and the Tory Hegemony" in Gifford, Douglas (ed.) *The History of Scottish Literature, Volume 3: Nineteenth Century*. Aberdeen: Aberdeen University Press. 125–52.

Noble, James Ashcroft. 1895. "Ian Maclaren at Home" in *Woman at Home* III: 511–21;

Norquay, Glenda. 2002. "Introduction" to *The Collected Works of Lorna Moon*. Edinburgh: Black & White.

Ochiltree, Henry. 1895. *Redburn*. Paisley: Alexander Gardner.

[Oliphant, Margaret], 1889. "The Old Saloon" in *Blackwood's Magazine*. August. 254–75.

[—]. 1895. "The Looker–On" in *Blackwood's Magazine*. June. 902–929.

Ormond, Leonee. 1987. *J.M. Barrie*. Edinburgh: Scottish Academic Press.

Paterson, Lindsay. 1981. "Scotch Myths – 2" in *Bulletin of Scottish Politics* II: 67-71.

—. 1994. *The Autonomy of Modern Scotland*. Edinburgh: Edinburgh University Press.

Paton, David. 1896. "'Ian Maclaren' at Home" in *Sunday Magazine* XXV: 37–42.

Pearson, Cora B. 1901. "Ian Maclaren. A Study of the Man and His Work" in *Temple Magazine* V: 659–64.

Petrie, Duncan. 2000. *Screening Scotland*. London: British Film Institute Publishing.

Phelps, Elizabeth Stuart. 1895. "'Afterwards': A Study of a Story by Ian Maclaren" in *McClure's Magazine* V: 329–32.

Power, William. 1935. *Literature and Oatmeal*. London: Routledge.

Quiller-Couch. A.T. 1892. "J.M. Barrie" in *Bookman* I: 169–71.

Rainey, Lawrence. 1998. *Institutions of Modernism: Literary Elites and Public Culture*. London and New Haven, Yale University Press.

Ramsay, E.B. [1857] 1861. *Reminiscences of Scottish Life and Character*, seventh edition. Edinburgh: Edmonston and Douglas.

—. [1857] 1872. *Reminiscences of Scottish Life and Character*, twenty-first edition. London: Gall and Inglis.

Reid, J.M. 1945. *Modern Scottish Literature*. Edinburgh: Oliver & Boyd.

Riach, Alan. 1995. "Introduction" in MacDiarmid, Hugh. *Contemporary Scottish Studies* (ed. Alan Riach). Manchester: Carcanet.

Ritson, Joseph. 1897. "The Maker of Modern Idyllism" in *Primitive Methodist Quarterly Review*. 577–91.

"Rix", 1897. "The Slump in Kailrunts", *Glasgow Evening Times* (January 6, 1897).

Robb, David S. 1983. "The Year's Work in Scottish Literary and Linguistic Studies 1981, 1840–1900" in *Scottish Literary Journal Supplement* 19: 25–32.

Robertson, David Ogilvy. 1872. *Long Ago Legends of Clova*. Edinburgh: [n/p].

R[obertson], D[avid]. 1890. Preface to *Whistle-Binkie; a collection of songs for the social circle.* Glasgow: David Robertson & Co.

Roy, James A. 1937. *James Matthew Barrie: an appreciation.* London: Jarrolds.

Royle, Trevor. 1993. *The Mainstream Companion to Scottish Literature.* Second edition. Edinburgh: Mainstream.

Schwend, Joachim and Horst W. Drescher. 1990. "Introduction" in *Studies in Scottish Fiction: Twentieth Century.* Frankfurt am Main: Peter Lang. 7–12.

Scott, Dixon. 1927. *Men of Letters.* London, New York and Toronto: Hodder & Stoughton.

Scott, Paul. H. 1988. "'The Last Purely Scotch Age'" in Gifford, Douglas (ed.) *The History of Scottish Literature, Volume 3: Nineteenth Century.* Aberdeen: Aberdeen University Press. 13–22.

Sharp, Elizabeth A. 1912. *William Sharp (Fiona Macleod): A Memoir*, 2 vols. London: Heinemann.

Shepherd, Gillian. 1988. "The Kailyard" in Gifford, Douglas (ed.) *The History of Scottish Literature, Volume 3: Nineteenth Century.* Aberdeen: Aberdeen University Press. 309–20.

Simpson, K.G. 1981. "Immortal Make-Believe: Burns and Scottish Values" in *Scottish Review* 21: 4–10.

Simpson, Kenneth. 1988. *The Protean Scot: The Crisis of Identity in Eighteenth–Century Scottish Literature.* Aberdeen: Aberdeen University Press.

Smith, Anthony D. 1991. *National Identity.* Harmondsworth: Penguin.

Smith, G. Gregory. 1919. *Scottish Literature: Character and Influence.* London: Macmillan.

Snell, K.D.M. 1998. *The Regional Novel in Britain and Ireland.* Cambridge: Cambridge University Press.

Speirs, John. [1940] 1962. *The Scots Literary Tradition: an essay in criticism.* London: Chatto & Windus.

Stevenson, Robert Louis. [1883] 1950. "A Note on Realism" in Elwin, Malcolm (ed.) *The Essays of Robert Louis Stevenson.* London: MacDonald. 376–82.

—. 1995. *The Letters of Robert Louis Stevenson* (ed. Bradford A. Booth and Ernest Mehew). 8 vols. New Haven and London: Yale University Press.

Stirton, James. 1896. *Thrums and its Glens: Historical Relics and Recollections.* Kirriemuir: W. Jolly & Sons.

Stoddart, Jane T. 1903. *William Robertson Nicoll: Editor and Preacher.* London: S.W. Partridge & Co.

Strathesk, John. 1882. *Bits from Blinkbonny, or Bell o' the Manse: A Tale of Scottish Village Life Between 1841 and 1851.* Edinburgh: Oliphant, Anderson and Ferrier.

—. 1886. *More Bits from Blinkbonny.* Edinburgh: Oliphant, Anderson and Ferrier.

Sutherland, John. 1988. *The Longman Companion to Victorian Fiction.* London: Longman.

Swann, Elsie. 1934. *Christopher North (John Wilson).* Edinburgh: Oliver & Boyd.

Swinnerton, Frank. 1956. *Background with Chorus: A Footnote to Changes in English Literary Fashion Between 1901 and 1917.* London: Hutchinson.

Terry, R.C. 1983. *Victorian Popular Fiction, 1860–80.* London and Basingstoke: Macmillan.

Tyler, Samuel. 1849. *Robert Burns as a Poet and a Man.* Dublin: James M'Glashan.

Tytler, Sarah. 1893. "The Realistic Novel. As represented by J.M. Barrie" in *Atalanta* VII: 60–3.

—. 1900. *A Young Dragon.* London: Chatto & Windus.

[unsigned]. 1893. "The Journalist in Fiction" in *Church Quarterly Review* 36: 73–92.

[unsigned]. 1896a. "Ian Maclaren at Home. Interesting Interview" in *Glasgow Evening Times* (September 28, 1896).

[unsigned]. 1896b. "Dr John Watson – 'Ian Maclaren'" in *McClure's Magazine* VII: 387–400.

[unsigned]. 1897. "A Cockney's Estimate of Crockett" in *Glasgow Evening Times* (4 February 1897).

[unsigned]. 1898. "The Domination of Dialect" in *Literature* (14 May 1898).

[unsigned]. 1900a. "The Irish Peasant in Fiction" in *Literature* (5 May 1900).

[unsigned]. 1900b. S.R. Crockett, "A Romancer's Local Colour" in *Windsor Magazine*, XII (June 1900), 3–14.

[unsigned]. 1900c. "A Day with Ian Maclaren" in *Sunday Strand* 1: 32–9.

[unsigned]. 1901a. "Ian Maclaren" in *Bookman*, 20: 6–10.

[unsigned]. 1901b. "Ian Maclaren. A Character Sketch" in *Young Man* XV: 217–20.

Veitch, James. 1952. *George Douglas Brown.* London: Herbert Jenkins.

Walker Hugh, 1910. *The Literature of the Victorian Era*, Cambridge: Cambridge University Press.

Walker, Marshall. 1996. *Scottish Literature since 1707.* London and New York: Longman.

[Wallace, William], 1894. "Scottish fiction to-day" in *Scottish Review* 23: 42–58.

—. 1900a. "Coming Scottish Literary Developments" in *Bookman* XIX: 137–8.

—. 1900b. "J.M. Barrie" in *Bookman* XIX: 40–4.

Wallace, Gavin. 1987. "Compton Mackenzie and the Scottish Popular Novel" in Craig, Cairns (ed.) *The History of Scottish Literature, Volume 4: Twentieth Century.* Aberdeen: Aberdeen University Press. 243–57.

Watson, John. 1896. *The Cure of Souls.* London: Hodder & Stoughton.

—. 1897. *The Potter's Wheel.* London: Hodder & Stoughton.

Watson, Rev. John. 1905. "The Church Crisis in Scotland" in *Hibbert Journal* 10: 237–252.

Watson, Roderick. 1984. *The Literature of Scotland.* Basingstoke: Macmillan.

Waugh, Joseph Laing. 1912. *Robbie Doo: His Reminiscences.* Dumfries: Standard Office.

—. 1914. *Robbie Doo: His Reminiscences.* London: Hodder & Stoughton.

Weber, Carl J. (ed.). 1954. *The Letters of Thomas Hardy, transcribed from the original autographs now in the Colby College Library.* Waterville, Maine: Colby College Press.

Whigham-Price, A. 1994. "William Robertson Nicoll and the genesis of the Kailyard School" in *Durham University Journal* 86(1): 73–82.

Wilson, John. 1819. "The Radical's Saturday Night" in *Blackwood's Magazine.* December. 257.

[—], [1840] 1857. "The Genius and Character of Burns" in *Essays: Critical and Imaginative*, Vol. III. Edinburgh and London: Blackwood. 1–211.

Wilson, Rev. Samuel Law. 1899. *The Theology of Modern Literature*. Edinburgh: Clarke.

Wittig, Kurt. 1958. *The Scottish Tradition in Literature*. Edinburgh: Oliver & Boyd.

Wright, T.R. 2003. *Hardy and his Readers*. Basingstoke: Palgrave.

Young, James D. 1978. "The Kailyard Myths of Modern History" in *New Edinburgh Review* 44: 3–5.

Young, James D. 1979. *The Rousing of the Scottish Working Classes*. London: Croom Helm.

Index